About This Book

Why is this topic important?

All organizations have access to basically the same technology and financial resources. What sets winning organizations apart is the depth and breadth of their leadership talent. Bluntly stated, organizations that develop their leadership talent are most likely to be winners in our highly competitive, global economy—and that's why this book was written.

What can you achieve with this book?

What you will get out of the *2008 Pfeiffer Annual: Leadership Development* is first-hand information about where the field of leadership development is headed, from experts closest to the action—practitioners heading up leadership development in leading organizations. You will also read in-depth case studies on leading organizational leadership development programs and processes and thought-provoking chapters from leading thinkers (academics, consultants, and practitioners) on key issues such as leadership development strategies and systems, metrics, developing high-potential talent, engaging top executives, today's most effective learning methods, developing global leaders, and other critical topics. You'll take away best practices, practical ideas, innovative approaches, and lessons learned that will guide you in your efforts to use high-impact leadership development to help your organization achieve its strategic objectives through exceptional leadership talent.

How is this book organized?

This volume is divided into seven sections. Section 1, History of Leadership Development, is an overview of how the field of leadership development has emerged, where our roots are, where we are today, and perspectives on charting future directions. Section 2, Defining the Field, contains provocative chapters designed to challenge your organization's strategic perspective on leadership development. Section 3, Developing Global Leaders, addresses, through case studies and practical examples, the critical question of how today's organizations can develop global leaders. Section 4, Approaches to Leadership Development, gives insight into leading efforts around the world to solve key leadership issues. Section 5, Methodologies, reviews some of the most powerful methods for developing leaders that includes timely discussions of coaching that changes behavior, combining assessment and development, the role of leadership competencies in development, practical suggestions for transitioning leaders into new roles, and action learning. Section 6, Creative Approaches to Develop Leaders—Pushing the Boundary, is our attempt to offer some creative new insights and tools available to professionals who develop leaders. Section 7, A Look to the Future, is a view on how leadership development could look and feel like in the not so distant future. The section closes with some interesting questions that have the potential to encourage new thinking and innovation in the field of leadership development.

About Pfeiffer

Pfeiffer serves the professional development and hands-on resource needs of training and human resource practitioners and gives them products to do their jobs better. We deliver proven ideas and solutions from experts in HR development and HR management, and we offer effective and customizable tools to improve workplace performance. From novice to seasoned professional, Pfeiffer is the source you can trust to make yourself and your organization more successful.

Essential Knowledge   Pfeiffer produces insightful, practical, and comprehensive materials on topics that matter the most to training and HR professionals. Our Essential Knowledge resources translate the expertise of seasoned professionals into practical, how-to guidance on critical workplace issues and problems. These resources are supported by case studies, worksheets, and job aids and are frequently supplemented with CD-ROMs, websites, and other means of making the content easier to read, understand, and use.

Essential Tools   Pfeiffer's Essential Tools resources save time and expense by offering proven, ready-to-use materials—including exercises, activities, games, instruments, and assessments—for use during a training or-team-learning event. These resources are frequently offered in looseleaf or CD-ROM format to facilitate copying and customization of the material.

Pfeiffer also recognizes the remarkable power of new technologies in expanding the reach and effectiveness of training. While e-hype has often created whizbang solutions in search of a problem, we are dedicated to bringing convenience and enhancements to proven training solutions. All our e-tools comply with rigorous functionality standards. The most appropriate technology wrapped around essential content yields the perfect solution for today's on-the-go trainers and human resource professionals.

Pfeiffer   *Essential resources for training and HR professionals*
www.pfeiffer.com

The Pfeiffer Annual Series

The Pfeiffer Annuals present each year never-before-published materials contributed by learning professionals and academics and written for trainers, consultants, and human resource and performance-improvement practitioners. As a forum for the sharing of ideas, theories, models, instruments, experiential learning activities, and best and innovative practices, the *Annuals* are unique. Not least because only in the *Pfeiffer Annuals* will you find solutions from professionals like you who work in the field as trainers, consultants, facilitators, educators, and human resource and performance-improvement practitioners and whose contributions have been tried and perfected in real-life settings with actual participants and clients to meet real-world needs.

The Pfeiffer Annual: Consulting
Edited by Elaine Biech

The Pfeiffer Annual: Leadership Development
Edited by James Noel and David Dotlich

The Pfeiffer Annual: Management Development
Edited by Robert C. Preziosi

The Pfeiffer Annual: Training
Edited by Elaine Biech

Michael Allen's 2008 e-Learning Annual
Edited by Michael Allen

Pfeiffer™

THE 2008 PFEIFFER ANNUAL

Leadership Development

Jim Noel and David Dotlich, Editors

John Wiley & Sons, Inc.

Published by Pfeiffer
An Imprint of Wiley
989 Market Street, San Francisco, CA 94103-1741
www.pfeiffer.com

For additional copies/bulk purchases of this book in the U.S. please contact 800-274-4434.

Pfeiffer books and products are available through most bookstores. To contact Pfeiffer directly call our Customer Care Department within the U.S. at 800-274-4434, outside the U.S. at 317-572-3985, fax 317-572-4002, or visit www.pfeiffer.com.

Pfeiffer also publishes its books in a variety of electronic formats. Some content that appears in print may not be available in electronic books.

ISBN: 978-0-7879-9521-8
ISSN: 1046-333-X

Acquiring Editor: Martin Delahoussaye
Director of Development: Kathleen Dolan Davies
Development Editor: Susan Rahmeler
Production Editor: Dawn Kilgore
Editor: Rebecca Taff
Editorial Assistant: Julie Rodriquez
Manufacturing Supervisor: Becky Morgan

Printed in the United States of America

Printing　　　　　10 9 8 7 6 5 4 3 2 1

CONTENTS

Acknowledgments   xi

Introduction: What's Next in Leadership Development?   1
Jim Noel and David Dotlich

SECTION 1: HISTORY OF LEADERSHIP DEVELOPMENT   5

1   Where We've Been: Leadership
    Development in the 20th Century   7
    Jim Noel and David Dotlich

SECTION 2: DEFINING THE FIELD   21

2   Why Are There Not Enough Leaders in Companies Today?   23
    Stephen H. Rhinesmith

3   Who Really "Owns" Leadership Development?   34
    Robert A. Stringer

4 Developing Leaders of Substance   45
Ram Charan

5 Why Is Leadership So Important and Formal Leadership
Development Not?   51
Tim Sullivan

SECTION 3: DEVELOPING GLOBAL LEADERS   69

6 The Evolution of Leadership Development at Novartis   71
Frank Waltmann

7 Achieving Success in the Globalization of
Leadership Development   81
Eric Olson

8 Developing Global Leaders Through Action Learning   89
Alice Portz

SECTION 4: APPROACHES TO LEADERSHIP DEVELOPMENT   99

9 Developing Customer-Centric Leaders   101
Thomas R. Knighton

10 Building Marketing Excellence   109
Jean-Claude Larreche, Mario Castaneda, and Zohra Jan Mamod

11 Time Warner Creative Leadership Summit   126
Vera Vitels

12 Be the One: The LEADToshiba Experience   135
Anthony V. Codianni and Terry Kristiansen

13 The Quest for 20:20 Vision: Developing
HR Leaders at Luxottica   141
Ken Meyers

14 What Women Executives Need from Leadership
Development Programs   150
Marijo Bos

15 Creating Real Employee Engagement   162
Alaric Mostyn

16 Leading Across Boundaries: Adventures in the "White Spaces" at General Mills   176
Kevin D. Wilde

17 Bank of America: Winning the Growth Challenge   187
Brian Fishel

SECTION 5: METHODOLOGIES   197

18 Coaching Leadership Transitions   199
Jim Sutton

19 Executive Assessment for Succession Planning and Development: A Sequenced Process and a Few Helpful Hints   208
Adam Ortiz

20 Do Leadership Competencies Define Effective Leadership?   220
Jill Conner

21 Transition Support: Best Practices from the Field   230
Stacey E. Philpot

22 Action Learning: Creating Leaders Through Work   239
Jim Noel and David Dotlich

SECTION 6: CREATIVE APPROACHES TO DEVELOPING LEADERS— PUSHING THE BOUNDARY   249

23 Leader as Storyteller   251
Chatham Clarke Sullivan

24 The Leader as Poet: A Consideration of What Poetry May Have to Offer Organizational Leadership   261
Juan Mobili

25 Choices in Work and in Life   268
Neil M. Johnston

26 The Leading Brain: An Exercise in Self-Coaching   275
Agnes Mura

27 Leading in the Matrix of Today: Integrating Body/Mind/Spirit   283
Ginny Whitelaw

28 Somatics and Leadership   293
    Susan Nichols

29 Learning from World-Class Athletes in Managing Performance:
    Achieving Personal Leadership Excellence Through P^{6}PROP   304
    Christian Marcolli

30 The Shaping of Successful Careers   314
    Norman Walker

SECTION 7: A LOOK TO THE FUTURE   323

31 The Future of Leadership Development   325
    Jim Noel and David Dotlich

Contributors   334

About the Editors   337

How to use the CD-ROM   339

ACKNOWLEDGMENTS

The best ideas and approaches in leadership development are often developed by people who are too busy to write about them. That's because they are so involved in designing, teaching, researching, and working with other leaders. Producing a book of best practices from the best practitioners requires a knowledgeable and skilled support team, willing to give up Sunday mornings and late nights to meet deadlines.

On our team, we want to thank Martin Delahoussaye, who as our editor has been supportive and patient upon hearing too often those four words, "How about next week?" We also want to thank Michaelene Kyrala, who served as project manager for this edition, and who was able to cajole, whip, and praise without losing her good humor. Amy Davis has been an exceptionally skilled interviewer and writer, translating broad concepts and ideas into concrete words and paragraphs. Brenda Fogelman, Christine Whitteaker, and Heather Schraeder have served as coordinators, schedulers, and champions.

We also want to thank three outstanding groups of people without whom this book could not have been completed. First, our clients, colleagues, and friends in great companies around the world make us proud every day—of the field of leadership development, how far we have evolved as a discipline, and how central our role has become in most organizations. Second, the Partners, colleagues, associates, and faculty network of the Oliver Wyman Delta Executive Learning Center have inspired us through the years and throughout the production of this edition, and many of them are represented in these pages. Finally, our families, and the families and friends of all those who contributed to this book know firsthand that writing is never easy, especially on the weekend. We thank them for their indirect, but important, contribution to this book.

As a reader, we hope these pages enlighten and perhaps inspire you, and most importantly, encourage the development of good leaders and great organizations

David Dotlich
Portland, Oregon
Jim Noel
Rindge, New Hampshire

INTRODUCTION: WHAT'S NEXT IN LEADERSHIP DEVELOPMENT?

Speculating about the future is always risky business, but trends indicate that a growing emphasis on performance and accountability for leadership development professionals is a reasonably safe bet. As we start to develop models to address current and future trends, we offer some thoughts about the issues we'll need to consider:

1. *The new leadership development model is outcome driven:* This idea isn't really new, but companies have finally reached the point where they are going to demand tangible results from resources invested in executive development. In days past, a rating of "five" was considered the hallmark of excellent leadership development experience. The performance of business people is linked to business results. So too should the work of professionals in leadership development.

We see several business measures affecting growth and profitability that can be linked to leadership development:

a. The number of "ready now" candidates for big executive positions.
b. The ratio of internal hires to external hires for key leadership jobs.
c. The diversity of the senior leadership team around gender, ethnic origin, and nationality.
d. The success rate of new leaders in their positions.

2. *The primary developer of people is the work they do:* By giving people big jobs to do where they will learn new things, we can drive new behaviors and begin to look at work as the primary mechanism for developing leaders. Through work, we can develop leaders who know the business—the business model and strategy, the ability to select the right people and build them into a team. We can use work to assess performance, give honest, candid, and helpful feedback, and coach potential leaders around both business issues and interpersonal skills. If we think of work as a primary developer of people, then every day when work is assigned it is a potential development experience. So how can we increase the probability that an assignment becomes a development experience?

First, we need to question the old generic university model of bringing people together in a classroom to learn. It's time to shift the focus from classroom teachers to using managers as "teachers." Managers can be taught to assess people, assign work on the basis of development need, provide coaching and feedback, and share their experiences.

Second, we need to employ action learning experiences designed to use real work in developing business leaders. Companies such as GE have considerable experience in testing potential leaders by giving them real business issues to solve, holding them accountable for the results of their learning.

3. *Successful leadership development requires assessment and feedback to the organization:* Companies are starting to ask us more and more to help them assess their talent, rather than just invest in the development of leaders. In the past, the client was the individual, not the company, and what happened during training and coaching was treated almost as privileged information. This kind of development is no longer sufficient; in order to create good, measurable outcomes for the organization, leadership development professionals may be asked to provide assessment and feedback to the company. This new model changes the scope and nature of leadership development models. It also changes the skill set required of professionals in leadership development by creating a fundamental need to understand the business in order to make competent assessments about the effectiveness of business leaders.

4. *Leadership occurs at all levels of the organization:* Gone is the day when we can think of leadership as being the prerogative of a small handful of senior executives; the old model of leadership development focusing on the top down is obsolete. The digital age has produced a whole generation of people accustomed to having a vast amount of information at their fingertips, and these people require a new leadership model. These young, emerging leaders want to participate actively in the organization, requiring professionals in leadership development to think about what it means to develop leaders at all levels of the organization. What does it mean to have individual contributors, first-line managers, and middle managers act as leaders?

For one thing, it would mean serving our customers better and faster. Several years ago the New York Yankees baseball team had a well-known Japanese pitcher. One of the editors of this *Annual* happened to be behind the Japanese pitcher at the branch of a well-known bank. The Yankee hurler, a customer of the bank, wanted to make a transaction, but the bank employee said she could not conduct the transaction without identification—a valid driver's license. The pitcher was sent away angry and frustrated. Having watched the transaction, the editor thought the bank employee didn't know who the customer was. However, the first thing she said to the editor, who was the next customer, is "Do you know who that was?"

When asked why she did not serve the customer, she said she did not want to get in trouble with the branch manager, who always insisted on identification.

How many times have we seen employees at lower levels of an organization frustrate customers because they are not sufficiently trusted to make decisions or exceptions to rigid policies? How would an empowered associate have handled the situation? Think of the benefit to an organization in which all employees see themselves as leaders and feel empowered to act. How we achieve this is the work of leadership development.

5. *The future requires leadership skills that make people effective in lateral relationships:* Traditionally, we have focused on the leadership skills that enable people to succeed in vertical organizations. Today's reality is that much of the effectiveness of leaders is their ability to harness resources of an organization that exist outside of their direct authority.

We were recently asked to do a study for Nike that contrasted its most successful leaders with those who are average performers. In the world of athletic and leisure wear fashion and style, trends move very quickly around the world. Information on these trends must be shared and manufacturing and marketing decisions made quickly. A fashion trend spotted on the streets of Sao Paolo must be quickly surfaced, evaluated, and acted on. Traditional organizational structures and leadership frameworks do not move this information fast enough. Nike has adapted by creating a network of informal relationships that allow leaders at all levels of the organization to move information quickly and make critical decisions fast. The most successful leaders are the ones who harness the energy of these lateral relationships and use them to create business results that keep shareholders, analysts, and customers smiling.

6. *Successful organizations of the future will use all available leadership resources*: Organizations need to learn to use their full human leadership resources. No company would ignore half of the available financial resources. Women are well-represented at lower levels of the leadership pipeline. Yet we look around at senior leadership levels and are amazed that there are still so few women in senior leadership

positions. It is time that we understand why this situation continues to exist and develop specific steps that will close the gap. Solutions will likely require new thinking that may challenge our traditional thought on leadership and leadership development.

Also, as companies continue to expand their global reach, they should open up their leadership pipelines to a flow of global talent. We know that intelligence and ability are equally distributed across all populations. What makes a difference is experience and opportunity. The challenge is to open up the leadership pipeline to include all talent. Novartis, the Swiss pharmaceutical company, for example, sees China as a pillar for future growth opportunities. To develop the Novartis leaders who will build the Chinese market, Novartis has established a leadership center in China to develop future generations of Novartis leaders. It is anticipated that graduates will develop not only the Chinese market but participate fully in Novartis.

All of these trends and observations add up to one conclusion: As leadership development professionals, we have a tremendous opportunity to step up into our role and help create leaders who can meet the challenges of a global economy. This is our time—*if* we can step into the gap and understand that the leaders we help develop must produce results that please the shareholders, analysts, and customers.

As you read this edition of the *Pfeiffer Annual: Leadership Development,* we hope you will look to the past to recognize some of the development methods that still work—and those that do not. We hope you'll find some innovative solutions to challenges all companies face. And we hope that, ultimately, you will come away equipped to help create the business leaders who produce results.Introduction: What's Next In Leadership Development?

HISTORY OF LEADERSHIP DEVELOPMENT

With the strong current focus on growth, performance, innovation, and new markets, the demand for leaders who can meet the challenges of the new global environment has never been stronger. This is why talent has become such a pressing concern for both CEOs and boards of directors. As professionals in leadership development, we will need to recognize and address the concerns of CEOs who believe that leadership development is critical to filling their pipelines, but are deeply skeptical over the ability of current practices to deliver results, think it is not worth the investment, or don't want to dedicate the time and effort required. In the only chapter in this section, we want to pose some tough questions, review the current state of affairs, and revisit our rich legacy of the last century to decide what we can learn as we go forward.

Where We've Been: Leadership Development in the 20th Century, by Jim Noel and David Dotlich

CHAPTER 1

WHERE WE'VE BEEN: LEADERSHIP DEVELOPMENT IN THE 20TH CENTURY

Jim Noel and David Dotlich

In order to understand where we are going, it is important to understand where we are and how we arrived at the present situation. How has executive development evolved over the past four decades? What is our legacy? What successes can we build on, and more importantly, what distinguishes breakthrough innovation from incremental improvements? While it's tempting to skip this historical perspective, having a sense of our collective past can inform our future choices and investments.

Post-War Leadership Development: Uniformity and Structure

In the immediate post-World War II era, U.S. businesses, largely enjoying a global market without competition, looked to business schools, long-term executive development programs, and MBA programs to develop leaders from an educational rather than applied perspective. In response, business schools designed programs that mirrored the organizational structures they studied, defining functional leadership and general management as the sum of the functions consistent with the work of Alfred P. Sloan. Because there was so little competition, there was plenty of time and money to invest in broad-based learning, and the challenge was defined primarily as one of business skills development. When we look at the business skills developed in the 1950s, 1960s, and 1970s at top business schools such as Harvard, Wharton, Stanford, and Northwestern, the emphasis for executives was on developing the hard skills of business—strategy, financial drivers, and operations, among others. These skills were considered not only essential, but also sufficient.

Many of the basic concepts of organizational structure were first developed during the late 19th Century, but the basic principles of organizational management were refined in the United States during the 1950s. Fields such as strategy and business planning, marketing, corporate finance, production, and human resources took shape from both contemporary business practices and the thinking of academics.

The core MBA curriculum was developed in the 1950s to prepare people for general management positions, but MBA programs did not become seen as a path to advancement, and thus enormously popular, until the late 1970s. Concurrent with formal degree programs, business schools were shaping business practices by offering "executive" programs to mid-level and senior executives. Participants in executive programs were often "high potentials" selected for the purpose of building business and general management skills.

Change on the Horizon: The Debate Between Hard and Soft Skills

Insights about how managers actually develop and what they require in order to perform were also developed during this period. The work environment typically reflects trends shaping society, and beginning in the 1950s and accelerating during the 1960s, there was a growing emphasis on the individual as compared to the organization—"The Man in the Grey Flannel Suit." Today, because we are so focused on the concept of "leadership," it is hard to imagine a time when a major area of academic research interest was "motivation." Researchers focused on key questions such as, "What is motivation?" "How does it differ across individuals?" "How does it appear in groups?" "How can a knowledge of motivation help a manager to maximize performance?" This was a period of great intellectual activity, and researchers like David McClelland, Abraham Maslow, and David McGregor provided strong insights into what motivates individuals and drives human behavior.

So the pendulum began to swing from solely "hard" business issues, and thus began the debate of whether to focus on tasks or people in driving performance. Two researchers popularized this debate during the 1970s, and their ideas were included in most management training programs. McGregor described two types of managers, a "Theory X" manager who focused primarily on tasks, processes, and outcomes, and a "Theory Y" manager who was focused on people, teams, and relationships. The work of Robert Blake and Jane Mouton also described the convergence of a focusing on task and focusing on people in The Managerial Grid—a set of boxes in which the ultimate manager was described as "9, 9" because he or she focused on both task and people with equal importance.

Other ideas emerged during this period that impacted the work of development professionals. Peter Drucker described The Effective Executive as a combination of the "hard" and "soft" in terms every manager could relate to. Hersey and Blanchard's seminal work on *Situational Leadership* did not prescribe a consistent approach to leadership but argued that situations required different approaches or the application of unique skills. What served the leader in one set of circumstances may fail under a different set of circumstances.

Ken Blanchard extended his earlier work on Situational Leadership by identifying the essence of what good managers do in the shortest period in *The One-Minute Manager*. This book popularized the impact of engaging individual employees and the power of the "soft" approach. A best seller that has been amazingly resilient, the "one-minute manager" spends time with people and tries to find people "doing something right" so he or she can acknowledge them.

IBM

Probably the paragon of leadership development in this post-world war era was IBM. In the IBM of the 1950s and 1960s, the issues were clear: Grow with the market, deliver a reasonable return, invest in the community, and provide life-long employment for satisfied employees. IBM created a leadership development model that leaned heavily on prescribed training. The idea was to spend a minimum of forty hours per year in leadership training that would produce exactly the type of leader previously produced by the same training. IBM was in the business of making high-tech machines that people bought; the customer had little real power to choose, and the organization worked well as a top-down, disciplined, and hierarchical company. In the 1970s, we both taught leadership seminars at IBM with at least sixty people. With only one exception, every person in the room wore a dark blue suit, white shirt, and tie. Women obviously didn't wear this because there were none in the program. IBM, along with much of the corporate world at the time, had a corporate uniform; leaders attended the corporate university and learned to adhere to the corporate line.

In 1960, at the end of his tenure as CEO, Tom Watson, Jr., gave a series of lectures on leadership at Columbia University that were later published. To read these lectures today is to be taken back in history to a much different time. It was a period when manufacturers could rely on their unique technologies to create demand wherein a sense demand exceeded supply. International meant selling your products around the world by having a sales force in major business centers. Watson spends the better part of one chapter describing the power of "corporate culture" and training to shape a company and its leadership.

General Electric

Another positive example of effective leadership development during this period is GE. In 1956, GE created the first corporate "university" in America at Crotonville, New York, to meet the company's growing demand for general managers. Early attendees were a reflection of that time period. All were men and many were veterans. The knowledge required to lead a GE business was found in seventeen "Blue Books" (so-called because of the color of their hardbound covers). The format for instruction was borrowed directly from Harvard and other business schools. Based largely on lecture and case study methods, it taught the GE approach to a multitude of problems. Perhaps nothing exemplifies the culture of post-war organizations so much as the length of the Crotonville program—three months, during which time participants were expected to visit their homes and families on only one weekend. This was a disciplined group!

A Changing Reality: The Emergence of the "New" Leadership Model

The period of the 1970s and early 1980s was altered by a new business reality. It was a time of "oil shocks" and a rising tide of competition for American manufacturers from Europe, and especially Japan. Some of the first industries to feel the new global competition were textiles, consumer electronics, and automobiles. This challenge led to a questioning of leadership practices. New ideas coming out of Japan, such as quality circles, lean manufacturing, "just-in-time" inventories, "Theory Z" and consensus-driven management, cross-functional integration, and Six Sigma began to impact how we developed leaders. The insight that corporations also create a culture that influences and shapes leadership behavior, rather than vice versa, was first described by Terrance Deal and Alan Kennedy in their book *Corporate Cultures*. Strong leaders, with an understanding of an organization's culture, could take leadership action to change the culture, but it was not easy. Many American companies had evolved stagnant cultures that inhibited change and adaptation to new competition.

Thus was born the idea of a "heroic leader"—one that could create transformational change in an organization. As iconic U.S. companies suddenly went adrift, a new generation of business leaders emerged who were celebrated in the media and focused attention on the role of the leader as a visionary and transformational change agent. Among these visionary leaders were Lee Iacocca, Jack Welch, Roger Enrico, and Lou Gerstner.

Perhaps Welch best defined this generation of visionary leadership. At first scorned by business schools and the popular business press as "Neutron Jack," he became their darling and the source of numerous articles, case studies, and books (including two of his own). At one point, it was unusual to sit through a discussion on leadership without someone pointing to what "Jack" would do in this situation. But the reality is that this was a rich period in executive and leadership development. GE experimented with large scale strategic and cultural change, the "boundary-less" organization, "work-out" as a form of employee empowerment, thoughtful career planning through the "Session C" process, action learning, and linking performance and values to individual assessments.

The GE of the 1990s under Jack Welch was revolutionary in developing leaders; the leadership school focused on strategy, change, developing people, 360-degree feedback, action learning, lateral relationships, networking—major contributions that continue to have an impact today. In many ways, the leadership development models of this "softer revolution" have so impacted the current field of executive development—and much of what we considered state-of-the-art from GE, PepsiCo, and other pioneers in the field—that we are now missing the next revolution that may be happening around us.

What We Can Learn From the Past

When confronting the complexities and challenges of today, the revolution of the 1980s is considered old news. In past eras, when companies sent leaders to school, either external university-based or internal, they sent the individual. Such training may have helped the individual, but it wasn't necessarily focused on the company's systemic issues, business drivers, execution challenges, leadership tradeoffs, or even growth challenges. In some cases, executive development became so focused on programs, events, and the softer side of business that it produced leaders with great people skills and very little business acumen. In one company, an annual senior leadership program became regarded as a mark of a certain level of achievement—something that a senior leader was entitled to attend at a certain point. Attendees saw it as a great opportunity to network—something that can be very positive, certainly, but an activity that may not provide a lot of impact to the business. One CEO of a Fortune 50 company, catching this trend and wanting to keep up, sought us out to design and deliver a senior executive program he termed "Wart Removal."

His goal was to produce more nice people who could get along with each other in the increasingly contentious atmosphere his industry was facing.

The truth is that much of leadership development today does tend to remove warts and in the process stamp out the character and uniqueness that made leaders stand out and produce results in the past. Winston Churchill or Harry Truman probably wouldn't make it today at Wells Fargo, General Motors, or IBM. Such entities have a tendency to expect their leaders to be codified—uniform. Global monoliths like Toyota, IBM, and Wal-Mart now struggle with a core paradox: How to gain adherence to the culture while constantly challenging it. Conformity enables speed, discipline, and alignment—and may ensure that the unchallenged business model dies.

In our experience, most large companies still err on the side of conformity. Walk into any global company's senior executive leadership program and look around: People dress alike, talk alike, and even think alike. Thirty years ago, such an approach enabled a company to grow and thrive; today, it can be dangerous. Leaders who don't want to be codified will leave. They'll drop out of a huge corporation (especially women) and do their own thing, start up a new company, or find a company with a more attractive culture. Challenges to the business that allow a company to jump on the next growth curve will go unspoken.

The New Revolution

This is the new revolution we are facing in leadership development today: Business models and technology are changing so fast, customers have so much more power, and people have so many choices, that our old approaches to defining competencies, putting people in classrooms, uncovering their flaws, and fixing them seem increasingly disconnected to what is happening in business. Our challenge is to discover how we as executive development professionals take our rich intellectual, theoretical, and practical approaches and mold them into revolutionary changes in leadership, innovation, and execution that respond adequately to the various needs and drivers of today's business.

Most boards and CEOs today recognize that everything is for sale: Technology, market share, brand, scale—and virtually all companies have access to the same capital. The one thing that can't be bought is a cadre of committed, capable leaders who uphold a company's values. That must be built. What differentiates the winners is a strong leadership pool with the ability to attract, develop, and retain talent. We're invited to help shape the next revolution in business and leadership—provided we can become contemporary, real, and driven by results, growth, and returns.

What is the shape of this third revolution we're facing? How can we be part of the action and not living in a parallel universe? How can we develop the business instincts that create effectiveness while maintaining a focus on leadership success? How can we acknowledge the strengths and weaknesses of our field without becoming defensive and pretending we have more answers than we do? Some of these issues are contained in the articles in this book—real dilemmas and paradoxes that are at the heart of our profession. Can real leaders be "made," or not? How can we be effective going forward, so we're contemporary, real, and contributing in valuable ways?

We are the recipients of a large reservoir of practice and experience. One of the criticisms often leveled at development professionals is that we constantly jump from trend to trend—"the flavor of the day." So let's look back and investigate what our legacy is—what practices and experiences we can use as we go forward into this new global economy. While there can be a lot of debate as which tools or perspectives should be highlighted, we offer six for your consideration.

The Work Done by the Center for Creative Leadership

Anyone working in the field of talent and executive development today is shaped by the research conducted by the Center for Creative Leadership in the early 1980s. How do people develop and learn the skills they need to be successful? They learn by doing. How do you develop people? You develop people by giving them challenging work that stretches them. Work is developmental, but some work, like "start-ups," "fix-its," and moves to new geographies working with new people and new cultures, are powerful developers of people. The conclusions drawn from this study were the need to plan and manage careers through "talent review" and succession planning and influenced the creation of many succession planning processes in large companies.

Feedback and 360-Degree Feedback

Writing in the *Harvard Business Review* about five years ago, the late Peter Drucker spoke on all of the fads and trends he had seen in his long career. Many were just plain silly, he said, but providing feedback to people, especially 360-degree feedback, could be very helpful. Feedback can cause us to address issues that we may not even be aware of because hierarchical organizations tend to stifle honest upward communication. No one wakes up in the morning with the intention of doing a bad job. We go to work, often with the best of intentions, yet things do not always happen the way we would like. It is feedback that makes us aware of these gaps and allows us to address them.

Coaching

Coaching has become a mini-revolution in delivering learning to the learner "just in time, just for you." In the late 1990s coaches proliferated because they could customize feedback and learning and because they provided a more efficient way to learn than sitting in management training programs. Coaching was also tied to work assignments, because challenging assignments could be made more valuable by providing coaching, and the best coaching opportunities are frequently from the immediate supervisor. Effective coaching provides support for reflection and attention to what is being learned. By listening, asking probing questions, and sharing experiences, a good coach or supervisor helps turn work into a developmental experience.

Action Learning

Action learning is learning by doing. If the best learning happens on the job, you may not be able to give executives all the experiences required through formal job moves. It is possible, however, to structure learning experiences in such a way that people do have a significant experience that will shape them as leaders. Action learning creates learning by setting up a unique environment in which learners must model behaviors and values needed back on the job. Learners are encouraged to reflect on their actions, to develop a point of view on what needs to change in themselves or their companies, and to determine how those changes can be accomplished.

In the late 1980s and early 1990s, GE realized that its future growth depended on markets outside of the United States. At the time only 17 percent of gross sales were outside the U.S. market. The irony is that this transition would be lead primarily by leadership within a U.S.-based company. At that time, nearly all executive development was done outside of the United States by giving participants action learning projects (e.g., How do we enter the lighting market in Western Europe? How do we enter the medical imaging business in India?). Projects were done in teams of people who were held accountable for their recommendations. Today, over 50 percent of GE's sales are outside the United States. Over time, GE systematically developed global leaders and a global mindset. Action learning was a part of this process of developing a "global mindset."

Emotional Intelligence

More recently, leadership development has been significantly impacted by the idea of emotional intelligence. Building on the earlier work of McGregor and Blake and Mouton, Daniel Goleman defined specific attributes that he proved were equal or more important than innate intelligence in getting things done in organizations and in life. He raised the question: Why do really intelligent people sometimes fail miserably in organizations? His explanation of emotional intelligence is a reminder that leadership begins with a personal understanding of one's self and the impact we have on others.

The Work of Ram Charan

To the ideas cited above we would add the work of Ram Charan. Charan, the co-author of *Execution* and author of *What the CEO Wants You to Know* and most recently *Know How*, reminds us to stay focused on the reality of business leadership—creating a profitable business. In his practical, common sense approach, Charan keeps us focused on the business side of leadership. While acknowledging the importance of people and "social architecture," he continually brings us back to the need to understand the core of business and especially how it makes money. According to Charan, the fundamental question for leaders is: "What is the business engine? At the gut level, how are we going to make money?" He suggests that the leadership pendulum may have traveled too far in the direction of people issues and must now swing back more in the direction of an understanding of the business and its key drivers.

We have only highlighted a few of the research tools, books, and ideas that have shaped the field of executive development today. What belongs on the list can be debated. But what we should not forget is that professionals in the field today have a legacy of practice and experience—a "theory of the case" that rivals that of Finance and engineering. It has been a field with a changing perspective, shaped by the requirements of the day—from a beginning focused on "hard" business tools to the inclusion of softer issues focusing on leading people, managing change, and understanding cultures. The common theme has been finding an advantage that leads to increased performance. The trends and influences that will shape executive development in the future are now altering the work environment and shaping the nature of global competition. It is to these transformational forces that we now need to turn our attention.

Creating Leaders for a Changing World

The turn of the millennium has introduced leadership challenges never before faced by business professionals. The spirit of the day is one of performance, of meeting expectations quarter after quarter. No CEO can feel secure from demanding analysts and shareholders. The focus today is on growth, performance, innovation, and new markets, and the demand is for leaders who can execute. In fact, one of the most successful books of this new era is *Execution* by Larry Bossidy and Ram Charan.

CEOs are in a bind when it comes to leadership development. There is no question that they value their leadership pipelines. When all companies have access to basically the same technology and financial resources, leadership is a competitive differentiator and is often the difference between winning and losing. But when it comes to leadership development initiatives and programs, what proof do CEOs have that current programs are effective? For many there seems to be a weak link between company performance and resources expended on leadership development.

CEOs today believe that leadership development is critical to the success of their organizations, but have a deep skepticism about the ability of current leadership development practices to deliver results. Let us illustrate with an example. One of our clients, a $5 billion global company, has seen dramatic changes in recent months. As part of an initiative to upgrade the talent in this organization, the new CEO began a search for a "Global Head of Talent and Organization Development." The CEO hired one of the best search firms in the world, and the firm presented three candidates. Two have Ph.D.s in organizational psychology from good universities and backgrounds in consulting, academics, and training. The third candidate has a BA in business and is a senior HR person with a track record as a proven generalist. Although this third candidate may appear to be the least qualified on paper, this is the candidate who caught the CEO's eye.

Why did this CEO select the third person over more highly qualified professionals in the field of leadership development? This candidate has proven line experience, a demonstrated ability to assess people as members of a business team, and an understanding of business issues from a strategic perspective.

This company's selection has broad implications for executive development as a whole. As a field of professionals, we need to develop a reputation as business partners—people who understand the strategy, the business model ("How do we make money?"), and can make difficult assessments of talent. Business is about results.

In this second edition of the *Pfeiffer Annual: Leadership Development* we want to ask some tough questions of ourselves as practicing professionals: Where are we as a profession today? What are our strengths? What are our weaknesses? What new tools and techniques will help us develop future leaders? What tools do we currently use that are worth holding onto? More than thirty experienced practitioners, academics, and consultants have contributed their insights.

Leadership development occurs in a context; it is a reflection of the business demands of the day. Next we want to explore some of the emerging trends in business and speculate on their implications for development professionals.

Some Observations About the Current State of Leadership Development

In our experience with global companies who want to develop leaders at various levels in the organization, we've noticed a trend: Leadership development initiatives are often—even usually—undertaken by very professional people who do excellent work—but fulfill the wrong agenda.

Leadership development professionals are often people who have degrees in psychology or a related field (for example, organizational psychology or industrial psychology) who have become unusually competent in organizational change theory and individual, professional development practices. However, what these professionals lack is something that is at the center of their client's world: An innate desire to make money, grow a business, and win. Many people are attracted to HR and leadership development because they "like people," not because they like "making money." As a result, leadership development experts often operate in a parallel universe. In their world, learning theory, the latest trends in management thinking, and incremental improvements in behavior and communication are valued. In their client's universe, what matters is an in-depth knowledge and understanding of business as an enterprise and a focus on competitive advantage—what works, now—with little investment of time and money. We have noticed that when this gap prevails, investments in leadership development most often go awry. Without a real anchor in the "business engine," leadership development is tolerated, but not embraced. Commitment is acted out, but not internalized. Leaders learn, but don't really change.

Why does it matter whether leadership development professionals have the business instincts, experience, and drive to match the right degrees and publishing credits? Because in business, it's always been about results, and as global competition intensifies, demand for effective leaders, not "textbook approaches to leadership programs," is trumping everything else. If leadership development and talent initiatives are to gain investment and support, the business as an enterprise, the board of directors, the CEO, and the team all need to see measurable impact on growth, execution, globalization, and financial performance.

As a field with deep roots in social science research, we've emphasized talking to each other about our best practices. We've excelled at going to conferences, reading about each other's success, and focusing on competencies. We become good at helping people understand their personalities, their strengths, and their flaws and at helping them to resolve conflict and interpersonal issues. When we're really confronted with the one question on the mind of business leaders today—"How do you measure your results?"—we demur, even fumble. "Trust us," we say. "We know this works; it just takes time."

What we aren't so great at is helping people understand the basics of business, selecting leaders who have the instinct to win, and helping organizations solve business issues first, rather than social science engineering.

In today's business climate, there is a greater focus on performance than ever before; shareholders and analysts are demanding that leadership teams perform and deliver consistently and in acceptable numbers. Leaders are being held accountable in greater numbers than ever; CEO tenure is shorter than ever, primarily due to impatience at insufficient results. In the recent past, CEOs of Merck, BMS, BP, Ford, Morgan Stanley, Home Depot, HP, and many others have faced the judgment of shareholders and been shown the door. CEOs feel the pressure. In most leadership development programs we run today, one characteristic seems to trump all others: Accountability. Even a large pharmaceutical company in Europe includes in its corporate vision a goal of providing a return to shareholders—right along with its vision to improve, extend, and save the lives of people. In an industry in which there is a focus on helping people, the dynamic importance of performance is still recognized.

Emerging Business Trends That Influence Our Industry

To understand the parameters of the current revolution in business, we think it is important to look around and see the most important signals coming from the environment. We see six major trends that are revolutionizing business and leadership today:

1. ***Digitalization:*** People worldwide download music, news, and various media from the Internet; trade stocks and manage investments online; and interact through blogs and online communities in ways that leaders of even ten years ago could not imagine. The result is summed up in *Time* magazine's "Person of the Year" for 2006—every person who creates, reads, and contributes to online content around the world. Corporate executives have begun blogging, providing a new method for interaction between levels of an organization and even the customer. In three years, Google has become a verb, a noun, and one of the highest market cap companies in the world. Companies such as American Express are buying real estate on Second Life for avatars to conduct business. Communities of interest are new constituencies for banks, pharmaceutical companies, car drivers, and almost every other type of end-user imaginable.

    Unfortunately, some leaders are unequipped to respond to this kind of worldwide digitalization and global community. Today's workforce expects to be involved, engaged, and empowered to make changes, and leaders who don't understand that they don't control information or events and embrace this digitalization will fail.

2. ***Globalization:*** As markets, economies, and companies continue to global-ize, leadership requirements become more complex, nuanced, and demand-ing. Now, many senior leaders in large companies have experience working outside their countries of origin. In the United States, recent immigrants con-stitute large segments of the entrepreneurial, customer, and employee classes. Leaders must be equipped to respond to the great variety of cultures and communities of a worldwide economy. They have to be able and willing to work across cultural differences with confidence. Culture is inextricably linked with business and will be an inescapable component of effective leadership in almost any setting. Without acknowledging it and learning to leverage it, leaders will fail.

3. ***Customer Power:*** The Internet has given the customer real power through the ability to acquire more information and opportunities to compare and choose. In the post-war world, demand exceeded supply and business didn't have to be as responsive. Now, supply exceeds demand; customers have access to research tools and information in greater quantities than ever, resulting in an upended organizational pyramid. At the top now sit shareholders, custom-ers, and clients—all of whom have the final say on any substantial course of action. The power of the customer is changing the old command/con-trol structure, creating a workforce that does not want to be part of an old bureaucratic organization and a customer base that is truly calling the shots. Organizations that don't respond by empowering their employees to genuinely take care of customers have no future.

4. ***Emphasis on Performance:*** In a throwback to an earlier era, we see a renewed emphasis on performance, results, and accountability in companies, but not in a command-and-control environment. Shareholders and analysts want to see results; they scrutinize expenditures, including executive compensation, with new information and vigor and challenge leadership development investments that aren't linked to business strategy and don't demonstrate results.

5. ***More Lateral, Complex, Adaptive Organizational Contexts:*** With the rapidity of information today, much of what is done in the business world is lateral—across organizational, cultural, and even time boundaries. The old metaphor for an organization was a machine: Organized, rational, planful, and disciplined. The new metaphor is an organism: Growing, adapting, problem solving, even shape-shifting. Hierarchy isn't disappearing, but it is becoming less important, and more lateral structures where people come together regardless of rank or status to solve problems and do the job are emerging. Increasingly, it's the information that's important—not the title of the person who has it.

6. ***Involving More Women and People of Color in the Upper Levels of Business:*** While women are being more effectively used in management today than in the past, we're still not seeing them climb to the levels we should expect to see. As in decades past, we still see that we're cutting ourselves off from a very valuable supply of talent by not effectively using the unique strengths and talents of half the world's labor supply—women and people who don't look, act, and think like the dominant culture. This trend requires some analysis: What isn't happening that needs to happen? We posit that many women may feel unable to find outlets for integrating their whole life experiences into the corporate world, and many simply start their own businesses to find careers that provide the rewards they are looking for.

All of these trends have contributed to creating a world that moves very fast in which leaders have to make decisions in an instant and workers are expected to do what needs to be done without waiting for instruction or delegation. Increasingly, we need leaders at all levels of the organization—people who can act intelligently, understand strategy, take tactical steps that help the organization win, serve customers in rapid way, and are at home anywhere in world.

SECTION 2

DEFINING THE FIELD

To define the field of leadership development, we first have to define leadership. In this section, our contributors discuss what it means to be a leader and how leadership development fits into that picture. Stephen Rhinesmith asks, "Why are there not enough leaders in companies today?" Robert Stringer discusses who "owns" leadership development. As Ram Charan points out, leadership is about results and outcomes, not just style, and this frequently requires a focus on basics. Tim Sullivan asks a key question (and answers it): We know that leadership is important, but why isn't the profession of developing leaders more central to the action in companies today?

Why Are There Not Enough Leaders in Companies Today? by Stephen H. Rhinesmith

Who Really "Owns" Leadership Development? by Robert A. Stringer

Developing Leaders of Substance, by Ram Charan

Why Is Leadership So Important and Formal Leadership Development Not? by Tim Sullivan

CHAPTER 2

WHY ARE THERE NOT ENOUGH LEADERS IN COMPANIES TODAY?

Stephen H. Rhinesmith

Complex times require complete leaders. Partial leaders struggle during an era of paradox, ambiguity, and unpredictability. To employ a one-dimensional leadership approach may have worked in simpler times, but in an environment of moral complexity and rapid shifts in attitude, social and political circumstances, economic conditions, and technology, leaders must be capable of using their head, their heart, and their guts as situations demand.

Business leaders have been extremely savvy in delivering short-term results, but they have not demonstrated the inner fortitude and courage to consistently do the right thing in the face of competing stakeholder needs, the constant pressure for performance, and the requirement to keep people engaged and motivated at work. In other words, our leaders often rely exclusively on a single quality—head *or* heart *or* guts. If all leaders are trying to do is demonstrate their analytical rigor, they may come across as insensitive and unethical.

The Mercer Delta Executive Learning Center conducted a recent survey with the Economist Intelligence Unit to learn the primary concerns of 223 global executives throughout the world. They reported increased competitive pressures, lack of capacity to respond to changing market conditions and a failure to innovate to meet customers' demands as key issues. These are not surprising results.

What was surprising was that 90 percent believed they did not have the leadership bench strength to meet competitive demands, and more than 75 percent said they did not believe they had the leadership talent to meet the remaining challenges. Seventy-two percent said they had plans to develop a new cadre of leaders, but had not yet done so.

Drivers of Whole Leadership

There are a wide range of reasons why companies face difficulties finding competent leaders to deal with a world characterized by complexity, diversity, and ambiguity. Five issues that I and my colleagues at Mercer Delta have seen as key to the leadership crisis are growth, innovation, global interdependence, execution, and rising expectations. Consider the following:

Growth

A good strategy (**head**) goes nowhere without leaders who are willing to balance the risks and rewards of bold competitive steps (**guts**). Many leaders who assumed their positions in the mid-1990s when cost-cutting was seen to be the key antidote to the excesses of the 1980s found themselves paralyzed by the risks they were required to take in "reinventing" their companies for growth. Furthermore, many companies that had grown through acquisitions also faced the challenge of organic growth, requiring leaders who not only had good strategic instincts for M&A, but who were also tough enough to determine which products and which customers were not profitable enough to grow the company at the pace required by Wall Street. The demand for continuous top and bottom-line organic growth has raised the bar dramatically on leadership skills in the last decade.

Innovation

Creativity is having a unique perspective on a situation (**head**). Innovation is driving a new perspective through a resisting system (**heart** and **guts**). Many companies have found in recent years that, to be competitive, innovation must extend beyond the R&D group. Innovation today requires the reinvention, resizing, and reprocessing of all aspects of a business. Leaders must make complex tradeoffs between retaining those elements of the business that will be key to the future while jettisoning those assets that will hinder its growth.

When I was CEO of one organization, people used to ask the proverbial question: What kept me up at night? My response was that I knew that I had to change an organization that over fifty years had been built on five basic principles.

I knew that three of the five had to change and had made a decision. What kept me up was that I didn't know whether I had made the right decision—and if I was wrong, the organization would probably face a very dire future.

Tough decisions with complex tradeoffs in uncertain times requires guts—the ability to make decisions based on clear vision and values—and less than perfect data.

Global Interdependence

Leaders must appreciate the knowledge, skills, and attributes valued by different societies (**heart**). In addition to managing the ambiguity of change and innovation, today's leaders must also be sensitive to the demands of multiple stakeholders throughout the world. There is hardly a company of any size that does not have some global dependence on foreign markets for sales, new product development, or cost saving strategies of outsourcing and offshoring.

Developing leaders with a more "global mindset" has been one of the most challenging tasks of CEOs and boards of directors. There may be an increasing number of young leaders (those under forty) with a global mindset, but many leaders over fifty who are candidates to lead global companies lack the depth and experience in foreign markets and global management necessary for today's worldwide marketplace.

While having a global mindset requires a good strategic sense of the global business (**head**), the real key to global success is understanding and appreciating the perspective of customers, suppliers, and employees from different cultural traditions. Leading a business in a global world requires the empathy to identify with many different viewpoints—key characteristics of "global" emotional intelligence (**heart**), or the ability to understand one's self and others within the global context. (See our article titled Developing Global Emotional Intelligence).

Complexity of Execution

Getting things done requires understanding the details of the business (**head**), standing up for what one believes is right (**guts**), and supporting other people to change their behavior (**heart**)—the whole leader.

There was a period during the 1970s and 1980s when there was a debate about "leadership" versus "management." "Leaders" were characterized as people with vision who stayed above operations and articulated the values and direction for the company. "Managers," on the other hand, were "operational" people who were to "get the job done" and keep the place running.

All that changed in the 1990s when growth strategies needed to be accompanied by cost reductions and the winning strategy changed to businesses that could do "more with less." When this happened, CEOs needed to be on top of the details. No longer could a leader afford to "stay above the business."

Rising Expectations

Most people today expect more than one-dimensional leadership; they expect intellectual challenge (**head**), emotional support (**heart**), and clear vision and values (**guts**) from their leaders. From Wall Street to boards of directors to employees, people are asking for whole leaders who can effectively meet the challenges of leadership in today's complex, diverse, and ambiguous world. These expectations reside not just in the United States, but in countries throughout the world, as technology enables people to participate in global discussions and cross-fertilization of ideas and lifestyles change expectations and requirements for leadership in country after country.

Companies will need to "raise the leadership bar" not only for their CEOs, but for leaders at all levels of the leadership pipeline. Leaders who have the capacity to use their heads, hearts, and guts appropriately will be in great demand. Let's look at some of the skills and characteristics needed.

What Is a "Whole" Leader?

Leading with head, heart, and guts requires a set of leadership requirements that are difficult to develop. It demands more than mastery of skills; it requires a leader to act with character as a human being. Becoming a mature, whole leader doesn't mean becoming one-third head, one-third heart, and one-third guts. Everyone has a different leadership style. It does, however, mean considering options that might not fit naturally with one's own style, in order to gather all the intelligence, empathy, and courage necessary to make decisions.

Whole leaders are able to anticipate and quickly respond to the needs of their companies and colleagues because they'll have simultaneously mastered how to use their heads, listen to their hearts, and act with guts.

The head, hearts. and guts framework accelerates an otherwise lengthy maturation process, and produces leaders who

- Are smart,
- Possess good people skills, and
- Have the courage of their convictions.

Being "smart" has traditionally been viewed as the most important element of leadership. This one-dimensional approach may have worked in simpler times, but as Jeff Skilling and the Enron culture has proven, being smart does not necessarily provide guidance for ethical decisions. Whole leaders with the right combination of cognitive skills, emotional intelligence, and decision-making knowledge are the only ones who will succeed in managing the rapid-fire challenges of businesses today and tomorrow.

The three mission-critical management qualities—head, heart, and guts—are described in more detail below:

Head

The "head" can be described as "intellectual intelligence" (providing strategy, direction, and purpose). Business leaders have led primarily with their heads. These types of leaders analyze a situation, absorb the data, and decide among rational alternatives. But today the necessary head skills are

- Rethinking the way things are done around here,
- Reforming boundaries when necessary,
- Getting things done, and
- Developing and articulating a point of view

Heart

The "heart" can be described as "emotional intelligence" (understanding, working with, and developing others). Leaders who have used their hearts to manage have traditionally possessed emotional maturity, the capacity to create trust, and the flexibility to work with a range of people. But today this must be augmented by:

- Balancing people needs with business requirements,
- Delivering integrated solutions though trust,
- Working with and developing people from diverse cultures, and
- Overcoming potential personal derailers when working with others

Guts

"Guts" can be described as "courage" (doing the right thing based on clear values). Guts leaders have demonstrated tenacity, persistence, and the ability to overcome obstacles that get in their way. They make tough, but necessary, decisions regarding everything from people to product lines and do what is right, even when it might not be the most expedient or popular solution. Today, the traditional "guts" leaders need to also exhibit:

- Taking risks with little or no data,
- Balancing risk and reward, and
- Acting with unyielding integrity

Putting It All Together

Many a fast-track CEO career has been short-circuited by the lack of one or more "head," "heart," and "guts" traits. Heart-oriented managers, for example, are often seen as "soft," not tough enough to make the really difficult business decisions and are shuffled off to a "safe" position in human resources. Gut-oriented leaders like Al Dunlap eventually self-destruct because they lack the long-term strategic view and tend to alienate too many influential constituents.

Partial leaders can succeed in the short term:

- **Head** leaders use analysis and logic to dominate a business.
- **Heart** leaders inspire people through personal connectivity to obtain loyalty and commitment.
- **Guts** leaders make bold moves that excite their people and attract the attention of shareholders.

In the long run, however, there are risks to using only one approach:

- **Head** leaders fail to understand the impact of their actions and under-value the people side of the business.
- **Heart** leaders develop people, but may lose sight of tough choices that need to be made for success in the marketplace.
- **Guts** leaders become too caught up in the drama of bold moves, or stay the course long after it is relevant.

Integrating head, heart, and guts into leadership will provide mature, whole leaders who are capable of making flexible, situational, and effective leadership decisions.

The Problem with Partial Effectiveness

I do not want to convey the impression that partial leaders are incapable of succeeding. We have worked with many brilliant senior executives who have led teams that formulated and implemented highly profitable strategies.

Smart people can often come up with innovative ideas that result in successful products and services. They can analyze data, devise partnerships and alliances, and use raw brainpower in a hundred different ways to lead their organizations.

Sometimes the context dictates head leadership. For example, companies may be market leaders that (for the moment, at least) need a CEO who is a strong strategic thinker and is financially astute. Or it may be that the situation dictates another type of partial leadership. Not-for-profits, for instance, used to be run by heart-focused CEOs because they strived to be people-oriented companies first and money-making companies second, with the result that fund raising and other expenses went up and credibility went down.

If situations never changed, partial leadership would be fine. As we all know, however, things change faster than we could ever have imagined. Because our current environment is rife with change and complex demands, the partial approach exposes a leader's Achilles' heel. When people are weak in one or two of the three areas of whole leadership, they eventually end up in situations in which they lack the range of options to deal with their challenges effectively.

Recognizing That Different Combinations of Head, Heart, and Guts Are Needed in Different Situations

Some jobs require more heart than guts; some assignments demand more head than heart. The mix of head, heart, and guts is different for a leadership team that is resizing a business than it is for a chief executive expanding into new markets. It's important to design a process with these situational requirements in mind.

In *The Leadership Pipeline* by Ram Charan, Steve Drotter, and Jim Noel, the authors make the point that, as people move thorough different levels in an organization, they must adjust their behaviors and their value orientations accordingly. The skills and values at an individual contributor level, for instance, are quite different from those at a first-time manager level.

One change a first-time manager needs to make is to value the contributions of others rather than focus on his or her own performance. The authors emphasize that it is not just acquiring a new group of skills and values that is necessary, but letting go of skills and values that made the manager successful at an earlier level.

To develop people effectively, consider how head, heart, and guts manifest themselves at different organizational levels:

Head

- Level 1 (first-line supervisor): Learning technical skills
- Level 2 (manager of managers): Coordinating horizontal people and projects
- Level 3 (executive): Creating strategy

Heart

- Level 1: Managing one-on-one relationships
- Level 2: Coaching, nurturing talent, and aligning teams
- Level 3: Managing complexity, dealing with personal derailers, handling ambiguity

Guts

- Level 1: Giving tough feedback and dealing with other tough performance-management issues
- Level 2: Managing conflict among units, allocating resources, taking the risk to speak up
- Level 3: Making the tough calls (closing plants, redeploying assets and resources, and so on)

These descriptions of levels are clearly generalized, and you may find that you need to make adjustments based on a more detailed delineation of levels or the particular requirements in your company. Although the general development goal is to help people integrate these three types of behaviors, the more specific goal is to help them integrate the right mix of behaviors.

Developing Whole Leaders

Guts is an umbrella term for the quality that has been missing: a willingness to do the right thing, no matter how difficult that is. It became clear to us that leaders who combine the capacity to exhibit courage with cognitive and emotional intelligence are best able to deal with the complexities that organizations face today. It isn't guts in the sense of reckless risk taking that is important; rather, it is the willingness to take risks, based on strong beliefs and values.

This insight is not new or unique, but it is needed now more than ever. Executives in all types of companies facing all types of different situations quickly saw that the head, heart, and guts ideal, however described, was worth trying to select for, coach toward, and develop.

How can companies effectively develop whole leaders? A "head-only" leader won't become a whole leader by taking a course in ethics or receiving coaching on integrity. A "heart leader" isn't going to start taking the right risks by going through a rocks-and-ropes course. Development must be ongoing and multifaceted—a combination of experience, training, and coaching.

Leaders who want to grow beyond their "leadership comfort zones" must use a variety of methods to enhance and develop their skills as whole leaders. Standard executive education programs that use case studies and other methods to focus on building analytical skills are valuable in developing executives who are smart and understand what needs to be done to enable their companies to compete effectively in the marketplace. At the end of a course, we can measure how smart they are through tests of knowledge.

Over the last twenty years, we have developed 360-degree-based training, testing, and coaching to help executives develop emotional intelligence—to listen to themselves and others and be able to respond to changing needs around them in ways that are constructive rather than destructive. Emotional intelligence can be learned. We are not born with basic emotional intelligence like IQ—we can develop EQ through focused diagnosis and personal development.

However, very little has been done from a leadership perspective to develop "guts," which is increasingly receiving focus as a key leadership factor in today's complex and multifaceted world.

Finding the "Edge" Beyond Leadership Comfort Zones

The development of "guts" is largely uncharted territory because conventional wisdom has held that courage and values can't be taught. These traits are generally believed to be formed through overcoming adversity. Overcoming adversity in the workplace and in one's personal life may provide transitions that can make or break a leader, which are often viewed as character-building experiences. Take, for example, Rudi Giuliani. His defining moment as a great leader was his management of New York City following 9/11. Known before 9/11 as a "head" leader, he rose to the occasion and was able to use his heart and guts to guide the city and world through a time of fear and uncertainty. He became a symbol of courage and compassion.

In the end the most important part of "guts" is *character*. Leaders with strong character know who they are, what they stand for, as well as what values they are willing to articulate and defend. Kevin Cashman, author of *Leadership from the Inside Out*, distinguishes between persona and character as follows: "Persona is acting based on what others expect of you, and character is acting based on what you believe is right. Integrity, then, is all about character and transparency—letting people see the real you." In companies in which leaders exhibit integrity, the result is a high level of confidence and commitment that energizes the entire workplace.

The Mercer Delta study revealed that companies use different methods to reach the three leadership qualities.

Training for Head

I have already noted that traditional business education has stressed the development of analytical rigor and basic business knowledge. This kind of training is still relevant and important. Business executives today must have a grasp of all aspects of a business, from finance to IT, marketing and sales, R&D, manufacturing and HR.

In the Mercer Delta study, 65 percent of the companies responding used custom-designed programs to broaden the knowledge of their executives. These are programs developed by business schools and usually aimed at senior executives involved in developing company strategy.

At lower levels of the organization, 68 percent of the companies use self-directed learning for employees and managers to work at their own pace in courses that are relevant to their particular business or functional area.

These knowledge and skill-building courses remain key to all companies in the development of leaders at all levels who have the requisite abilities to carry out their organizational and functional responsibilities.

Coaching for Heart

With Daniel Goleman's introduction of "emotional intelligence," most leaders of major companies have begun to understand the need for more empathy and ability to relate to their customers, employees, and suppliers. The interpersonal side of business has become increasingly important, especially in the international arena, where relationship-oriented cultures place a premium on working with people they enjoy and trust.

As a result, 360-degree feedback has grown as the primary methodology for enabling executives to understand how their leadership is viewed by others. Over 65 percent of the companies surveyed deploy some form of 360-degree feedback as a means of sensitizing their executives to their behavior and the impact it has on others.

On a more personal bass, 51 percent of the companies report using executive coaches. This is a trend that has grown enormously over the last decade. In the early days of executive coaching, it was seen as a remedial activity to save an executive from failing, but today many well-known companies are offering executive coaches to members of their executive committees and their high potentials.

Experiences for Guts

As I noted earlier, there is general agreement that "guts" cannot be taught in a classroom. It is a quality that is developed through career planning and some action-oriented real-life experience.

Of the companies in the Mercer Delta survey, 62 percent used action learning and coaching to develop more clearly defined values for decision making. These activities, in which teams of executives work on the most pressing strategic issues facing their companies, are focused on increasing their understanding of the complexity of executive decision making and the difficult tradeoffs that come with increased scope of responsibility.

The second and equally popular way of developing leaders with broad experience and clear values has been through stretch assignments. In the survey, 55 percent of the companies use career-pathing and stretch assignments to push leaders to operate outside their comfort zone and learn from experience.

It is clear that there is much work for training professionals to do to develop leadership strategies that are "wholistic." The increasing need for leaders with head, heart, and guts demands that new methods be developed to help executives deal with a world of complexity, diversity, and ambiguity. This will require everyone, including the human resource community, to examine how it has been meeting the leadership challenges and how it will meet the staggering demand for leadership that is emerging in a more globally integrated world.

Stephen H. Rhinesmith is a senior partner with Oliver Wyman Delta Executive Learning Center and is one of the world's leading experts on global leadership development. His recent book, *Head, Heart, and Guts: What Leading Companies Are Doing to Develop Complete Leaders,* co-authored with David Dotlich and Peter Cairo, is being used in management and leadership development programs throughout the world to help executives gain a more complete view of their leadership skills. He is a frequent speaker at major international conferences on globalization and conducts executive seminars on how to develop the mindsets and skills necessary for managing in a globally competitive world.

CHAPTER 3

WHO REALLY "OWNS" LEADERSHIP DEVELOPMENT?

Robert A. Stringer

Ever since 1997 when McKinsey & Co published its ground-breaking study about the "war for talent," business leaders and development gurus have agreed that talent—especially leadership talent—is a company's most important source of sustainable competitive advantage. However, there has been an ongoing debate about who should "own" leadership development. What person or group of people should be held accountable for seeing that companies have the leadership talent that they need? Since it is a strategic priority, should it be the province of human resources, the CEO, or even the board?

"Owning" leadership development is more than just being held accountable for it. Ownership implies a feeling of personal responsibility, which parallels but is not the same as being held accountable by an external person or group. It's an emotion as well as an explicit part of a job description. Ownership, at bottom, implies a sense of commitment made real only by actions that demonstrate that commitment.

Developing the next generation of leaders has long been considered the province of the HR function. Beginning in the 1970s, progressive corporations began investing heavily in human resource management systems that helped companies identify "high-potential" talent and arrange for this talent to be exposed to an ever broader array of development opportunities. Led by companies such

The 2008 Pfeiffer Annual: Leadership Development.
Copyright © 2008 by John Wiley & Sons, Inc. Reproduced by permission of Pfeiffer, an Imprint of Wiley. www.pfeiffer.com

as AT&T, GE, Citibank, and PepsiCo, HR departments sponsored leadership development initiatives that included assessment centers, more sophisticated psychological profiling, corporate-wide leadership training built around subordinate feedback, leadership development institutes or campuses, and human resource planning (HRP). Dave Ulrich's work, beginning in the 1980s and culminating with the publication of *Human Resource Champions* (1997), presents the strongest argument for the proactive role for HR.

By the late-1990s, however, it was becoming clear that leadership development had to become the province of the CEO if it were to be successful. Observers noted that unless the CEO "owned" the executive talent management process, it was likely to be either highly politicized or a mystery—what Pepsi managers called an "HR black box." All of the most effective HRP systems were endorsed, championed, and often controlled by the chief executive. Jack Welch claimed in 1996 that he spent 33 percent of his time thinking about talent management and leadership development. Experts such as Ulrich, Noel Tichy (*The Leadership Engine*, 1997) and Morgan McCall (*High Flyers*, 1998) started to refer to the CEO as the "chief talent officer." Ed Michaels, Helen Handfield-Jones, and Beth Axelrod, authors of the McKinsey report, stated that "In our five years of conversations with hundreds of companies, we have never seen a company that has developed a pervasive talent mindset without the CEO's leadership and passion" (*The War for Talent*, 2001, page 23).

But now there seems to be another shift in our thinking. According to data reported in both *Fortune* and *BusinessWeek*, CEO tenure has been shortened significantly. This increase in turnover at the top suggests that CEOs may no longer be the best custodians of leadership development. At the same time, boards of directors are more concerned about growing their own executives rather than having to look on the outside. This concern is leading them to focus more attention on the quality of the "bench strength" of executive talent. Accordingly, boards today are less hesitant to insert themselves in the people decisions normally made by the CEO and his or her HR advisors. For example, Coca-Cola's board was actively involved in the series of decisions that led to the appointment of Neville Isdell as CEO, and the ConAgra board has made executive talent development one of CEO Gary Rodkin's top strategic priorities.

So the question becomes: Who really should take responsibility for developing leaders and leadership talent? Who should "own" this critical aspect of corporate life? I believe that none of the current candidates for ownership of leadership development can hope to succeed. HR, the CEO, even the board—all will have to play secondary roles. Four emerging realities make it increasingly clear that leadership development must be "owned" by the individual leader.

Reality Number 1: Personal Development Is Mostly Self-Development

The key to personal development is self-development. Outsiders are support players. Research conducted at the Center for Creative Leadership and my own personal experience with adult learning have demonstrated that the formula illustrated in Figure 1 is roughly right.

Adults will grow and learn new skills when they see that their current skills are inadequate to get them where they want to go. Period. Awareness and motivation are at least 75 percent of the story. And although others can create opportunities for self-awareness, only the individual can "own" the insight and the energy—the motivation—to change.

In many ways it has been a myth that HR or the CEO can own an employee's development or his/her career path. This myth has often been perpetuated by training and development practitioners eager to sell and deliver the latest program or intervention or development "experience." Michael Feiner, the dynamic head of HR for the Pepsi-Cola Company in the 1980s, took great pride in crafting and managing Pepsi's HRP system. For better or worse, many Pepsi executives came to feel that he "owned" their development and their careers. Given the sense of power and control this gave the HR function, it is easy to see why perpetuating the myth became part of Pepsi's culture.

FIGURE 1. HOW DEVELOPMENT HAPPENS

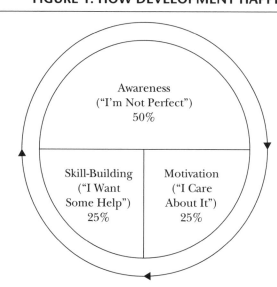

Ironically, the more skilled and talented the employee, the *less* control the company has over his/her personal development. That is because ambitious and upwardly mobile future leaders are less inclined to follow prescribed career paths or passively acquiesce to leadership development programs—no matter how well designed and implemented. What makes them skilled and talented is that they are self-motivated and can see what is needed to add value, both for their own development and for the good of the company. They intuitively understand the equation represented by Figure 1. They are inventive, resourceful, and self-aware. Rising stars are self-developers—passive acquiescence to somebody else's idea of what's good for them does not count for much in their success formula.

The bottom line: Even if boards of directors or CEOs or forward-thinking HR professionals had big budgets and sophisticated leadership development tools at their beck and call, they would have a limited impact on the course of the real learning and development that happens in their organizations. You simply can't force people to learn what you want them to learn if they don't see its value and don't want to learn it!

What are the immediate implications of this reality? A much larger part of our leadership development systems and budgets should be devoted to providing future leaders with more tools for *self-development* and greater opportunities to *choose* career options.

Reality Number 2: Companies and Their HR Professionals Miss the Locus and Timing of Development

When we look at those aspects of leadership that make the most difference (and, therefore, are the most important things to be developed), it is increasingly clear that they are not very easily developed by the CEO, the Board or the HR function – or any "employer." Lominger, Inc., has conducted research into the specific competencies that are associated with executive success. Although these will vary from company to company, Lominger has found that there are what they call "five killers"—competencies that are critically important but that few people possess:

- Creativity
- Dealing with Ambiguity
- Strategic Agility
- Planning
- Managing Vision and Purpose

Lominger has also studied how easy or difficult it is for people to acquire these kinds of skills. Not surprisingly, their research found that most of the killers (all but planning) were rated as being very hard to develop.

And guess what? These skills and competencies are most often developed *early* in a person's life and often *outside* of a person's work experience. What this means is that by the time a future leader is in his or her forties, company-sponsored and controlled experiences do little more than hone or polish skills that an employee already possesses. Since most leadership development systems focus on senior managers, one can argue that it's too late to do much significant development. Leadership skills—or the lack of them—are hard-wired by the time a mid-career person gets on the radar screen of most HR departments or CEOs or the most proactive of boards. When it comes to executives, Lominger's Bob Eichinger and Mike Lombardo put it bluntly: "You have to begin to develop executive skills long before they get there" (Lombardo & Eichenger, 2001, p. 36).

What does this reality mean? Not only can't the HR department, the CEO, or the board "own" leadership development, but the leader herself can't do much about development once she reaches a certain point in her career.

Reality Number 3: Career Expectations Have Changed

Career and personal growth expectations have changed radically since the 1980s. As was emphasized by McKinsey, the career equation has shifted—especially for the most talented future leaders. Today, talented employees know that companies will not provide them with lifetime employment. In return, their loyalty to any particular company is for sale. This represents a profound change. It makes future leaders even more selfish about their careers and their own development. "I trust only myself to look out for me," remarked a high-ranking executive from Merrill Lynch not too long ago. Between 2003 and 2005 Merrill downsized, laying off over 30,000 people.

Even if HR managers, CEOs, or members of the board were to *try* to orchestrate career and development experiences for the current generation of younger high-potential leaders, it is unlikely that such experiences would be automatically accepted. The next generation of leaders of most large corporations will not be linear thinkers when it comes to their careers. They don't trust their employers to look out for them. If pressed, they will tell you that they believe that they know what they need to do to get ahead—and "getting ahead" may not mean what it used to mean. Nobody is going to force them to develop or prescribe a path to the top.

Reality Number 3 is not easy to deal with. Mobile and ambitious future leaders probably won't spend all of their careers with one company, but the more they know about the growth opportunities within the company, the better. If high-potentials do leave, the company should keep in touch with them and stay on good terms. Who knows? They may return, having acquired new and improved skills and maturity.

Reality Number 4: More Tools for Self-Development are Available

Technology today has put many powerful self-development tools in the hands of future leaders. When I started my career with The Forum Corporation back in the late 1970s and 1980s, giving people personal feedback on their leadership skills was revolutionary. It was new, different, and exciting. Today, if executive education programs don't use at least one or two personal development feedback instruments, they are viewed as terribly old-fashioned. The reason is obvious: self-development tools—especially well-designed feedback instruments—work. People gain insight and learn from them.

More and more personal assessment tools are now being offered by reputable organizations. Many are online and readily available to people who want to learn about themselves. I have had very positive experiences with our company's own Leadership Derailment Report, Caliper (a lengthy but fascinating self-assessment of a person's personality and social style), the Conflict Dynamics Profile, as well a couple of oldies-but-goodies tools such as FIRO-B and the Myers-Briggs Personality Indicator (MBTI). As awareness and familiarity with such tools increases, it will be impossible for organizations to "control" or dictate the flow of personal development information and insights. Even if they wanted to, HR managers, CEOs, or directors of companies can no longer decide who will learn what, when, or how.

In response to this reality, enlightened companies should provide future leaders with as much career development technology as possible. Whenever possible, development tools should include company-specific information so that talented people can see the growth opportunities that are available within their current organizations.

What's to Be Done?

Rather than bemoan this turn of events, progressive organizations should accept the reality of individual accountability for leadership development and take steps to influence the process and manage what they can.

How can organizations respond to this shift in mindset? If the company can no longer be viewed as primarily responsible for the development of its future leaders—if this job is left up to each employee—how can we hold today's executives accountable for building a bench filled with future leaders? Must we simply throw up our hands and pray that the right future leaders will appear when they are needed?

No.

Winning organizations will respond to the new reality of employee-centric leadership development. If they are smart and flexible, such companies will win the "war for talent"—they will start to make their organizations attractive to an ever-larger group of selfish, immature, impatient, independent, diverse, and empowered future leaders.

Eight Employee-Centric Leadership Development Strategies

Leadership development in the 21st Century will be most successful when companies engage in eight strategies. Not all will work. As a matter of fact, not all of them will appeal to many companies today. But the new realities demand new approaches, and winning the war for talent will mean implementing as many of the eight as possible.

Strategy One: Make Leadership Development a Priority from Day One

Let every new employee know that his or her development is part of the culture of the company. Make it clear that the primary responsibility for development rests with the individual, but that the company will do its part and expects all employees to be aggressive in seeking out developmental opportunities. Communispace Corporation of Watertown, Massachusetts, is a rapidly growing marketing software company that has successfully implemented this strategy. It has a remarkable track record of growing future leaders and a corporate culture that is the envy of all of its competitors.

Strategy Two: Expand the Leadership Talent Pipeline to Include More People

Too often the pool of future leaders is limited to only the top fifty or top one hundred or even the top 250 executives in the organization. Thus, developmental opportunities are limited to those populations. If companies are to establish any lasting bonds with the younger generation, they must pay more attention to a much larger talent pool. Of course, new technology and approaches will have to be employed if thousands of employees are to be considered to have leadership potential, but this is exactly what the younger generation expects. Starbucks has invested significant dollars in such development for its front-line "associates." This admired and well-managed company has found that expanding the leadership talent pipeline not only enlarges the talent pool, but it sends a highly motivating message to the entire organization.

Strategy Three: Expand Career Options

If companies are going to be attractive places for today's workers to develop themselves, they are going to have to change the way they think about managing—including the way they think about managing leadership development. Thomas Malone, professor at the MIT Sloan School of Management and author of *The Future of Work* (2004) very forcefully makes this point. He believes that Google is the wave of the future and that command-and-control management practices will drive away the best and brightest leadership talent. "Workers will be doing more things on their own. . . . They'll have more freedom as well as more responsibility." Companies will not be able to dictate precise career paths for the most valuable members of their workforce. But even in Malone's employee-centric world, they can provide their people with multiple development options, a variety of new challenges, and a much broader array of possible learning experiences. This will require a significant shift in HR practices, leadership development policies, and management expectations. It will undoubtedly tax the patience of old-line development professionals and executives. But it just might energize, excite, and grow the current generation of future leaders.

Strategy Four: Turn More Managers into Feedback Machines

There is no better way to grow future leaders than to provide them with candid feedback on their performance, their behavior, and their impact on others. High-quality feedback, delivered by a trusted source, helps people gain insight and learn. Unfortunately, most managers hate giving candid feedback. Furthermore, they are lousy at doing it, and they know it. (Which, of course, is why they don't do it.) Somehow, we need to turn managers into feedback-giving machines. Telling people where they stand, how they performed, what is expected, and so forth, has to become a critical part of every manager's job. It can be done. Pepsi is perhaps the most feedback-rich corporate environment I've ever observed. I can't say it was always a pleasant place, but employees—especially those who wanted to be future leaders—received multiple doses of feedback from multiple sources all of the time. Future leaders complained, but they grew. Over the years Pepsi has an enviable record of producing talented leaders. Jeff Carney, one of Fidelity Investments' most talented executives and the current head of its retirement business, has made a point of attracting and developing talented people. In the Fidelity culture, Jeff isn't always seen as the most tactful executive. But his development track record and strategy is clear: "If people don't get straight feedback, they'll never develop. We have to coach our people if they are going to make their careers here, as opposed to another company."

Strategy Five: Get More Personal

The Center for Creative Leadership, Lominger, Inc., and other development experts have found that the most memorable developmental experiences are highly personal and most often involve what are called "personal hardships." These include such events as divorce, the death of a loved one, the lost of a job, or a severe personal sickness or accident. Most personal hardships are outside of one's work experience and, therefore, outside of the normal scope or control of the company. However, there are ways for companies to turn an employee's personal hardship into a valuable learning experience. Development usually requires reflection and perspective. If the company can offer high-quality close-in counseling to an employee going through a personal hardship, insights and learning may result. Such counseling has to be invited, of course, and this requires a high degree of trust. But if companies and development professionals have the desire and the capability to be more personal with people—so they are aware of when personal hardships are occurring and are invited to help—they will provide future leaders with an invaluable sounding board and an opportunity to grow and develop.

Strategy Six: Extend the Boundaries of the Organization

Given the realities of today's talent marketplace, it may be impossible to keep the most promising future leaders in the company "from cradle to grave." But don't give up on them. What organizations need to do is extend their boundaries by creating outreach programs for former employees, even when they go to work for competitors. Make it easy for high-potentials who decide to leave the company to keep in touch, to stay engaged, and to communicate with their peers who were left behind. Scholastic often recruits future leaders from the ranks of its alumni, and my own company, Oliver Wyman, has an explicit program aimed at keeping tabs on talented people who have left to seek other challenges.

Strategy Seven: Invest in Self-Development Technology

Rather than fight the trend toward more self-development, support it. Invest in providing all high-potential employees with the latest technology. Every month new assessment tools are being invented and tested. Many of these are available on the web. The HR department of an enlightened company should figure out how to put these tools into the hands of their future leaders. To the extent these tools can then be customized to fit the company—so that internal learning development opportunities are showcased—employees can be influenced to grow within the boundaries of the organization. An excellent example that supports this strategy is CareerDNA, an innovative new service provider that markets a series of online self-assessment and career planning tools. CareerDNA's leadership development system is meant to be customized so that companies can use it in just the way I am suggesting.

Strategy Eight: Create More Realistic Expectations

The new realities of leadership development must be reflected in the messages companies send and employees hear. Companies need to communicate more clearly what they can—and cannot—do to further a person's career. And employees need to know how much personal responsibility they will have to assume for their own development. Companies should spell out the skills and experiences that they deem critical for success. More often than not, these will be competencies such as creativity, personal courage, integrity, self-awareness, critical thinking, dealing with ambiguity, and managing vision and purpose. Future leaders should be told *how* these skills are normally acquired and then provide as many development options as possible. But the expectation should be very clear: Actual development is the employee's job.

Conclusion

One of the best ways to motivate constructive and entrepreneurial behavior in an organization is to tell people who are in charge of a business or a project or a department to "pretend that it is yours" and "run it as if you owned it." A genuine sense of ownership leads a person to do whatever is necessary to accomplish the desired goal. That's why it is so important to understand who really "owns" leadership development. While the CEO and the board are ultimately responsible for the success of the company, and this success depends heavily on leadership development, they can't "own" it. All they, along with the HR function, can really do is to create the support systems and the climate that make it clear that leadership development is "owned" by the individual future leader. It is time for leadership development professionals to take a hard look at the new realities. They should back off some of their old strategies and adopt a few new ones.

References

Bianco, A., & Lavelle, L. (2000, December 11). The CEO trap. *Business Week*.

Lombardo, M., & Eichenger, R. (2001). *The leadership machine: Architecture to develop leaders for any future*. Minneapolis, MN: Lominger Limited.

Malone, T. (2004). *The future of work: How the new order of business will shape your organization, your management style and your life*. Boston, MA: Harvard Business School Press.

McCall, M. (1998). *High flyers: Developing the next generation of leaders*. Boston, MA: Harvard Business School Press.

McCall, M., Lombardo, M., & Morrison, A. (1998). *The lessons of experience: How successful executives develop on the job*. Lexington, MA: Lexington Books.

McKinsey & Company. (2000). War for talent: 2000 corporate officer survey. New York: Author.

Michaels, E., Handfield-Jones, H., & Axelrod, B. (2001). *The war for talent*. Boston, MA: Harvard Business School Press.

Tichy, N. (1997). *The leadership engine: How winning companies build leaders at every level*. New York: HarperCollins.

Ulrich, D. (1997). *Human resource champions: The next agenda for adding value and delivering results*. Boston, MA: Harvard Business School Press.

Robert A. Stringer is a partner with Oliver Wyman Delta Executive Learning Center. He has led a wide range of research and consulting assignments in the U.S., the U.K., Australia, and New Zealand in the areas of organization design, executive coaching, leadership effectiveness, organizational climate, and business strategy. He has published numerous articles on business strategy, motivation, career development, innovation, and corporate integrity. He has served on the faculty of the Harvard Graduate School of Business Administration. He has co-authored three books: *Motivation and Organizational Climate* with George H.Litwin, *Men in Management* with J.B. Kassarjian, and *Strategy Traps and How to Avoid Them* with Joel Uchenick. His fourth and most recent book is *Leadership and Organizational Climate*. He received a bachelor's degree (with honors) from Harvard College and an M.B.A. degree (with distinction) from the Harvard Business School.

CHAPTER 4

DEVELOPING LEADERS OF SUBSTANCE

Ram Charan

Change is always with us, but at the current magnitude, speed, and depth, more than ever, we need leaders who know what they are doing. This is an environment in which a Google can come out of nowhere and grow into a multi-billion-dollar business in a few short years, presenting new challenges and opportunities to the advertising, broadcasting, and publishing industries, to name just a few. Emerging-nation players with clear industry advantages now become world-class competitors thanks to mobility of talent, capital, and knowledge. Companies need more than just leaders with style—they need leaders with substance.

What makes a leader of substance? It's not just raw intelligence, education, or great charisma. I've seen leaders with little formal education succeed handsomely and leaders with Harvard Business School degrees fail. Often, there's a temptation to rely on superficial leadership traits and assume that, because a leader has great presence or a bold vision, that person is a leader of substance. How often have you seen a leader take command of a room and deliver a PowerPoint presentation that has everyone eating out of the palm of his hand? But that same leader, despite his commanding presence, may make terrible decisions as time goes on. Soon the people who report to him lose focus, the organization loses direction, and the business flounders.

The real issue is confusing style with substance. Far too often, the people who identify, develop, and appoint leaders focus on the appearance of leadership.

They miss the most important aspect of it: knowing how to run a business. Many traps that cause us to put the wrong people in leadership positions, with terrible consequences for the person and the business.

Are They Really Leaders?

Certain types of leaders aren't necessarily equipped to lead a business. Don't assume you've found a leader when you find one of the following:

The Pedigree

Be careful of leaders who try to impress by virtue of where they've been rather than by what they've done. If a leader makes frequent references to a prestigious alma mater ("When I was at Harvard . . .") or a big, successful company he or she used to work for ("When I was at Toyota . . ."), be skeptical.

I'm not against education (I'm a proud Harvard grad myself) or valuable work experience. But some people are taken in and choose such "leaders" either because they assume something good must have rubbed off, or because they think it's safe.

It isn't. You have to look at the person's skills and record of actual accomplishment to have any sense of the person's capability as a business leader.

The Spiritual Leader

Some leaders can stir up energy and excitement in other people, conjuring visions of something great and appealing. They have extraordinary communication skills that fire up emotion. People believe them, and want to go where they're going.

The ability to inspire others is indeed a wonderful trait in leaders, but not every person who can arouse emotion can link her vision to the practicalities of business, and emotion alone cannot get an organization where it needs to be.

When a spiritual leader, rather than a business leader, runs the show, the initial burst of excitement can be uplifting. But it inevitably fades when results fail to materialize.

The Brain

One way people gauge a leader is by how smart she is. We can't help but be impressed by the person who reacts quickly, gets to the answer fastest, can speak knowledgably on a breadth of topics, and has instant recall of names, quotations, and numbers.

Sometimes such people let you know how well-read they are. But being quick on your feet is not the same as intelligence, and intelligence is not the same as being a leader. Do we want intelligent leaders? Absolutely. Just don't choose leaders based on raw intelligence alone.

The Savior

A leader is running a troubled division. Margins are shrinking, quality is deteriorating, and customers are defecting. But he is undaunted by every piece of bad news. In every review, he assures his superiors that change is right around the corner.

He has a plan, meticulously detailed in charts and graphs. He wants you to trust him, and because he seems so confident and sincere, you do.

Optimism and confidence are appealing, but make poor substitutes for the know-how of addressing problems. And we all know that problems neglected have a way of growing. The person who promises the answer but never delivers on it is not a business leader.

Focus on Substance

What makes a leader of substance? I have observed over the years that there are certain personality traits that deeply influence how leaders develop and deploy the know-how necessary to run a business well.

- *Ambition:* A great leader needs a healthy dose of ambition—that desire to achieve something visible and noteworthy—to push themselves and others to reach their potential.
- *Drive and Tenacity:* Some leaders will drill for specific answers and push to get to the heart of an issue to find solutions. They have a highly infectious energy and an "inner motor" that drive their priorities throughout the organization.
- *Self-Confidence:* These leaders have that tough inner core or emotional fortitude that helps them endure the lonely moments when important decisions fall on their shoulders. They speak their minds and act decisively, knowing they can withstand the consequences.
- *Psychological Openness:* Leaders who are psychologically open welcome diverse opinions so that they can see and hear more and factor more information into their decisions. Such openness enhances candor and communication within a social system.

- *Realism:* Realism is the mid-point between optimism and pessimism. A realist wants to obtain unfiltered information that can be weighed, measured, evaluated, and tested to determine what step to take next.
- *Appetite for Learning:* A leader with an insatiable appetite for learning will build know-how faster than one who prefers not to be exposed to new challenges or situations.

Of course, these traits are not enough to create a leader of substance. There are lots of personal traits we want in our leaders—things like confidence, intelligence, and communication skills. But if we want our organizations to be in good hands, we have to focus primarily on the substance of leadership—whether the person really knows what he or she is doing.

The real substance of business leadership comes down to the eight "Know-How's" I've identified:

1. *Positioning and repositioning the business to make money:* A leader of substance can find a central idea for the business that meets customer demands and delivers the fundamentals of moneymaking. In today's tumultuous world, leaders may have to reposition a business four or five times in their careers.
2. *Detecting the patterns of external change:* Leaders of substance can make sense out of the complexity of the world and put their businesses on the offensive.
3. *Managing the social system of your business:* Designing the mechanisms that link actions and energy to business results, while enforcing the right behaviors, is a crucial capability for a leader of substance.
4. *Judging people:* The ability to get to the truth of a person and unleash that person's natural talents is a vital skill for leaders who would expand an organization's capacity.
5. *Molding a team of leaders:* It takes true skill to get high-powered, high-ego people to work as a team.
6. *Setting goals:* Finding the right balance between realism and reach in setting the organization's destination is more important than you think. Many leaders set goals by looking in the rearview mirror.
7. *Determining priorities:* You need to define a clear, specific pathway to an organization's goals, aligning resources, actions, and energy to accomplish goals.
8. *Managing non-market forces:* There are many forces you don't control but that significantly impact your business. Leaders of substance can deal with those forces in creative, positive ways.

In Practice

When a leader has the know-how to run a business and the personal characteristics that best influence good leadership, a portrait of a substantial leader starts to emerge. In practice, a leader of substance can:

1. *Think big—and small:* Kay Krill, CEO of Ann Taylor, told a *Wall Street Journal* reporter that "You have to fly at 50,000 feet, but you also have to come down and mow the lawn every now and then." At 50,000 feet, a leader can see the total picture of the business, the industry, and the world economy. But stratospheric thinking can miss details. Great leaders can be incisive as well, drilling to the specifics necessary to create goals and priorities for the group.
2. *Reframe:* Reframing is changing a vantage point—looking at a phenomenon or problem from a very different perspective. This is how great leaders redefine markets and create new growth trajectories.
3. *Connect the dots*: Linear, analytic thinking is useful and important, but sometimes it's incomplete. Leaders of substance can take mental leaps in order to make sense of incomplete or seemingly unrelated pieces of information. They can use their imaginations and go beyond charts and graphs to connect the dots.
4. *Put purpose before self:* Leaders of substance aren't focused on the celebrity, fame, or fortune that comes with running a high-profile, growing business. Rather, leaders of substance care most about carrying out the mission of the business, delivering the promised results, and building an organization they can be proud of. They have a sense of purpose that goes beyond their own personal desire for wealth, status, self-aggrandizement, or power.

In 2005, a $20 billion company underwent a major reorganization, and one of the senior executives approached the CEO to tell him a portion of the executive's new job really should belong to someone else. What was he thinking? He was in a horse race to succeed the CEO and already had the smallest scope of all his peers and fellow contenders for the top job. Under those circumstances, many leaders would try to expand their span of control. But he believed the organization would work better if certain areas went to someone else.

This leader was not naïve or unambitious. It's just that he truly wanted the business to succeed. Of course he hoped that his thinking would be recognized and appreciated. When his boss and the board are close to the succession decision, no doubt they'll remember that this person revealed he's not a greedy empire builder.

The Winning Combination

Great leaders—those who deliver results consistently over time—aren't perfect human beings. But they have a winning combination of personality traits, thought processes, and know-how. Any one of them would admit to having made mistakes throughout his or her career, but along the way, he or she took sandpaper to the rough edges of his or her personality, and learned to compensate for inherent shortcomings. Most of them will describe experiences in which they expanded their range of thinking, learning to dig into more detail, to think more conceptually, or to broaden their lens, sometimes against their natural inclinations.

Ram Charan is a highly acclaimed business advisor, speaker, and author who has coached some of the world's most successful CEOs. For thirty-five years, he's worked behind the scenes at companies like GE, Bank of America, DuPont, Home Depot, 3M, and Verizon. His influential books include *Execution* and *Confronting Reality*, written with former Honeywell CEO Larry Bossidy. His other books include *Boards That Deliver*, *What the CEO Wants You to Know*, and *Profitable Growth Is Everyone's Business*. Charan has also written for *Harvard Business Review*, *Fortune*, *Time*, *Information Week*, *Director's Monthly*, *The Corporate Board*, and *USA Today*.

CHAPTER 5

WHY IS LEADERSHIP SO IMPORTANT AND FORMAL LEADERSHIP DEVELOPMENT NOT?

Tim Sullivan

The Value of Leadership

Leaders are essential to an organization, but most formal leadership development courses are not effective in developing leaders. Why is that so important? Unless we focus on the true value of talented leadership and how it is developed, we will waste critical resources and time investing in the wrong things, and mislead ourselves into believing we are addressing this critical need. This statement is not made casually, but is based on a career of observation.

Leadership, like an organization's culture, is a resource that cannot be duplicated by a competing organization—or even by the company itself in its next generation of leadership! And yet, the quality of a company's leadership team is a critical component in its valuation. This is easily verified in annual reports and proxies in which the quality, experience, and effectiveness of the management team at the top and in various competitive segments is profiled at length. It is prominently displayed there for only one reason: It is essential in valuing the company's current competitive position and it future prospects.

Another indicator of the importance of leadership in valuing a company is the role top executive search firms play in assessing the strength of management teams during the due diligence phase of acquisitions. Edward Speed, Global Head of the Consumer Packaged Goods Practice at Spencer Stuart in London, cites cases in which the firm has been engaged by potential acquirers to do such an assessment. If the quality is strong and deep, the acquiring company has room to negotiate upward in any takeover battle—because the leadership team is worth more.

That leadership cannot be easily duplicated by competitors is not an abstract idea, but something we know from our everyday experience. Examples can be found at Nordstrom and Allen-Edmonds, where we enter a store knowing we can find a choice of luxury items—but also that will be backed up by a superb shopping experience and customer service policies that guarantee that expectation. The unique and sustainable value of the leadership of these companies versus competitors adds to the value of the whole enterprise. Small surprise that the market puts a price premium on these companies over not only other retailers but over luxury goods companies as well.

Finally, leadership is not only difficult for competitors to duplicate, it is sometimes impossible for a company to sustain in its "next generation." There are a number of first-class family companies that were able to succeed only through one management generation. Then they are forced out of business or forced into selling out because the family could not replicate or develop a new class of leaders to follow up the strengths of the founders who brought the company to life and success. Without an intense dedication to finding, renewing, and developing the top leadership required for tomorrow's challenges, the valuation and vitality of any organization is at risk.

Please note, this statement applies to universities, governmental, and not-for-profit organizations as well.

The Current State of Leadership Development

Companies have invested considerable resources (time and money) in leadership development programs. The harsh reality is that *much of what passes for leadership development is not that effective.* "John" or "Joanna" attends a leadership development program sponsored by the company and returns to work pleased with the experience and enthusiastic. Within a month, however, there are no visible or observable changes in his or her behavior on the job. At about the same time, you receive a memo from the corporate education team that the recent leadership program has been vastly successful—receiving an overall rating of "5" from all participants. But based on your first-hand observation of John, you wonder whether any of this activity has really affected the percentage of "Ready-Now" successors for leadership positions throughout the company.

We know that the answer to that question is "no"—but why? First because most programs are intended to build insight and learning from the experience of others (in case studies or classroom exercises), but without a tangible link and use of these insights on the job, reinforced by executives around them, no leadership skills are developed at all. We know that leadership is developed facing real issues and opportunities with action and decisions taken in the real world and in the work of the business—classroom activity by itself will accomplish nothing.

Why do participants most often rate it so highly if it lacks impact? First, because all of us enjoy learning, and off-the-job sessions give us a break from everyday work and colleagues. It also helps build a network of other promising talents in the company. Finally, being selected for participation provides recognition that I'm a talent, too.

If our candidate for development is selected for a leadership development program outside of the company in a university or public session, the same limited benefits are received, but since those in the sessions are "outsiders," a strong network of talented colleagues in other companies is formed. No wonder that a number of these participants are poached in the months ahead by people met in the "new network" to join other firms. It is no surprise that executive search firms collect data from executive programs from major university MBA programs—the talent is clearly identified and often susceptible to being recruited in order to capitalize on the executive program degree or certification.

So What Do We Know That Works?

What really produces bottom-line results when it comes to producing "Ready-Now" successors for leadership positions? Here are eight actions that organizations can take that are proven to strengthen their leadership pipeline:

1. Clearly Answer the Question: Leadership Development for What?

Without knowing what the leadership is required for, the role it is to play, and the specific mission of leadership in your industry or business, you lack the criteria against which leaders can be selected and developed.

To begin, assess the status of current leadership. Don't assume that the incumbents model the shape of leadership required. Are they new to the organization or near retirement? The former may not be in position long enough to determine whether they have what it takes, and the latter may reflect the talent required to move us to the present, with no assurance it fits the organization's future needs. Another concern: How long in position? CEOs today rarely hold the position more than five years—and research shows that any leader in a key position for eight years or more rarely keeps a sharp edge in driving the organization forward and resists change.

The strategic purpose of the organization also has a big impact on leadership requirements: new markets, products, or competitors? Going global, industry change or consolidation, and new technologies can all have an enormous impact on the kind of leadership required.

There are also requirements that spring from the unique characteristics of the company itself: Is there a lack of successors—despite the current success of the business? Is the company evolving from a family ownership or sole founder environment to more structured professional management? Each of these situations shapes the kind of development effort required and, importantly, the starting point for development initiatives.

Timing is easy to establish if the business is prosperous and attractive to leaders building a career. In a crisis, there is an urgency requiring new leadership now while still incorporating provisions for leadership development on a long-term basis.

Finally, values and culture have a very large impact on whom and how leadership can be developed in any organization today. Top executive candidates and board of director prospects spend a lot of time in multiple interviews with prospective employers focusing on the culture and values of the organization. Instinctively they know that the financials, brands, and competitive position of the business are easy to assess. If they are joining a team for the long term, or even measuring chances for success for themselves and the firm as a whole, culture and values are as important as the numbers.

2. Select Talented Leaders and Bring Them "On-Board" Successfully

If you get this one, crucial step right, everything else will fall into place. In fact, choosing the right talent is so important that if you get it absolutely right, you can forget the rest of this article. Everything else is secondary.

Think about your own experience: If a leader has all the talent you need—and some surplus capacity for the future, she or he can do the job at hand readily and respond naturally to growth opportunities and development for the future. If you fall short in obtaining the inherent talent, all the career planning, executive development courses, and coaching will not have any value at all.

For a top position, I have never had any CEO or board member complain that the person nominated for a key job is too talented or too smart! Perhaps too expensive, too arrogant, or too ambitious—but never too talented.

If Job 1 is "to get the right person in the right job," why is it that most organizations do not do a thorough job in selection? In my experience, they don't devote sufficient time and energy to this most critical process—and they don't get the CEO and other top executives as recruiting champions. If "war is too important to leave to generals," then recruiting top talent is too important to leave to staff functions or line superiors alone to come up with nominees for a key job.

Selection has to begin with a thoughtful and detailed knowledge of what you absolutely must have in the position—and the behaviors you want in your leaders. It is essential to begin with what is critically required in the role at this time—and to be specific in terms of the desired behaviors that must be obtained. Keep in mind that the best predictor of future behavior is past behavior—so you can readily examine a candidate's experience to see whether he or she has a history of achieving what you need to do. That is where the rock solid proof is found—in a leader's history of achieving results.

Don't confuse the current rage for "competencies and values" for a diligent search for the essential talent, qualifications, and a track record of results required for the key position. For some reason, we are generating "competencies and values" at a ferocious pace—and in many cases, enshrining them in plastic desk monuments. In one European company, I have seen more than sixty-five competencies required for selection, leadership development, and performance management schedules. When asked how this all works, the reply was "Well, you can't expect any one person to have all of these—so, of course, we compromise." Which is precisely the point! Without some painstaking effort to focus on the skills, experience, qualities, and talent level essential in this position, it is impossible to ensure selecting precisely the right person.

Since this approach to selection sounds like a lot of hard work, and would require a lot of a top executive time ("which we don't have"), it would be logical to look for shortcuts. Unfortunately, there aren't any. If top executives will not become deeply involved in the process, you won't find the essential specifications, skilled "assessors" of talent in interviews, and powerful recruiters who can sell the prospective executives on the opportunity and the future. Only they can describe the future of the business and career opportunities because only they are the ones setting the strategy and direction for the future. Your top executive can also be useful in eliminating bureaucratic logjams in setting schedules and designing creative compensation packages once the right person is found.

For external prospects, executive search firms also look like highly skilled and useful resources to lessen the work and to serve as "shortcuts" themselves. Too many companies rely too much on search firms to do this important work. Unless you go through the same selection steps outlined above, and without deep executive involvement, search firms can't get the job done for you. Once you know what is essential, backed up by your own top team as recruiters, then search firms can do what they do best: bring talent otherwise unavailable to your attention and help ensure you have the widest net possible out there to source for the best fit. The best executive search firms have seasoned partners who can help you stay objective in evaluating talent, maintain an independent rapport with the candidate to help them chose your opportunity if it fits, and assist in designing and selling the compensation package—since they are in the executive marketplace every day. For a key position, however, none of those assets is useful unless it starts with the essentials: (1) a clear and focused description of key requirements and the mission, and (2) ongoing support, commitment, and involvement day-to-day from executives at the top.

One CEO I worked for over several years viewed selection as this important: "If there are ten crucial things for a CEO to accomplish, at least five of them have to do with people." Selection is the key to shaping great companies because, after all, the CEO must appoint her or his top team, who will form and populate the future for that organization. Why is this so difficult? Because it is very easy to accept those in place or nominated for top positions—and very difficult to make tough judgments about people. When you have been searching inside and outside of the company for a CFO for months, and someone nearly matching the requirements is identified, the simple solution is to accept him or her. Much tougher to hold tight, work harder, and struggle longer to not compromise—and keep looking for the best possible candidate and fit. Remember, too, there is often a great deal of pressure from the board of directors or the nominating committee to get on with the process, and, internally, the incumbent management team will prefer that you select from the last-written succession plan and choose a person well known by the organization. Despite the impressions given, even CEOs want to be loved, so it takes strong leadership to make the tough call and say "no" when required. It is okay to go along with the crowd in choosing the site of the next worldwide management meeting, but not okay to compromise on leadership talent at any level.

Some concluding thoughts on the crucial importance of selection: Without the right raw material, leadership development is not possible. In each assignment, know what you are looking for, and don't settle for less. Having a vacancy in a key position is awkward, but putting the wrong person in the job (without the capacity for further development) is a disaster. In our own experience, we all know it is just like getting married: better to be single than to choose the wrong marriage partner—the future with the wrong person is bleak.

In assessing key talent, be certain not to be entranced by the exquisite resume: All those dazzling degrees and leadership academies won't mean a thing if, in your judgment, it is the wrong person or a bad fit for your organization. Trust and integrity are more important than a great CV or superb references. On another level, it is easy to be seduced by highly articulate candidates who present themselves brilliantly—a clear record of verified results is a more solid foundation than PowerPoint skills, and sometimes we confuse the two. Always be able to answer a question: If someone is so sensational, why is he or she available? Be on guard if their "power suit" is worth more than your car and wonder: Is that meant to distract you from substance?

All of these principles apply to selection inside or outside of the organization—because someone is well known in the company only means that you can more easily verify performance. It is not a reason to compromise on essential qualifications of talent and the needed record of results. Another key point: Without more than one candidate (inside or outside), you cannot make a choice or selection. In fact, when you are under time and peer pressure, finding one potentially qualified candidate often "forces" a selection that is a compromise. Of course, that is not true—but it underlies the fact that excellence in selection requires both judgment and courage. You have to be willing to say "no" even when it hurts and there is no other candidate in sight.

Selection is a key role for executives at every level, but it has only become tougher in the past two years for two reasons: (1) Global requirements are putting a premium on talent that can serve customers and build effective teams that succeed across continents, language, and culture. Rusty French from high school and a year abroad in London during college will not cut it, and (2) Pressures on public companies and the bureaucratic demands of many large enterprises have caused some highly talented women and men to give up their promising executive careers and corporate life overall. The cost in human terms and on their families is simply too great—health and happiness is more important. Selection is tougher because requirements are growing and the talent pool is reduced—the truce is over in the War for Talent.

3. Give Talented People Big Jobs and Top Line Management Support

People grow into leadership roles when they are given the opportunity to lead. An everyday role of management is to assign work to people, and that is the way any business makes progress and achieves its mission. However, most often that work assignment is handed to someone who can get results quickly and efficiently. If the person carries out the task well, we repeat the assignment over and over. We believe that the person is doing a great job, but if he or she has further potential and fails to receive more challenging and complex roles to plan, he or she is in a career rut.

Instead, we should consider that each time work is assigned, it can be a tremendous development experience, too. Building stretch into assignments is the best possible way to grow and develop executive talent on the job. Even if the mission of the group is limited or constrained due to the nature of the business or industry, we can stretch by putting them in new environments working with new people. A couple of examples: When pitching a new account, take someone promising from customer service (or some other function responsible for integrating the client or servicing the account) and assign him or her to the "final pitch" with the prospective client. He or she can learn a lot about the potential client's business, people, and expectations. The person also can learn about your company's promises and commitment to the client once on-board. Finally, give her or him free reign to work across all departments of the business to make the integration successful. The development experience is exciting for the up-and-coming executive. He or she gains confidence seeing the "big picture" right from the start, and learning how to mobilize all the people and functions required for success across the company forces that person to learn about leadership by actually leading.

In that example, a great deal of development and learning can occur—but it is only one challenge. The key to successful executive development on the job is to continue to provide a variety of assignments with increasing complexity, more people in different functions and levels, and across geographies. Unfortunately, top executives are often too busy or preoccupied with the day-to-day urgencies in the business to carefully reflect on the impact of assignments on the growth and development of top talent in their company. Being challenged by a top-line executive to take on bigger assignments and more important work has enormous impact on emerging talent. To have a senior executive personally assign a tough task to me is empowering, encouraging, and sends a strong message that "You are important to us and we have important growth plans for you." All the paperwork in a career development office or in a locked-up succession planning document falls short in those growth and motivational aspects—no matter how brilliantly or cleverly those plans are created. Said another way, having the CEO throw a challenging assignment my way with the message, "This is important to our company and I have confidence you have the talent to pull it off" is a more memorable and exciting development experience.

Providing a variety of assignments will require new learning and pushes high-potential leaders to develop themselves. Linking leadership development to the real executive job-to-be-done links the executive to the work of the company in a more profound way—and that builds loyalty and reinforces dedication, which is a tremendous benefit for the company. Others outside of the company can offer bigger salaries and grander titles, but if I believe I am developing executive skills in my current company and that the top management of our group has a professional and personal interest in my development, it will be harder to recruit me away.

These real executive challenges on the job do more than just add to my skills and toolbox for the future. Because the development experiences are assigned by leadership at the top of the organization, the executive is linked not only to the senior team, but his assignments are linked to the "real career ladder" in the company. These are not theoretical skills that may be useful in the future; they are skills gained in a company needed for that company's future. By definition, this person is on the senior career path, and that is beneficial for everyone involved. Because my performance and results are being observed by top management, I become a nominee for added number of positions in the company's living succession plan—not just the book.

Keep in mind also that executive development on the job is powered by the energy, ambition, and aspirations of the individual. You don't need to invent extraneous tools to motivate and grow the individual—she or he brings talent and vision for the future as the tools for motivation and development. Look to your own experience: What was the most important leadership growth experience you ever had? For most, it was a challenging assignment from the top, starting a new function or operation, trying to fix a broken business or plant, etc. Notice, it is rarely a great course you took. The most promising executives grow themselves rapidly—given challenges and opportunities. Executive coaches and mentors can help, but so do smart colleagues, and the freedom to do whatever is required to do the job. From the experience, with inherent talent, and top management support, *executive development occurs from within.*

In a recent interview for a top marketing role, a candidate reinforced this message for me. In preparing for the interview, I noticed he pointed out that he worked for Al Dunlap, and I wondered how he found the experience (and why he mentioned it at all): "Don't knock Chainsaw Al. I worked for him for a couple of years, and that was the best development experience in my life." By definition, the team was working to urgently turn around a business on life support, and from Chainsaw Al he learned how to identify and tackle only the most essential problems and opportunities, and seize them quickly. Finding the best talent in the company had to happen quickly, too, and he learned how to identify those whom he could give "impossible" tasks to—those who wouldn't give up without succeeding. Most of all, he learned how to do these things and take decisions and choose people at "warp speed." Notice it wasn't "Chainsaw Al, my role model"—instead, it was "great things I learned about being an executive from him."

One final mention about giving talented people big jobs for development: It is not always obvious to promising executives why they should give up a relatively safe and secure role for something more dangerous and, perhaps, under hardship conditions or even a hardship location. One role that top executives in human resources or talent development are in a unique position to do well is to lay out for an executive (especially inside the company) all the developmental and career benefits that come from the challenge presented, and to "sell" the opportunity

in terms that are meaningful to the executive candidate and his family (if relocation is required). Many executives believe that they can stay in the location and
country they are quite comfortable in and still advance and grow in the organization. That fails to provide strong development for that individual and it creates a
"blockage" because high-potential executives at lower levels cannot move up to
a new challenge and role. Two disastrous results: Promising talent leaves the firm
seeking more career path and development opportunities, and, in many cases, the
firmly rooted incumbent is shocked to learn that he or she is no longer a candidate to "move up." He or she has grown stale and is of no use to the company at
higher levels.

4. Provide Honest, Concise, and Candid Feedback

Providing challenging assignments and development opportunities is a great
start, but there is a lot more to be done to ensure that the right development
occurs. In a new development role, individuals make decisions and take actions
trying to move the project or assignment ahead. Making certain that they receive
quick feedback on the consequences of those actions (good or bad) is extremely
important. Quick feedback can forestall a bad decision turning into a fiasco—so
the executive can learn without enduring all the pain. Especially when he or she
is supervising a new team of people, in a new function, a new location or country, there are faux pas that one can learn from quickly without alienating the
new team. Pointing out what the person did right or wrong ensures the learning
and growing, but it also requires a supervisor or mentor who is alert to what is
going on and one who stays involved and committed to this person's growth and
success.

The individual may know that something went wrong, but of course didn't
deliberately set out to make a blunder. What is needed is a line supervisor, mentor,
or coach who can spell out how to fix the problem and what skills will be needed
to prevent a repetition of the same difficulty. Emphasizing what went right and
wrong can lead to quick skills development and an agenda for executive development this person can build on.

The leadership development I have been describing is a contact sport, not
a classroom exercise. *Liking and learning are two different things*—painful experiences
and bad bosses have taught me more about being an effective executive than all
formal university programs combined. This kind of "in action" development and
coaching must be distinguished from more generalized 360-degree feedback or an
annual performance review. Those can certainly be enlightening and fulfill formal
aspects of learning, but nothing will substitute for an involved and caring superior
committed to the development of a potential leader.

One last comment on giving candid and clear feedback: Most executives are quite poor at this—and those who are the worst are "highly sensitive" executives who want to put a positive spin on everything around them. In the spirit of positive morale, they accentuate only positive aspects of performance, and the unfortunate subordinate never receives the needed candor and frankness required to become better. The most important virtue of great executives is that they have the courage to see their businesses, their performance, and their teams in clear and unvarnished terms. Translating that to executives developing around them, they are able to concisely, honestly, and clearly assess their performance and needed improvements. Blunt, clear, and concise feedback gives all the important benchmarks to members of their teams—and since they gain a clear picture of reality, they can rapidly adjust, improve, and develop. The individuals gain confidence (because they know nothing is hidden "in the file"), and the organization gains stronger performance in the marketplace, with more successors becoming qualified as "ready soon" because they have been tested on the firing line and given concise feedback on how to get better.

5. Support with Coaching

If all it takes is great selection and candid feedback annually or periodically, why don't promising talents quickly become great leaders? Because believing I have the capacity to lead, and then knowing on the job what worked and what didn't, is not enough to tell me *why* things worked (or didn't) and *what else* I might have done to lead more effectively. Until a potential leader knows what options and alternatives are available to solve business problems better in the future (the "what else"), he or she has only learned a lesson. The goal is to see a whole range of leadership choices and then pick the best one for success in the future. Those leadership choices become skills that are embedded in experience on the firing line—and that is what dynamic leaders have: skills based on experience that are "second nature" over time and lead to them being recognized as "natural leaders." Except that it isn't natural at all—it is learned and practiced until it becomes one's "style" as an effective leader.

That all sounds great, but how is that learned and practiced effectively on the job? By working for bosses who are effective coaches. Good coaches help emerging leaders discover their own strengths and development needs that are unique to them. They do it by being good observers and excellent listeners. They ask a lot of questions, provide feedback on a very frequent basis, and share their own experiences so the person learns new techniques and additional choices that would not have otherwise occurred to them. Most important, good coaches are supportive but honest in their relationships.

In one case I remember clearly, the developing leader had just completed a product launch in a new market—and in doing so forced his ideas about introducing and promoting the product upon local staff. At first, there were incremental gains (just due to the added investment, attention, and novelty in the market). However, once issues of affordability and resistance from competitors took hold, the launch was clearly unsuccessful. This promising executive's boss was tough minded but also a good coach. His feedback was concise about the failure (which was transparent), but in coaching this executive focused on the fact that this approach alienated the local team, disrespected their contributions, and, importantly, failed to capitalize on their local knowledge and experience. You can imagine that that lesson was painful and expensive but also enormously important. This executive spent a lot of time in the months ahead learning how to listen to his staff, incorporate their ideas, and take seriously their contributions. That lesson learned in the field has paid rich dividends for this executive ever since.

It is apparent why successful line executives are the best coaches; they utilize work underway as true "action laboratories" for rapid learning and development. Like a general on the battlefield, they cannot wait for classroom time to develop promising leaders. They take real life (and death) situations and force those in charge to build their skills while fully engaged in conflict. That is why I have always favored blunt-spoken bosses—they don't pull their punches and can teach important lessons as quickly as you can absorb them.

The most dangerous coaches are "people oriented" executives who are so interested in remaining popular that they sugar-coat every assessment and provide feedback couched in such positive terms that it is impossible to learn what needs improvement. Almost invariably, when they discipline or terminate a subordinate there is shock and anger: "He/she never gave me a clue I was in trouble!" Good coaches may make you wince when the feedback is painful, but they are actually more helpful. As one CEO told me while pointing out something I had to fix (as my face turned red), "Don't worry, it isn't personal—it's just business and something you need to learn."

Third-party executive coaches are highly popular and in vogue today. Those who are seasoned and skilled can be just as effective in coaching as senior line executives—especially when the promising executive has no internal coach she or he likes and trusts (emphasis on the latter point). These "professional coaches" can provide the kind of objective, blunt, and skilled feedback that accelerates rapid development—and this coaching can work just as well as that of a strong internal mentor. In addition, when there are issues of trust or conflicts within a team (or with a boss) that are hard to resolve, the third-party relationship can help give the promising talent strategies and suggestions on how to cope effectively within the organization. The coach can also help the individual gain confidence that he or she can develop skills and advance within the organization without giving up and going elsewhere. In those cases, an external coach can "save" a talent for the organization and keep the person from quitting, although there are cases where the coach must agree to "go elsewhere" to maintain the confidentiality and integrity required of any coach.

6. Make Good Assessments of Potential (for Key Appointments and for Succession)

Who is ready to take a top assignment, and who is capable of leading at the next level? These are always difficult judgment calls, and good judgment is based on sound experience and perceptive observations. For these reasons, organizations have developed formal processes to assess people. Assessment centers, performance appraisal systems, and talent reviews as part of succession planning are all core operating mechanisms in most organizations.

The reality is, however, that regardless of how objective the process seems or how large the machinery in place to help make these decisions, it is flawed and fallible individual human beings making these judgments. Consequently, the most important thing is to have individuals with a track record of success making these judgments in charge of the process. Don't leave it to technicians or academics, or to process people who fall in love with their own testing process or checklists that cannot be matched with living, breathing executives in the field.

It surely helps to take time to define what is considered excellent leadership behaviors for our business and at this point in time. There is also the need for a common language for discussing leadership and the values that support leaders in your organization's culture. Those things are important to ensure that the drive for leadership at the top is understood and supported with criteria and values applied consistently up and down the organization. The essential hope is that your organization can do this in a non-bureaucratic way that supports the very real people running the businesses in your company.

A closing thought: In making key appointments, humility often leads to better and sometimes surprising outcomes. Most successful executive search professionals admit that luck and their personal knowledge of a candidate is often more valuable than all their computer databanks and global networks. The best prospect may have, by coincidence, just sent a CV over the transom or showed up for coffee quite by chance. We need to be humble enough to accept the fact that the best candidate sometimes just appears.

Similarly, we need to be humble enough to recognize that a great leader can emerge in our organization outside of all the processes we set up to identify her or him. I recall an outstanding leader who was often overlooked for promotion by his company in his early years because he lacked the sizzle of his FMCG colleagues—who were more used to gold cufflinks and black limousines befitting their status. He made his own coffee and liked to share it with co-workers in the cafeteria in the morning—it was his "daily briefing" from across levels and functions in the company. His interviews always began, "Tell me about yourself . . ." and then he patiently and intently listened without interruption. When he was inevitably promoted to higher and higher levels, it was because he always had stronger and highly motivated teams. He spent a lot of his time figuring out *what they needed*—not how he looked! As a result, his teams got great results—they were thoughtfully armed, aimed, and rewarded when they went into the competitive battlefield. This leader developed a large number of talented executives—and everyone in the company benefited from his ability to recognize and appoint the best leaders.

7. Going Global Is No Longer Just an Option

Today everyone recognizes that leadership for the future must function and be developed on a global basis. That all sounds terrific, but who actually believes that they must leave "home" and take that assignment in a foreign country (or Third World environment) to be truly successful? Not many—and therein lies the opportunity for those who are willing to do so.

Keep in mind, there is growing and nearly universal pressure for "workplace flexibility" and "work-life balance"—and those are, of course, highly desirable things. There are also a number of professions and occupations in which one can work from home at least part of the time (law, accounting, and consulting, among others). There are also many business fields in which one can remain based in one place (investment banking, stock brokerage or trading, service occupations, or professions). In the world of business leadership, however, development must be for international opportunities and competition—and that means leadership development must be global, too.

This is so obvious there is no need to belabor the point. However, the implications of that reality may not be so clear. Most international corporations or firms are keen to create and market their best brands globally. To do so they must have international leadership, and this creates global marvelous career opportunities for the talent with the ambition, skills, and motivation to take advantage of them. In my view, these global opportunities are the "career portals" for the best leaders for the future. Those who have the vision and self-confidence to seize these opportunities will gain skills and experience that will set them apart from and above their domestic colleagues for a generation.

The main qualifications for these opportunities are the same educational and experience requirements any other promising leader must have, but in addition they must have the *mobility and language skills* to make the most of these possibilities—those are the tickets or the "passports" that allow leaders of the future to pass through the career portals for truly senior global positions. The language requirement speaks for itself, but in the global companies I have worked for, language was the single best predictor of who would take an international assignment and who would succeed in that assignment.

Mobility is the least understood requirement across most companies. It seems simple enough: Is the candidate for international development willing and able to move abroad for a new position? Most executives readily say "yes" unless health issues, aging parents, or some other family issue prohibits or postpones taking a position in another country. However, while the company tries to match the executive with a need abroad, until a specific position and country is identified, that mobility isn't really tested. Recently, a top executive position in Russia developed in a consumer products company, and a few qualified candidates were approached on a preliminary basis. Each declined the opportunity, although each agreed it was the best position for top management development across the business. Why? They said they were mobile—but really meant they and their families could move to London, Paris, Brussels, Dublin, Rome, or Munich. Moscow, Kazakhstan, Beijing, or Sao Paolo were viewed in a totally different way—even though they might provide more exciting growth possibilities for the business and a more substantial leadership experience for the executive. Mobility has to be tested well in advance of planning any assignment or career plan for the most promising talent in the company.

The other main quality global leaders must possess is cultural curiosity: to succeed as an international executive (and especially in consumer products companies), one has to have an interest in the culture, customs, values, and tastes of that global audience that consumer companies must serve.

Family considerations are essential in making international opportunities successful for the company and the executive. If the spouse and children are unhappy and cannot adjust to the new environment, it is only a matter of time before the expatriated executive must give up and go home. There is no such thing as an executive succeeding in an international base without his family gaining something positive in the experience, even if it takes some time and an adjustment period before stability and happiness emerge. Both the executive and spouse have to make a plan to help their children adjust and then thrive in the new country. One often overlooked benefit: Children who succeed in adjusting to a new culture and learn the language often are more sought after in the college admissions process—the expatriate experience can help get your children into better universities!

8. Succession: The Process Versus the Stark Realities

To wrap up this chapter, it is important to frame the context for leadership development within a company's specific business plans for the future. We are seeking to develop leaders to ensure the company has the executive leadership to achieve its strategic plan for the future. That is just as important as a company's patents, reputation, and financial resources. Without the essential leadership, it cannot achieve its purpose and plans.

The succession plan must become the dynamic and vital process to identify the company's leadership requirements well into the future and to present those requirements as leadership development opportunities for the company's best talent. All succession plans look good until they are tested by reality. You can write that you have two CEO successors who are "ready now," but when the board actually has to appoint the successor, there is often a moment of truth where the written plans are not accepted and there is a boardroom revolt.

Succession planning, just like sausage making, is really messy when key members of the board and line management become deeply involved in the process for top executive positions. Without that involvement, however, there is no actual commitment to successors as identified, and, increasingly, boards and management teams engage executive search firms to find someone outside of the company they can both agree on.

Far from the CEO position, succession plans are also hollow if they are never or rarely followed in making key appointments. Managers who believe they are "named in the succession plan" are shocked or angry to learn that commitment to their advancement was shallow—and in fact, another executive or an outsider was chosen. Therefore, all the leadership development investment will walk out the door unless career plans for the individual are committed to in the succession plan, regardless of the level. Unless one believes that he or she can count on a career plan with your company, the person must go elsewhere to pursue his or her objectives. A key test question for your organization: What percent of the time is our succession plan actually consulted or followed in making appointments?

Succession planning is often referred to in terms of retirement plans for key executives. It must be far more than that: Succession planning is also a powerful tool for an individual to help facilitate her or his own career. If I am successful, I must have at least one "ready now" successor ready to take my position or I am not free to move on (or up) to my next opportunity. Therefore, the real reason you may be trapped in your career may lie with your failure to develop a qualified person to follow you—you are "too valuable" where you are and must stay in place. So succession planning is readying the organization *for success*—not just planning backups for retirement.

Summary and Conclusion

These have been the thoughts of a seasoned practitioner around developing leaders. Leadership courses and programs can serve a valuable purpose, but never when they are used in isolation. They are appropriate when new skills are required (for example, transitioning into a general management position from a functional role); when you want to expose people to new ideas or directions; when it is important to communicate with managers during periods of great change; when people need to develop networks laterally across the organization and share best practices across an organization; or when a forum is required for senior leadership to communicate and model new direction or behaviors. So there are clearly times and reasons when such courses or programs are effective and important for the organization. At the end of the day, however, I believe the best developers of leaders are committed line executives in the field who take full responsibility for growing the next generation of leadership.

Let me close with one case study of an outstanding president whose career and development I contributed to and observed over the past two decades right up to today. Born in the Nordics of European and American parents, he finished secondary school in the United States and then, over time, graduated with an MBA from Columbia University. Selected as one of two "graduate interns," he served in the home office of a global company in Manhattan. It was a very informal program but offered him a brief rotation through key financial and marketing functions of a first-class organization. At the same time, just through the normal coffee break and lunch social contacts, he developed a large number of contacts who would become his "functional network" throughout his career. He was modest and low key, but his strong work ethic, smarts, and common sense and his candor, honesty, and reliability caught the attention of two senior executives in the same facility. He always delivered on what he promised, and when something went wrong, he quickly pointed out the problem and took responsibility for the mistake without excuses or prettying up the facts. Those qualities are essential for a top executive to be trusted and relied on in the field—"no surprises" is the mantra of all successful field executives.

From these informal "sponsors" he gained coaching almost daily—without any forms or formal processes. As key projects opened up or crises presented the need for problem solvers, he was quite naturally steered to join the project or team. As he delivered reports or presented solutions to issues, he received instant feedback on strengths or weaknesses in his analyses or his recommendations. All of this contributed to his development—without any formal interventions at all.

Soon he raised his hand to take an overseas assignment in Switzerland while still in a headquarters organization. More feedback and coaching followed, along with working knowledge of international economies and foreign currency. In the course of his informal interactions with colleagues in his new base, a second language developed easily. His early mentors in the world headquarters kept track of him, and as his success continued (although with quite a few bumps in the road along the way), he was identified as a successor for a number of international posts over the years. With each assignment he grew and built skills, and applying the same principles that worked for him, he has built very strong functional and line management teams that are very loyal and dedicated to him as a leader.

This successful blueprint for development can be replicated in any organization. Take care to bring on board promising talent and ensure that top management is involved in selecting each recruit. Make sure that those talented individuals receive an early exposure to your top functional and line executives to help them know each other, which will foster "networks" for the individual and coaching and mentoring opportunities for senior executives. Once identified and confirmed as potential leaders, give them jobs and assignments that are as big as possible with enough autonomy so they can find their own strengths and learn new skills to overcome their shortcomings. A personal prejudice of mine: Give them an international assignment as soon as possible—it develops leadership, adjustment, and language skills quickly, along with cultural and business knowledge in a whole new world for them.

Ensure there are "return trips" with some frequency, and schedule meetings on those tours, so that senior mentors and informal coaches can observe development progress while continuing to provide candid, timely, and relevant feedback and coaching on coping with successes and failures. Follow up these meetings with an assessment: Given the progress of this individual, what is the right next step for her or him? And reflect that in your succession and development plans right away.

Postscript for promising executives: As you read the development suggestions outlined above, you recognize that you can build your own tailored development program for yourself by simply applying the steps outlined here in your own "self-development plan." Don't wait for someone else to do it for you—take responsibility for your own career.

Tim Sullivan is senior vice president of human resource of Bacardi Limited. Prior to Bacardi, he served over ten years as vice president of human resources with Philip Morris International—with 55,000 employees based in more than 120 countries. Earlier in his career, Tim served as executive vice president in human resources for other global consumer products companies, including Diageo/Grand Met in the United States; as senior vice president of human resources for the Pillsbury Company; and as head of AMF Incorporated, Maremont Corporation, and units of United Airlines.

SECTION 3

DEVELOPING GLOBAL LEADERS

Companies faced with expanding their businesses around the world face challenges never before confronted in the history of business, primarily due to economic development and new competition throughout the world, but also due to technology—far-reaching parts of a company in diverse locations can be knitted together to work, connect, and create value. What this means is that everyone, at almost every level of an organization, is in some way impacted by globalization. Globalization has become a leadership issue and a leadership development challenge for everyone. The authors in this section discuss what globalization means to leadership development and ways to develop leaders who are equipped to meet the challenges of this global environment. Frank Waltmann from Novartis a large pharmaceutical company facing global competition and regulatory issues, describes how they go about developing global leaders. Eric Olson provides some concrete ideas in describing how leadership development has become a global challenge and opportunity. Finally, Alice Portz describes in detail how action learning can be used as a method to develop global leaders.

The Evolution of Leadership Development at Novartis, by Frank Waltmann
Achieving Success in the Globalization of Leadership Development, by Eric Olson
Developing Global Leaders Through Action Learning, by Alice Portz

CHAPTER 6

THE EVOLUTION OF LEADERSHIP
DEVELOPMENT AT NOVARTIS

Frank Waltmann

When Sandoz Ltd. and Ciba-Geigy Corp merged in 1996, one newspaper headline described it as the "mega-merger" of the year. And it was: the joining of the two Swiss companies into a new company known as Novartis created the second-largest drug conglomerate in the world.

Other newspaper headlines followed as business analysts discussed the challenges facing the new company. How would the merger affect shareholder value? Research and development? Marketing and sales?

The training department didn't generate any headlines, but it faced the same challenges. How could training best serve the new company?

During the first two years after the merger, the company focused on the logistics of merging the Ciba-Geigy and Sandoz training departments. While both companies shared the same Swiss cultural environment, the new training department inherited diverse and fragmented learning in each company. Overlaps needed to be eliminated, synergies needed to be created, and a crucial question needed to be answered: Should training in the new company be centralized or decentralized?

Novartis decided on a combined approach, with centralized learning for management and local and regional training for non-management. Novartis Corporate Learning was created to ensure alignment, eliminate overlaps, and drive strategic initiatives into the whole organization. Corporate Learning would also be responsible for the development and delivery of the programs for the company's management population, which represents 10 percent of all employees. Local and Regional Training and Development would be responsible for non-management and technical training.

From the start, Novartis sought to integrate development into the HR function. Corporate Learning, together with the Global Talent Management Department, forms one of the key components of Corporate HR.

Setting a Strong Foundation

In designing and delivering a new portfolio of management learning programs, the new Corporate Learning unit followed two principles. First, all learning must be aligned with the company's strategic agenda. Second, learning must be integrated into global talent management activities.

To ensure alignment between learning and the strategic agenda, Corporate Learning developed strong links between program offerings and the leadership of the company. Each program offered by the learning unit is sponsored by a member of the Novartis Executive Committee, and other top managers are also involved in the design and delivery of each program. On average, about sixty Novartis managers are involved during the design process.

Integrating learning into global talent management activities was accomplished with a set of management development tools and processes, such as definition of leadership standards and competencies, identification of high-potentials, career development and performance management processes, and an Organization Talent Review (OTR) system for development planning. In combination with Corporate Learning's portfolio of courses, these tools link individual and organization development needs in a systematic way.

Corporate Learning also established a program nomination process closely linked with the OTR system that requires collaboration between HR and line managers, which gives line managers a clear understanding of each individual's development needs so they can choose a program to match the needs.

Filling the Leadership Pipeline

A clear need after the merger was ensuring a pipeline of leadership talent. This became a priority of the new learning department as it planned the future of management learning at Novartis.

Again, developing a fundamental approach was the first step. Talent Management and Learning established three key components to leadership development: talent identification/selection, job experiences, and continuous learning.

To identify and select leadership talent, Novartis HR instituted a set of leadership standards in close cooperation with senior management and also designed functional competency models that define the essential core skills, knowledge, and abilities an individual needs to be successful in a specific role and function. To incorporate the standards and competency models into the culture, an *Executive Guide* and a *Manager's Toolkit for Assessing and Applying Potential* were developed.

Job experiences are viewed by Novartis as having a dual function: They drive the business and develop leaders. The company's OTR process provides a system that enables the company and individuals to focus on clear goals and set directions and priorities and to establish mutual expectations between Novartis and its associates. Career review meetings are held with each associate annually. These discussions result in a written, agreed-on development plan for which the responsible line manager gives feedback and outlines next steps to take.

Continuous learning processes provide feedback, rewards, and learning to reinforce the Novartis culture, improve performance, and ensure continuous development. A single company-wide 360-degree feedback tool is in place and programs offered through Corporate Learning are augmented with accelerated development programs to speed up the growth and development of potential leaders and mentoring programs to leverage top management experience and skills as they coach/develop young high-potentials in the organization.

A Two-Dimensional Model for Learning Programs

The portfolio of programs designed by Corporate Learning since the merger follows a two-dimensional model that provides a sharp focus, both in terms of target audience and subject matter.

The first dimension is adapted from the leadership pipeline concept championed by Ram Charan, Jim Noel, and Stephen Drotter. The leadership pipeline model (see Figure 1) views an individual's career as a series of transitions from one management stage to another. To keep the pipeline running smoothly, a corporation needs to help prepare the best talent to negotiate the next turn in the pipe. Novartis' adaptation of this model breaks management learning programs into three levels: first, middle and senior.

One practice Novartis instituted after some experience is to tie the learning level to an associate's actual job responsibilities, rather than his or her title. Programs have been expanded to include associates with management responsibilities

FIGURE 1. THE LEADERSHIP PIPELINE MODEL

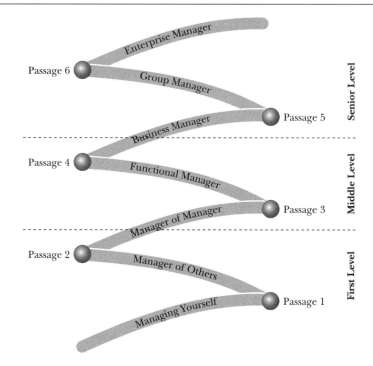

who do not necessarily have direct reports, for example, project managers who don't have formal authority over others in their groups.

The second dimension of the learning program model is core capabilities. In addition to levels, programs are positioned in terms of the core capabilities they develop: external focus, innovation, people or performance, as shown in Figure 2. The result is a portfolio of highly targeted programs in general management, marketing, project management, negotiation, IT, leadership, and finance.

The Leadership Development Curriculum

By 2007, Novartis' focus on filling the leadership pipeline resulted in a six-program leadership development curriculum that evolved from a single course, *Leading at the Frontline.*

Leading at the Front Line was developed in partnership with Mercer Delta. During its pilot phase in 2000, the program was used in part as a change management tool to impart the strategy of the new company to its five hundred top managers.

FIGURE 2. CORE CAPABILITIES

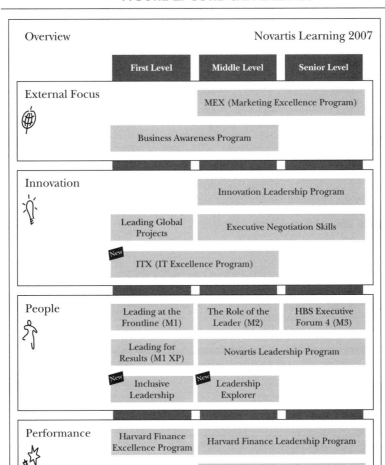

After the initial group was trained, the program changed its focus to providing basic leadership skills for first-time managers. The program is given in multiple languages to make the learning accessible to more people. By 2002, sixty-two programs were offered across all business units in six languages. In 2007, Novartis Learning expects to deliver eighty programs per year to employees worldwide—in twelve languages.

Leading at the Frontline emphasizes central corporate values, but is customized to specific regions. The program also takes a personal approach: Participants are asked to bring their own experiences and problems to solve during the course. The wide participation in this program has had multiple benefits: It encourages large numbers of managers to improve their skills, understand Novartis processes and culture, and foster synergies in the company. An unplanned but welcome benefit is a positive effect in inter-division cooperation. Two of the company's divisions have delivered the program to each other—a great example of how global learning can break down organizational silos.

As Corporate Learning developed its two-dimensional model, additional courses were added to the leadership curriculum. A middle-level program, *Role of the Leader,* was added in 2002. Targeted at managers of managers, *Role of the Leader* provides a broader view of leadership, showing participants how to manage in several dimensions: vertically, horizontally, across geographic and cultural boundaries, and across company boundaries.

Between 2002 and 2006, Corporate Learning added two more leadership development programs: *Leading for Results,* a program for alumni of *Leading at the Frontline,* and an *Executive Forum,* conducted at the Harvard Business School, for senior executives. Corporate Learning rounded out the decade with the addition of another two courses, *Leadership Explorer* and *Inclusive Leadership.* The programs focus respectively on the individual managing him/herself and supporting the current diversity and inclusion initiative at Novartis.

Figure 3 illustrates how the courses are overlaid on Novartis' Leadership Pipeline Model.

Refining Leadership Development

Throughout the last decade, Corporate Learning has assessed and revamped its course offerings as the company's priorities have changed. In 2003, the unit undertook an intensive self-assessment as preparation for applying for certification from the European Foundation for Management Development (EFMD). EFMD is an international organization dedicated to the continuous improvement of management development. The unit's hard work and dedication paid off when Novartis became the first pharmaceutical company to receive EFMD certification.

As Novartis celebrates its ten-year anniversary, Corporate Learning has turned its attention to new leadership development challenges. Some challenges are typical of any function that has reached maturity: keeping a sharp focus, ensuring continuing high quality programs and consistently realigning its activities with

FIGURE 3. LEADERSHIP DEVELOPMENT CURRICULUM

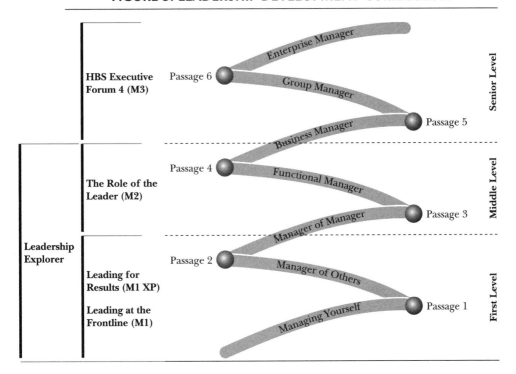

company goals. Other challenges are due to the changing environment in the pharmaceutical industry.

Case Example: The Role of Learning in Supporting Growth in China

One of these challenges is supporting leadership development in emerging markets such as China, which is expected to be the fifth-largest pharmaceutical market by 2010. Novartis is now the third-largest multinational pharmaceutical company in China, with an average growth of 30 percent since 2000 and fast employee expansion.

Operating in China poses significant management challenges. At one time, multinational companies filled mid- to senior-level management positions primarily with expatriates. The trend now is to hire local talent; in fact, about 99 percent of the Novartis China staff is Chinese.

While the proportion of college graduates in China is growing and competition for entry-level white-collar jobs is becoming fierce, fewer than 10 percent of graduates in China have the skills to work for a foreign company. Estimates are that China will need 75,000 mid-level managers with international experience by 2015, while the country now has only about 5,000 such managers. At the same time, the competition for skilled managers is becoming more intense as an increasing number of Chinese companies enter the market. There are currently more than 6,000 domestic pharmaceutical manufacturers in the country, and that number is expected to grow.

Retention of talent is also a challenge: the average tenure of mid- and high-level executives is eight to twelve months and turnover among skilled managers is in the 30 to 40 percent range.

To address the problem of filling the leadership pipeline in China, Novartis applied the same basic approach that has proved successful in other regions, tailoring its talent management to fit the specific needs of Novartis China.

Surveys of Chinese managers show that Chinese managers want to improve their practical skills and rank interpersonal relations as a greater factor than salaries in the decision to leave a company. This data suggested three areas to focus on in China: training, deployment of talent in "stretch" assignments with clearly defined career paths, and improving the connection between newer associates and experienced peers and other professionals.

In developing training for China, Novartis set a two-faceted goal: to help Chinese leaders become more effective both in China and in the global Novartis organization. To accomplish this, Corporate Learning created the Novartis China Leadership Development Center in 2005. The Center, which combines traditional education with on-the-job learning, offers programs provided by both the country organization and global learning. These include an intensive, highly customized accelerated development program at BiMBA in Beijing, localized corporate programs, a virtual training center, Corporate Learning programs, and marketing and sales programs.

The BiMBA Development Program is an innovative eighteen-month program that has been ranked by the Chinese versions of *Fortune* and *Forbes* as "The Most Valuable Business School in China" and "The Most Valuable Part-Time MBA Program in China." The program combines lessons on corporate finance, marketing, and leadership with local case studies. Forty-six of the company's most promising Chinese staff were selected to participate following a rigorous assessment of the local organization. These students attend the program for four days every month to two months.

Finding challenging "stretch" assignments means ensuring that the corporate OTR process provides each employee with a clear career path. Potential future assignments must be mapped out and the actions needed to move from one level to another defined.

Finally, to increase the Chinese staff's sense of belonging, the company instituted monthly lunches with senior management to discuss the latest business developments. The key messages from these meetings are then communicated immediately to all regions and offices. Longer-term business trips have also been instituted to help integrate Chinese hires into the global corporate culture while expanding their networks.

The intensive work that Novartis has done to develop its staff in China has already paid off: Not only does the company have lower turnover in its sales force than other companies, but it was also named one of the Best Employers in China in 2005 by Hewitt Associates.

The Decade's Key Recommendations

In the decade since the 1996 merger, Novartis has become one of the fastest-growing and most-respected healthcare companies in the world, with analysts often citing Novartis' strong pharmaceutical pipeline as a major factor in the company's success. Behind the scenes, Corporate HR and Corporate Learning contribute to that success by filling the company's leadership pipeline with skilled and motivated employees.

Based on what Novartis has learned about corporate learning and leadership development over the last decade, following are ten key recommendations:

1. Get the support of top management; this is essential. Novartis Learning programs owe much of their success to the participation of senior executives, who not only participate in the design process, but also show their commitment by their presence during the programs.
2. Focus corporate learning programs on key initiatives. Learning must be directly aligned with corporate strategy and business challenges.
3. Get the right people into the learning department; it is important to include people with commercial and business experience as well as people with HR experience.
4. Put quality, not quantity first: think of yourself as a specialty shop, not a shopping center. Choose areas where you can add value with high-quality programs for a selected number of employees.
5. If you combine centralized and decentralized learning, manage carefully and with consensus. Value your decentralized colleagues and establish an open communication process.

6. If you are a global organization, act globally. Be adaptable. Develop and apply intercultural skills.

7. Carefully select the best training providers and work with them as partners. Look beyond what is available locally; find the best providers wherever they are.

8. Take care when making changes in your learning team. Don't change your team too fast or too often. Learning is a strategic function: you need to build a sustainable team.

9. Fully integrate your learning activities into overall HR processes but spend 90 percent of your time with the business.

10. Assess learning results to make sure they meet changing corporate objectives. Use formal assessment tools as well as informal discussions with participants. Follow up with participants after the program. Obtain their input; listen, learn, and continuously improve your programs.

Dr. Frank Waltmann is the head of learning for Novartis International, where his responsibilities include strategic and global learning initiatives. Under his direction Novartis Learning was awarded with the European Foundation for Management Development (EFMD) Quality Label. His most recent project includes the creation of the Novartis Leadership Development Center in Beijing, China. Prior to joining Novartis in 1999, Dr. Waltmann served as a management consultant for Ernst & Young and as personal assistant to the German Minister of Transportation and Aviation. He also served in various marketing, finance, and HR roles at PUMA Sports AG. Dr. Waltmann is a member of the Steering Committee of the European Foundation for Management Development (EFMD), the Advisory Board of Credit Suisse Business School, the European Corporate Learning Forum and the U.S.-based Conference Board. Dr. Waltmann received his Ph.D. in economics, business administration, and international relations from University Albert-Ludwig in Freiburg (Germany).

CHAPTER 7

ACHIEVING SUCCESS IN THE GLOBALIZATION OF LEADERSHIP DEVELOPMENT

Eric Olson

The worldwide growth in leadership development programs is the direct result of numerous organizations trying to expand their leadership strategy in order to keep pace with the globalization of their business strategy. This linkage between leadership and business strategy is what defines the current understanding of the "globalization of leadership development" and it also defines its success or failure.

In a recent study (2005) of 223 executives from 44 countries, the Economist Intelligence Unit discovered that most companies defined success in this endeavor as "developing leaders who align and grow the business in ways that transcend geographic, political, organizational, and cultural barriers." Because of the complex, dynamic requirements for leading in a global (as opposed to local) world, the research found that leadership development that was globalized needed to address the notion of "whole leadership" in particular. The challenge of leading teams or organizations of culturally diverse individuals with conflicting values requires head, heart, and guts. Add the element of virtual or remote teaming as the primary mode of contact and the need for whole leadership becomes even more apparent.

Linking Global Leadership and Business Strategy

While the specifics of content and delivery vary depending by culture and circumstance, the general subject matter for learning initiatives that link global leadership and business strategy is often shaped by three levels of need: master the fundamentals of leading in a global world, improve personal and organizational performance in cross-cultural environments, and demonstrate strategic leadership in a complex, global world.

Mastery of the fundamentals typically includes three competencies: develop a global mindset, value diversity, and lead with global responsibility.

- Develop a global mindset typically includes elements like engage in lifelong learning, understand global challenges and opportunities, and transfer best practices across cultures.
- Value diversity includes such things as develop cultural self-awareness, respect cultural differences, and balance the needs of a diverse workplace.
- Lead with global responsibility involves knowing how to act with integrity, make decisions based on what customers' value, and persevere in the face of adversity.

The intermediate level of learning in many globalized leadership initiatives focuses on improving individual and organizational performance. Three competencies frequently addressed at this level include knowing how to drive for the broader picture, manage laterally, and balance paradoxes.

- Drive for the broader picture means to take a systemic view of the organization, synthesize knowledge from a global perspective, and to see local and global issues simultaneously.
- Manage laterally means that leaders develop global networks, manage virtual relationships, and leverage relationships inside and outside the organization.
- Balance paradoxes requires leaders to tolerate ambiguity, seek and appreciate competing interests (local/global customer focus; centralized/decentralized structures, etc.), and to take calculated risks.

The most advanced level of competencies for leading in a global world typically include the ability to articulate a point of view, manage global teams, and lead change globally.

- Articulate a point of view means leaders can develop insights about doing business globally, reassess strategy based on changes in the global environment, and articulate a compelling vision across cultures.

- Manage global teams challenges leaders to establish clear direction and norms for global teams, build open and trusting relationships across cultures, and leverage the unique skills and talents of the team.
- Lead change in the context of leading in a global world means to create new opportunities out of change and chaos, remove obstacles to allow for change, and to build capabilities to compete in a global environment.

The Expansion of Global Leadership Development

The phenomenon of leadership development's globalization is one of migration from a North American/European origin in the 1960 through the 1990s, to an expansion into non-Western geographies in the decade of 1990–2000, and most recently toward an increasingly omni-directional expansion. In the last five years, for example, the globalization of leadership development programs at the Delta Executive Leadership Center (ELC) has doubled every two years with the proportion of non-U.S. programs constituting slightly over 50 percent of all programs during this period. During a recent ELC leadership program in Budapest, another leadership program was taking place in the same hotel. That program was delivered to managers and supervisors of a Chinese shoe factory setting up East European operations, and the program was delivered entirely in Chinese by managers from Shanghai.

While there are many sources for tracking the globalization of leadership development, at ELC it is measured by the iterations to Stephen Rhinesmith's work in a *Manager's Guide to Globalization*. It is one of the most frequently cited works in the field and still guides discussions with the CLOs of multi-national companies in all parts of the world. The thinking and conceptual frameworks in the book have led to an ongoing globalization of leadership work at companies like Novartis, Groupo Santander, and Bank of America over the past decade.

Because of continued interest in the subject, a second generation of global leadership work is emerging in these companies. Features include: (1) ELC hire of partners with global work experience, experience in running business units that had multinational scope, (2) a mix of U.S. and international faculty, (3) a blending of consulting/learning engagements, and (4) emphasis on cost control and meeting learning objectives. Companies increasingly seek leadership solutions that successfully integrate learning and business objectives in a much more impactful way than has been done in the past, and the solutions must have relevance to a variety of business and cultural settings.

As the globalization of leadership development moves into a more business-based phase, it's important to acknowledge and understand the drivers of this change. Key drivers cited by clients who are expanding their globalized leadership development efforts often include:

1. Business: The business strategy needs globally savvy leaders.
2. Organizational: There are significant gaps in the leadership pipeline.
3. Geographic: New markets lag behind core markets in terms of local leadership.
4. Technology: Cost and travel constraints drive the need for more virtual work.
5. Diversity: From legal requirement to market driven need.

In addition to these universal drivers of change, regional drivers impact growth in various geographies. For example:

- North America (market penetration and Baby Boomer replacement)
- Europe (defend and grow position beyond the Eurozone)
- Brazil, Russia, India, China, or BRIC countries (talent gap and market development)
- South America (foreign investment)
- Asia-Pacific (market expansion)
- Middle East/Africa (energy industry growth)

Defining Success

With changes in the drivers for globalization of leadership development also come changes in terms of how success is defined. Within the CLO function, globalized leadership initiatives are often seen as successful if they adopt and implement an increased use of technology/learning systems. Travel is done when absolutely necessary to meet learning objectives, but otherwise many programs have gone virtual. Beyond the CLO's office there are more general measures. One is short-term, measurable impact, often achieved through global action learning initiatives (cost reduction, new product commercialization, market expansion, cycle time reduction, etc.). A second is organizational and business impact. Success in this case is seen through leaders who have learned how to open and sustain new market growth, strengthen organizational culture around key values and initiatives, and balance key global-local dilemmas.

A third measure of success is impact on the leadership pipeline. Companies invest in global leadership initiatives to increase in the number of leaders who can move from a "ready future" to "ready now" status in critical, global-oriented positions. Action coaching is a key component to achieving success.

A fourth measure is growth in the organization's leadership network. Some programs have no other stated goal than to bring together and deeply link networks of disparate leaders who can improve the way things are done by knowing each other better (break down silos, connect virtual teams, reduce frustration, enhance career development, improve communication, etc.). The degree to which measure of success is formalized depends on the strategic relationship between business units and functions.

Best Practices

Certain "lessons learned" or best practices emerge in the course of collecting evaluations on hundreds of leadership programs run in scores of countries. Most of these measures are cross-cultural, while others (noted below) are more specific to emerging markets outside the United States and Europe.

First, globalization is a dilemma to be balanced, not a problem to be solved. Companies that develop leaders who learn to differentiate between a problem to be solved and a paradox to be managed accelerate the speed of organizational learning and reduce costs by avoiding the extreme polarization that comes from seeing everything as a problem to be solved. Typical dilemmas that must be effectively managed include:

- Centralized learning AND decentralized learning
- Western-based messages AND local messages
- Corporate culture AND local business culture
- Global client expectations AND local responsiveness

Leadership initiatives that succeed in teaching how to balance global dilemmas often focus on the following key factors:

First, establish and follow due process where practical, balance integration and differentiation needs, and create a portfolio of solutions

Second, use variable formats to expand the leadership message into diverse populations. There is an art to selecting the optimal mix of academic, work, corporate, and world-centric formats for leadership initiatives. Academic formats excel at building a common, global knowledge base to leaders. Work-centered programs create the highest degree of relevance and knowledge retention. Corporate-sponsored initiatives bring the unique ability to infuse organizational culture to multiple parts of the company. World-centric formats have the greatest "life changing" impact on participants because of their immersion in the real-world of clients and markets, but they are prohibitively expensive for most organizations.

Third, use a design of mass customization where possible. In the past, globalized leadership initiatives have largely been "pushed" from a corporate center. Increasingly there has been a shift to acknowledge and incorporate the "pull" of ideas and needs from the field. To many organizations this means finding a way to preserve the core of any leadership offering and at the same time expand the edges of learning by promoting local interpretations of the initiative. This includes recognizing that even leaders with the same titles have different requirements for leading (that is, a country manager in a decentralized multi-national company has very different skills needs than one who is working in a functionally organized one), so adapt the content and delivery modes accordingly.

Fourth, learning goes both ways (top-down and bottom-up) when putting a globalized leadership initiative into action. Most globalized initiatives have board, CEO, or senior business unit leader sponsorship to guarantee gaining the attention of the organization. While sponsorship by the chairman, CEO, or board is critical, there's also a continuous learning loop for them in addition to the one for the CLO and participants. The best initiatives are characterized by "iterative learning" by the senior sponsor. This means that every time the senior sponsor(s) attend the meeting they dialogue with participants in such a way thatit's clear they have learned something from past programs and participants. Repeatedly, the highest marks on evaluations of global programs are given to the senior sponsor (especially the CEO) who can clearly communicate that he/she is also learning while leading in a highly complex business environment, and that the concepts and practices taught in the initiative make a difference in his/her world as well.

Fifth, action learning and action coaching continue to create some of the highest gains in learning and leading in a globalized initiative. These approaches consistently help to efficiently transfer the lessons learned from outsiders into the company's leadership DNA. Bringing the lessons learned from inside up through action learning projects gives a much more realistic sense of the participants ability to lead in the current business context.

Sixth, leadership architecture matters. There is a temptation to just build a program, either off of existing elements that are cobbled together or off the shelf. While initially attractive from an up-front cost, design, and development perspective, there are numerous drawbacks to this approach because of the complexity of global execution. Take the time to integrate into a strategic framework that respects the nuances and complexity of the firm's business strategy. Learning architects also examine whether the prerequisite components for success are present when designing their approach. Assess the context for any leadership initiative before beginning on an "importance" by "current performance" grid. Include items such as local business unit readiness, bandwidth for participants to commit to time required, integrated technology, and learning systems, etc.

Seventh, culture matters in learning and leading. Too often companies ignore or pay scant attention to the cultural bias inherent to their approach, and they are then mystified when encountering resistance from non-Western managers. The typical U.S.-based program often assumes the following values (which are not universally shared) about participants:

- Achievement-motivated
- Control-oriented
- Time-sensitive
- Action-driven
- Individually and team-oriented
- Ambiguity-tolerant
- Change-receptive
- Conceptually oriented
- Analytically skilled

These assumptions about participants' values and preferences can create hostility and sabotage the initiative's goals when exported to Europe or elsewhere. Outside of the United States, there may well be a need to pilot an approach to discover how best to communicate concepts like self, teamwork, alignment, etc.

Finally, there are different best practices to consider when working in non-Western environments. Senior leadership consultants with deep experience in Asian learning experiences cite these guidelines:

- There's no such thing as "Asia" when it comes to leadership initiatives. The region is too culturally diverse to embrace a single approach.
- The war for talent is paramount (brilliant people with technical skills in China and India outpace a similar-sized pool with experienced management practices).
- It is more expensive than it might seem at first to do business in these regions. Even virtual methods that rely on technology are not as inexpensive or as reliable as one could hope when trying to develop leaders.
- Decide on how much company culture to push, and what kind of flexibility is required for leading in the local culture.
- There will be unique ethical issues for leaders to face because of standard business practice differences between the U.S. and local custom (especially on the sales side); be proactive in your approach to this as a business issue.

Conclusion

Around the world there are thousands of solo practitioners, boutiques, and virtual networks of trainers, coaches, and consultants who aspire to contribute to globalized leadership development initiatives. However, to really provide a consistent approach to participants in multiple markets either requires a large internal staff or an external firm with global reach. In either case, there is a truism: Many believe they can do the work, but few have the unique combination of education, life experience, and corporate acculturation to work successfully in this arena. The design, development, sequencing, implementation, iterating, and evaluation of a globalized leadership approach is so nuanced and complex that it's important to talk with the best people before becoming too heavily invested in a particular approach or solution. Often key consultants or business faculty can offer current examples of how other companies are creatively handling a similar challenge. So first seek out wisdom from credible and diverse sources. Then begin the journey toward successful execution.

Eric Olson, Ph.D., is a partner with Oliver Wyman Delta Executive Learning Center. He is highly skilled at fostering leadership collaboration across divisional and cultural boundaries, as well as bringing together diverse teams for strategy execution/alignment, succession management, and leadership development. He has worked with companies such as Viacom, BP (ARCO), United Healthcare, Toyota, MTVNetworks, EADS/Airbus, and Sony. Formerly, he was CEO of an eHealth company that provided online specialty services between the United States and international medical centers. In addition, he served as a faculty member at various colleges and universities, including UCLA and UC Irvine Business School Extension. Dr. Olson holds a Ph.D. in clinical psychology from the Fuller Graduate School of Psychology, an MA in complexity and organizational change from the University of Hertfordshire, and an MS in counseling psychology from Central Washington University.

CHAPTER 8

DEVELOPING GLOBAL LEADERS
THROUGH ACTION LEARNING

Alice Portz

In early 2007, I was in China with thirty of Nike's emerging leaders from across the globe who were participants in a program conducted by Oliver Wyman Delta Executive Learning Center. These leaders were participating in a leadership development program, and this week in China was their second week-long learning program within the last eight weeks. At the end of each day, they were asked to reflect on what they had learned. On the last day, one team designed a reflection session that asked each participant to offer one word or short phrase to reflect on the whole week. As the participants passed around a sort of "talking stick" in the form of a Starbucks mug imprinted with the word Shanghai around the conference room of a large, multinational hotel chain with music from *Crouching Tiger, Hidden Dragon* playing in the background, a theme emerged. Over and over, we heard the words "context," "knowledge," and "perspective" combined with the word "global." Only two months into the program, and after only one week in China, paradigms were shifted and minds were opened to the future of a global business environment. What kind of program can develop this perspective so quickly? Action learning.

Leaders for a Global Environment

In 2005, Thomas L. Friedman chronicled the era of globalization in *The World Is Flat: A Brief History of the Twenty-First Century* and described how this new era of history has taken the world from being driven and shaped by corporations to being driven and shaped by individuals. This rapidly shrinking world offers new, tough challenges for the leadership development industry. In a 2005 study, the Globally Responsible Leadership Initiative estimated that "substantially less than 10 percent of the adult population of the developed world have reached a level of personal development wherein they have a genuinely global outlook." Similarly, the Global Leadership Imperative Study conducted in 2005 by Mercer Delta Executive Learning Center summarized the leadership shortages facing global businesses in the coming decades. Over 75 percent of study respondents revealed weaknesses in their organization's leadership pipelines, and competitive pressures alone revealed weaknesses in over 90 percent of pipelines. When it came to addressing the shortages, 72 percent of respondents said their companies were planning to take action to close the gap, but only half of the companies had made sufficient investments in that direction.

To address this severe shortage of leaders with a global perspective, more and more companies are turning to action learning, a methodology first introduced in the UK in the 1950s and 1960s by Reginald Revans. Action learning is based on the idea that, by working on projects of interest and importance to senior management and program participants, the participants will develop leadership abilities and business knowledge that will equip them to be valuable members of the leadership pipeline of a company.

As a method of developing executives, action learning is growing in popularity because it delivers immediate business results while the executives learn new leadership skills and behaviors. As a strategy for developing global leaders, action learning provides a tremendous advantage in the speed at which it develops perspective for participants—and as Alan Kay has said, "Perspective is worth eighty IQ points."

A Strategy for Developing Global Leaders

Action learning programs provide content and context at a pace that far exceeds that of other traditional ways of developing global leaders. Global business school programs and rotational assignments primarily provide content; the context can come, but it takes much longer than in an action learning program. Action learning gives participants the opportunity to learn the business from multiple functions, geographies, levels of expertise, biases, and conflicting priorities, and then examine business tradeoffs that must be made from country, regional, and global perspectives.

In 1998, David Dotlich and James Noel took the basic concepts of action learning and gave them a practical, approachable framework to guide companies through the process. Their book, *Action Learning*, provided a very useful, concrete model designed to develop high-potential, high-performing people into executive-level leaders. The framework is outlined in twelve steps:

1. Sponsor
2. Strategic Mandate
3. Learning Process
4. Selecting Participants
5. Forming Learning Teams
6. Coaching
7. Orientation to the Issue
8. Data Gathering
9. Data Analysis
10. Draft Presentation
11. Presentation
12. Reflection

While we use the same basic framework in developing global leaders, we make three important distinctions to adapt the framework for our purposes. These distinctions involve the participants, learning content, and projects.

Selecting Participants

Selecting the right participants for a global action learning program is critical to the program's success. They are typically emerging or high-potential leaders, which is usually defined as someone who is a consistent high performer and has potential for more senior leadership positions. Specific definitions of who is a high-potential leader are slightly different from company to company.

Often the company embarking on an action learning program selects participants with the intention of improving candidate pipelines for different levels. At Sun Microsystems, for instance, the company wanted to develop its high-potential employees to increase their capacity for vice president positions. At Nike, global action learning programs focused on growing the company's general manager capacity.

A third perspective on participant selection comes from another global client. When the company began selecting participants for a global action learning program, it had just acquired another company and doubled its size. In recognition of the talent present at the acquired company and in the interests of accelerating global perspective for everyone, the company selected half of the program participants from the legacy company and half from the acquired company.

Finally, when choosing participants for a global action learning program, companies must look across functional, cultural, and geographical boundaries. To really accelerate the perspective and cross-cultural learning potential within the program, companies must bring the diversity that represents their global presences into the program.

Selecting participants is only half of the equation. Once participants are chosen, teams must be formed to work together on the chosen projects. They must be given the opportunity to work across the cultural boundaries, language boundaries, and time zones that represent how the company is organized and/or competing in the marketplace. Often this kind of work involves virtual team work, when people aren't actually sitting in a room together and must communicate via e-mail, web conferences, and virtual collaboration sessions. This kind of work builds lateral networks across the organization.

Choosing Learning Content

Another critical element of global action learning programs is the learning content. The idea behind learning content in any action learning program is to balance the time spent doing actual work on the business project with more traditional learning. Within the learning programs, participants will work on developing critical skills and business acumen required of developing senior leaders. The difference with a global action learning program is that everything within the learning content is given a global perspective and context.

Several best practices go into creating the learning piece of a program that will successfully create global leaders and have a good output of people who are ready for global positions. First, before participants begin the program, they engage in a fair amount of pre-work that can take a variety of forms. Participants undergo interviews with sponsors and a series of assessments. They are assigned reading material as well, usually in the form of items that will develop both company perspective and global perspective. Along with analyst reports, participants are asked to read texts that help begin the development of global perspective. We often assign Friedman's book along with *The Manager's Guide to Globalization* by Stephen Rhinesmith and articles from *The Economist*. All of this reading helps participants begin the learning process and start to get a sense of what the street is saying about their company and industry.

Once the program begins, participants go through three to five days of content work before the teams part to perform project work. After spending some time working virtually, the teams come back together for additional learning content work. The learning content sessions provide instruction from external experts on topics such as strategic thinking, leading laterally, worldview, and innovation, and internal experts on topics around company strategy and goals. Sometimes the learning can take the form of content around the specific project as well, and usually includes sessions specific to managing cultural differences, influencing across boundaries and cultures, leading global teams in a matrix environment, leading virtual teams, balancing global paradoxes, and developing a global mindset.

Within these learning content sessions, it's critical that participants have visibility and interaction with executives and coaches. Coaching and opportunities for reflection are key elements in developing a global perspective rapidly. It's also vital to have internal experts available to offer instruction around strategy, goals, and values of the company. In a global environment, it's often the company values that hold people together; when people from different countries and different cultures share the values of the company, it gives them a connection that transcends the globe. Exposure of high-potentials to executives throughout the process also allows them to see how executives debate issues and consider tradeoffs.

Finally, external experts are an important element of learning content within a global action learning program; they can provide instruction on lateral leading, innovation, and business areas such as strategy and finances from a global perspective.

Picking Projects

The final critical element of an action learning program is the project. First, projects must involve working on real issues that require the organization to make tradeoffs and resource allocation decisions. The projects can involve global, regional, or local perspective, and tradeoffs can be country-specific, enterprise-specific, or business-unit-specific and have an impact on the results of the business.

First and foremost in any action learning program, global or otherwise, we need to be sure that the projects involve important business issues that are linked to the company strategy and an enterprise-wide view. The projects need to expand participants' knowledge beyond their areas of the business, and they need to include actions that link to company goals with metrics such as growth, enhancing brand image, delivering profitability, incremental revenue, cost savings and/or efficiencies improvement, customer experience, entering new markets, developing new products and services, and so on.

Sun Microsystems, for example, wanted to link and integrate all project teams into an overarching enterprise issue by having teams work on various elements of an "uber issue" and integrate their recommendations. At Nike, the programs were split into two focuses: short term and long term. For the two short-term projects, the teams looked at issues from a country level and an enterprise level and made recommendations that resulted in cutting costs and adding incremental revenue. For the long term, the teams looked at a strategic plan for a specific business. These projects enabled participants to think like general managers.

Another global organization took a different approach. In its quest to build future senior leaders, the company asked participants in the action learning program to choose their own projects, but the projects had to be business challenges that were linked to strategy. As part of the pre-work, participants submitted project ideas to the entire participant group and came up with a list of over twenty projects. From that initial list, they narrowed the list down by dividing it by local, regional, and global issues. They then took the global issues back to the team and asked them to vote with their money. We posed the question, "If you were a member of the executive committee and wanted to invest the company's money, what would be the top three projects you would pick?" The question forced participants to think about what projects would offer the best return on investment and ultimately helped them narrow the list down to seven projects that went before the executive committee.

Ways to Ensure Success

In the action learning programs I've led, I've noticed that there are several ways to increase the chances of success with an action learning program. One company I have worked with did some formal measurements of their action learning programs, and they found certain early indicators that were predictive of successful outcomes:

1. *Interaction with the right people:* Direct interaction and exposure to the executive committee was a significant factor in the success of participants, as was exposure to effective coaches. In addition, by putting participants in contact with each other across the business, when later lateral openings came up, participants had a higher rate of success in making those moves because their lateral networks were already in place.
2. *Taking an enterprise-wide perspective:* The most successful projects should require participants to take an enterprise-wide perspective.
3. *Specific solutions and actions:* The projects that fared the best and were the most successful were the ones that presented specific, focused questions on very

specific business issues. The recommendations also fared better when they were presented as specific solutions with clear actions.

4. *CEO delegation of actions:* The recommendations that had the best outcomes were those in which the CEO delegated actions to particular groups within the organization.

Measuring Success

In measuring the success of a global action learning program, we look at three key areas: the individual, the team, and the organization.

On an individual level, we develop for each person a leadership action plan that defines leadership issues, behaviors, and actions that are measured and time bound. The actions of the plan increase leadership effectiveness and often result in speed decisions, execution, and innovation.

To measure success at a team level, we look at things such as lateral network speed, success at implementing global initiatives, and effective team building to facilitate cross-boundary communication. These are the measures that build a strong company network for future problem solving, and these skills link disparate leaders and enable them to break down silos, connect virtual teams, improve communication, and get things done more efficiently.

Finally, at the organization level, we look at a variety of measures that relate to the company as a whole. First, we look at return on investment of the action learning projects. A successful program can produce cost reduction, new product commercialization, market expansion, cycle time reduction, and incremental revenue from the team recommendations. It can also open and sustain new markets, strengthen the organization's culture around key values and initiatives, and balance key global-local dilemmas. And in a broader organization context, participants can learn to guide their leadership decisions and recommendations through the program content, assessments, feedback, and coaching. Other success measures include speed of execution on a global level, retention of high performers, and acceleration of an organization's global leadership pipeline.

There are some specific areas where we can see success at an organization level as well. For example, at the end of an action learning program, participants present their findings to the executive committee in a formal presentation. A successful presentation can often act as an objective method to surface issues that are difficult for executives to fully understand because they tend to see the view and biases from limited perspectives. Successful presentations with quality work behind them will create the conversation at the senior level of the company and sometimes bring up conflicting tradeoffs that haven't been made, but need to be. Also, since the proposals and presentations are strategic in nature, they save consulting dollars for the company. Finally, the presentations represent the diversity of perspectives within the company and create organizational alignment around an issue.

The Benefits

Global action learning programs provide a wealth of opportunities and benefits to global companies. First, this type of organizational learning populates ideas faster across the globe; innovation and best practices can be shared quickly in the context of the projects, allowing those global best practices to be fully leveraged. Second, these programs surface endemic problems and questions that haven't been asked or answered. Third, the call for action and a sense of urgency builds change agents across organizational boundaries. Finally, by charging a global action learning team with these kinds of projects, the company brings fresh, bias-free thinking to strategic issues and encourages objective recommendations.

Drafting Success: An Analogy from Nike

I had the privilege of sitting in on the final presentation that Nike's global action learning team gave to the executive committee. This team came in with a freshness and approach that made everyone sit up and take notice, and being Nike, they came up with a sports analogy that really sums up the globalization of the business environment as a whole.

The Nike team presented its recommendations in the context of drafting in a sport. Cyclers and swimmers know about drafting—the idea that they can use the current from the cycler or swimmer in front of them to make their own journey faster, more powerful, and more productive for the same amount of energy. The Nike team suggested that by "drafting" off of their existing investments, best practices, worldwide brand, and growth, they could meet the strategic goals of the company. Every innovation, every project, every idea that someone has should play off the speed and momentum the company already has.

The idea of drafting plays so well into the environment of globalization that we are facing today and in the future. The world will only get smaller; companies need to address strategic issues faster than ever. By harnessing the power of high-potential employees within a global action learning program, companies can take a big leap toward meeting the growing challenges of a global business environment.

References

Dotlich, D.L., & Noel, J.L. (1998). *Action learning: How the world's top companies are re-creating their leaders and themselves.* San Francisco, CA: Jossey-Bass.

Friedman, T.L. (2005). *The world is flat: A brief history of the twenty-first century.* New York: Farrar, Straus and Giroux.

Globally Responsible Leadership Initiative. (2005). *Globally responsible leadership: A call for engagement.* European Foundation for Management Development.

Mercer Delta Consulting, LLC. (2006, January). *The global leadership imperative: Capturing competitive advantage.* Portland, OR: Author.

Washington Mutual, Inc. (2006, November). *At-a-glance: What happened to 2001–2006 chairman's challenge graduates.* Seattle, WA: Author.

Alice Portz is a leadership development consultant with over twenty-five years of experience in the field. As president of Alice Portz & Associates in Medina, Washington, she focuses on leadership development strategies and building the leadership capacity at companies such as Old Castle Materials, Concur Technologies, Washington Mutual, and Safeco. She is also an affiliate to Oliver Wyman Delta Executive Learning Center and focuses on delivering action learning programs for them with companies such as Nike, Sun Microsystems, Group Health Cooperative, Washington Mutual, and Cemex. She is an adjunct faculty member with the University of Nevada at Reno. Ms. Portz has an M.S. in human resource development from National Louis University and an Executive Certificate in Business Strategy for Development Professionals from Northwestern University.

SECTION 4

APPROACHES TO LEADERSHIP DEVELOPMENT

From developing human resources leaders to developing women, developing market excellence to creating employee engagement, companies face myriad functional issues and challenges when developing leaders. In this section, our authors address some of those issues and discuss how some companies have met those challenges successfully, presenting a range of methods and tools for developing leaders around issues as broad as marketing and customer service to risk management, HR, and helping leaders through transitions.

Developing Customer-Centric Leaders, by Thomas R. Knighton

Building Market Excellence, by Jean-Claude Larreche, Mario Castaneda, and Zohra Jan Mamod

Time Warner Creative Leadership Summit, by Vera Vitels

Be the One: The LEADToshiba Experience,
by Anthony V. Codianni and Terry Kristiansen

The Quest for 20:20 Vision: Developing HR Leaders at Luxottica,
by Ken Meyers

What Women Executives Need from Leadership Development Programs, by Marijo Bos

Creating Real Employee Engagement, by Alaric Mostyn

Leading Across Boundaries: Adventures in the "White Spaces" at General Mills, by Kevin D. Wilde

Bank of America: Winning the Growth Challenge, by Brian Fishel

CHAPTER 9

DEVELOPING CUSTOMER-CENTRIC LEADERS

Thomas R. Knighton

In March 2007, Scott Burns, a columnist on MSN's Money Central board, wrote about his experiences with Home Depot over the years. He recounted the many home improvement jobs he and his wife had completed in sixteen years together, and recalled a note he had left his wife at one point: "Carolyn: I've gone to Our Store. Be back soon. Love, Scott." Home Depot was the place they could count on for well-trained, knowledgeable, and helpful staff who would quickly and easily answer any question, "even a silly one." He recalled the store's "amazing inventory" and the staff that always helped access inventory, make choices, and purchase items quickly.

"But that was then," he recalled. As of March 2007, Burns and his wife "don't shop much at Home Depot anymore. Indeed, we generally try to avoid it and grieve for the loss," he wrote. Recounting Home Depot's 28 percent drop in earnings for the fourth quarter of 2006, he acknowledged that some of the loss was due to the housing slump and some due to the "egregious compensation of [Bob Nardelli] and his high-handed treatment of shareholders." But, Burns says, the larger reason for Home Depot's fall from grace is that it is "a consistent abuser of its customers' time." In short, the customer experience at the Home Depot of 2007 failed to live up to the expectations that had set it apart in previous years, and customers were leaving in droves.

The 2008 Pfeiffer Annual: Leadership Development.
Copyright © 2008 by John Wiley & Sons, Inc. Reproduced by permission of Pfeiffer, an Imprint of Wiley. www.pfeiffer.com

Burns' column generated thousands of responses on the MSN discussion board. Former customers chimed in with experiences similar to Burns'; many wished for a return to the glory days when they could get timely, competent help on home improvement projects.

Complaints and dissatisfaction with companies, even in a public forum, are nothing new or unusual. What *was* unusual was the response of Home Depot to the column and subsequent postings. Frank Blake, newly appointed CEO of Home Depot, posted his own responses on the MSN Money board. Rather than issuing excuses through a PR department or simply ignoring the complaints expressed, Blake stepped up and spoke from the heart about the steps the company would be taking to win back its customers. He complimented Burns on his "insightful and revealing" column and thanked the many posters who offered comments in response. "There's no way I can express how sorry I am for all of the stories you shared," he said. "We let you down. That's unacceptable. Customers are our company's lifeblood—and the sole reason we have been able to build such a successful company."

Blake understands a basic and fundamental rule of business first expressed by legendary marketing guru Ted Levitt, that the "purpose of business is to get and keep a customer." Through this public exchange and his subsequent actions, Blake exemplified customer-centric leadership; he now has a chance to reestablish Home Depot's position as a leader in customer loyalty and achieve the marketplace and economic success that a customer-centric strategy can deliver.

A New Brand of Leadership

There's no way to deny the business imperative for customer-centric leadership. Gone are the days when a company could rest on its laurels and still reap the benefits of customer loyalty. Look at JetBlue. After poorly handled delays and cancellations left passengers stranded in New York on Valentine's Day 2007 and prompted the cancellation of 1,200 flights, the company was dropped from a *BusinessWeek* ranking of twenty-five companies considered customer service champions. Rival Southwest Airlines made the list, and JetBlue is still feeling the effects. In fact, the company acknowledges that it may lose up to $30 million due to that one event (JetBlue Adds . . ., 2007). When a single customer-service fiasco can cost a company millions of dollars, the business imperative for customer-centric leadership becomes obvious.

What do customer-centric leaders have in common? Research and experience suggest that customer-centric leaders share a common passion for the customer, common beliefs about business, and some uncommon practices. First and most important is that customer-centric leaders are passionate about customers. Jeff Bezos, CEO of Amazon.com is a self-proclaimed fanatic. "I'm a fanatic about the customer experience," he states. He goes on to explain his view about the pervasiveness of the customer experience. "The customer experience is bigger than customer service in that it is the full, end-to-end experience. It starts when you first hear about Amazon from a friend and ends when you get the package in the mail and open it" Leaders like Bezos put the interests of customers ahead of other stakeholder interests. They have the courage of convictions about the customer experience and ensure that their companies follow through on the promise of their brand. Bezos is legendary for putting his executive team in the warehouse during the holidays to ensure that customers get their merchandise as promised, before the holidays. His passion for customers is contagious and shapes every aspect of Amazon's culture and operations.

Second, customer-centric leaders share a common belief about business. They believe that a relentless focus on the customer will enable them to achieve and sustain market-leading revenue and profit performance. The jury is in on the economic benefits of customer loyalty—that a 5 percent increase in customer loyalty can increase profitability by as much as 25 to 85 percent, depending on the industry. It's not by accident that Southwest Airlines has outperformed its competitors for ten years straight and continues to win awards for its customer experience and employee experience. What's intriguing about customer-centric leaders is that customer focus is not simply a pillar in their strategy or corporate values—it *is* the strategy. Customer-centric leaders see their brand, the customer experience, and their strategy as inseparable parts to the strategic whole. Together, they drive the performance of people, processes, and products.

Finally, customer-centric leaders share some "uncommon practices." These are practices that on the surface may appear to be common sense, but in fact they are not common practice. Gary Loveman, CEO of Harrah's Entertainment and a former Harvard professor, will tell you that the "service-profit chain" is the magic behind Harrah's extraordinary business success. The service-profit chain theory states that leaders create an employee experience that drives a customer experience that produces business results. Loveman and other customer-centric leaders believe that the employee experience and the customer experience are inextricably linked, and their human resource practices and leadership practices reflect it.

Customer-centric leaders align employees and operations to ensure that they are consistently delivering a loyalty-building customer experience. Managers at all levels know what to do to create and keep customers. The organization is characterized by high levels of accountability and empowerment. Jeff Bezos will not allow his managers to make the artificial tradeoff of customer focus for operational excellence. "I'm a broken record on the customer experience," he says. "I've spent a lot of time making sure people understand that there is no tradeoff on the customer experience. One of the things you have to be constantly on guard about is either/or thinking—if you apply enough problem-solving skills you can often get both."

Employees at Harrah's know that for every day that they meet or exceed their metrics for customer satisfaction that money is added to a bonus pool that they will share. Leaders like Bezos and Loveman know that their job is to align their organization with their customer strategy and then remove the obstacles to performance—giving employees the freedom to exceed customer expectations.

The core tool of a customer-centric leader is customer information. The voice of the customer permeates their organizations, informing their decision making and driving both people and process performance. FedEx publishes its customer satisfaction and operational metrics every day so that employees have immediate feedback on how well they performed the night before. The executive team of Wachovia Bank pores over customer satisfaction metrics each month and drives accountability for improvement and sustained customer-keeping performance. It's no wonder that they consistently lead their industry in customer satisfaction and loyalty. It is this combination of passion for customers, an unwavering belief in their customer-centric strategy, and uncommon practices that set customer-centric leaders apart.

How to Develop Customer-Centric Leaders

Our experience has shown that there are four key strategies for developing customer-centric leaders.

Strategy 1: Develop a Belief in the Economics of Customer Loyalty

Encourage leaders to explore the economic rational and develop their own "proof of concept." There are several frameworks one can use to help leaders get their heads around the benefits of a customer-centric strategy. The "net promoter" metrics first developed by Frederick Reicheld can be used to create a compelling picture of how a focus on customer loyalty can drive growth, profitability, and competitive performance. Simply helping executives to see the cost of customer defection or to calculate the lifetime value of a customer can open their eyes to the economic impact a customer-centric strategy can deliver. One doesn't have to venture too far afield to see the impact of failed customer strategies.

Strategy 2: Connect Leaders to Their Customers

This strategy is easily overlooked and surprisingly absent in many leaders' experience. Jeff Bezos says that the Amazon.com mission "is to be the earth's most customer-centered company." This means three things: listen, invent, and personalize. By listening to what customers say and don't say, creating innovative customer solutions, and then personalizing those solutions to reflect individual customer preferences, Bezos has created and sustained Amazon.com's "customer obsessed" culture.

Of course, to listen to customers, a leader must first have contact with them. Many companies with call centers require senior leaders to listen to a certain number of customer calls per month to hear what customers are saying and gain personal experience about the customer experience they are delivering. At Chick-fil-A, every corporate employee from the top down is required to spend at least one day each year working behind the counter of one of the chain's restaurants. Dan Cathy, president and chief operating officer, regularly works the counter at his stores in order to stay in touch. When he introduces himself to waiting customers, he shakes their hands and says, "I'm Dan . . . I work in customer service" (Salter, 2004).

I coached a CEO who admitted that he had not spoken to a customer in five years. "I wouldn't know what to say," he told me. So I made a deal with him. If he would invest a week, we would reintroduce him to his customers. We took the company jet and spent one week flying around the United States to meet with customers. We created a survey for him to use to gather data about his customers' experience. Each night he wrote an email back to his entire organization chronicling his encounter with customers that day. The experience profoundly changed his view of his role in the company. In addition to being chief "deal-maker," he also viewed himself as chief "customer advocate."

In this era, there are innumerable ways for senior leaders to be in touch with customers. Consider Frank Blake's example; he didn't hesitate to jump onto a message board and post responses to disgruntled customers. Other CEOs and senior executives are turning to blogs to stay in touch with customers. David Neeleman, CEO of JetBlue, keeps an online "Flight Log." His blog's header tells customers, "Each week I fly on JetBlue flights and talk to customers so I can find out how we can improve our airline. This is my flight log."

Jeff Immelt, CEO of GE, spends four or five days every month with customers in various settings. Twice a month, he holds town-hall meetings with hundreds of customers at a time to share the direction of the company and hear feedback from the customers. He also holds what he calls "dreaming sessions" with smaller, key customer groups to explore a common vision for the next several years. "I've spent my lifetime working with customers, and I love customers," says Immelt (Irish, 2005).

Strategy 3: Immerse Leaders in Best Practice

We worked with the executive team of a large hotel chain that was trying to breathe new life into a tired brand by reestablishing its unique legacy of providing family-friendly accommodations at a reasonable price. To help them understand the challenge of reviving a legacy brand, we took the entire team to Fenway Park in Boston. By playing up its history as one of American's great ball parks, Fenway has re-created a true, historic American ballpark experience. The hotel chain's team connected with the management at Fenway, and they came away understanding the best practices of a legacy brand—best practices that they could translate into their own customer experience. One executive looks back at that experience as a powerful point in his brand-building career. At the end of the visit he shared with us and his team, "I didn't really know what we were trying to accomplish until I saw it being implemented at Fenway."

Often, immersing leaders in best practices involves finding a customer experience that mirrors the kind of experience they want to create. A company that wants to create an upscale customer experience, for example, might study the best practices of the Ritz Carlton Hotel, whereas a company focusing on differentiation in the mass market might study the best practices of Southwest Airlines.

Strategy 4: Integrate Customer Centricity into Your Leadership Development Curriculum

The fourth strategy for developing customer-centric leaders is to coach and train them to model the behaviors needed to lead a customer-centric organization. Frank Blake has taken that development into his own hands. After his appointment to the Home Depot helm, Blake enlisted the help of Home Depot co-founder Bernie Marcus. Marcus took Blake on walking tours of several stores, offering advice on how to build a good store experience for the customer (Waters, 2007). He sought out his own coaches and trainers—the very people who made Home Depot famous for the customer-centered experience.

A large retailer in the UK needed to develop three core skills for their store leaders as part of a rebranding effort. In order to lead the change to a more customer-centric organization, they knew that they needed to embrace teamwork across the stores and not just within the store, improve their leaders' coaching skills, and improve in-store communication. However, their store leaders were tired of the usual workshop format and demanded something more engaging. What they got was team development while racing sixty-foot yachts, coaching training in Wembly stadium, and communications training in a local theatre, where they interacted with actors who stimulated their communications challenges. As a result, the retailer beat their competition on all aspects of the customer experience.

Pitfalls to Avoid

While most leaders would readily admit that creating a customer-centric culture is critical to company success, there are still a significant number of companies that fail to deliver the results they anticipated when they began their customer journeys. Implementing a customer-centric strategy is easier said than done. Here are some common pitfalls to avoid:

1. *All talk, no (or wrong) actions:* Leaders can give lip service to being customer-centric, but when actions communicate conflicting priorities, the culture reflects what they see and not what they hear. Leaders who abandon their customer strategy when company performance is not meeting expectations make "withdrawals" from their credibility accounts that are hard to repay.
2. *Lack of leadership alignment:* Likewise, if the managers are excited and willing to develop a customer-centric culture, but the executive team is not aligned with that strategy, the initiative will fail. Developing customer-centric leaders has to begin at the top.
3. *Under equipping managers to implement the strategy:* Customer-centricity is an "all hands" strategy and requires leaders at the front line who are empowered to exceed customer expectations Without the requisite tools and skills, front-line leaders will lack the competence, confidence, and commitment to perform.
4. *Failure to remove obstacles*: The best intentions of leadership are usually "trumped" by processes and policies that inhibit performance. Leadership training must be accompanied by a dogged determination to remove the obstacles that get in the way of customer-keeping customer.
5. *Not actively leading change:* Many customer-centric strategies fail because leaders fail to anticipate the amount of change that will be required to realize their aspirations. A systematic leader-led change process must accompany the implementation to mitigate the risk of a false start.

As companies face the new era of increased globalization and competition, creating a customer-centric organization will become more important that ever. The customer-centric leader who can permeate a company culture the way Jeff Bezos or Gary Loveman has will be well on the way to creating a customer experience that brings results to the company's bottom line.

References

Blake, F. (2007, March). Home Depot CEO: Sorry we let you down. MSN Money Central. http://articles.moneycentral.msn.com/Investing/Extra/HomeDepotCEOWeLetYou Down.aspx

Burns, S. (2007, March). Is Home Depot shafting shoppers?" MSN Money Central. http://articles.moneycentral.msn.com/Investing/Extra/HomeDepotShaftingShoppers. aspx

Irish, L. (2005, July). The Fast Company interview: Jeff Immelt." www.fastcompany.com/ magazine/96/jeff-immelt.html

JetBlue adds operations chief after service fiasco. (2007, March 9). USA Today.com. www .usatoday.com/travel/flights/2007–03–09-jetblue-coo_N.htm

Salter, C. (2004, October). Customer-centered leader: Chick-fil-A." FastCompany.com. www .fastcompany.com/magazine/87/customer-chickfila.html

Uncommon Practice Research. (2001). CITY: The Forum Corporation.

Waters, J. (2007, March 30). Blake's blueprint for Home Depot remodel. MarketWatch.com. www .marketwatch.com/news/story/new-home-depot-ceo-wins/story.aspx?guid=%7BA586A765– 4B8E-40C6–81C7-FE3EC12EA875%7D

Thomas R. Knighton is a partner with Oliver Wyman Delta Executive Learning Center. For over twenty years, he has helped companies such as Citigroup, Disney, American Express, and Black and Decker implement strategy, improve market effectiveness, and increase customer loyalty. He is lead author of the book, *Managing the Customer Experience*, and a frequent speaker on a variety of business issues and has been quoted in national publications such as *FORTUNE, The Wall Street Journal, Human Resources Executive*, and *FastCompany*.

CHAPTER 10

BUILDING MARKETING EXCELLENCE

Jean-Claude Larreche, Mario Castaneda,
and Zohra Jan Mamod

The purpose of this article is to share our experience at StratX in helping lead-ing global firms increase the performance of their marketing performance through Marketing Excellence initiatives. These endeavors represent significant opportunities for companies, but also a number of risks and challenges. To guide those considering the creation of such initiatives, we address the following ques-tions: How does Marketing Excellence differ from traditional marketing training? What organizational capabilities and individual competences require develop-ment? What key factors drive success? In the process of answering these crucial questions, we also illustrate the structure, contents, and deployment strategy of such initiatives with specific cases from our practice.

Most companies reach a point when top management sees the value in creating a management development initiative to build Marketing Excellence in their organization. Usually the request is passed on to both the marketing and human resources departments to develop the initiative, contact suppliers, make proposals and organize it. Over the years we at StratX have been involved in many of these projects and have helped clients with Marketing Excellence initiatives in a variety of sectors, including business-to-business, consumer goods, services and pharmaceuticals. The context varies, but the requests are usually due to one or more of the following factors: expansion of the company into new markets, changing competitive environment, lack of growth, or lack of new products in the pipeline. However, all of these factors usually lead to management's realization that, for the firm to achieve its objectives, investments have to be made in the capabilities of the marketing department.

The challenges can be very different. In some companies, the marketing department is weak, staffed with people who do not have the discipline or the passion for marketing. But most companies who have called on us to help them develop Marketing Excellence already have a significant competence in marketing. Such clients have included global leaders such as Boeing, Canon, GE, L'Oreal, Novartis, Pfizer, and Philip Morris.

When deciding to invest in a Marketing Excellence initiative, each company faces a unique situation determined by its leadership, its culture, and its market situation. It is therefore essential that such an initiative be defined and executed after thorough analysis, as opposed to transplanting a successful program implemented by another company in a very different context. We will, however, extract from our experience some specific advice that could help companies considering or already deploying a Marketing Excellence initiative.

The Nature of Marketing Excellence

One of the first priorities is articulating what Marketing Excellence means to the executives sponsoring such an initiative. This is more difficult than it appears. The fact is that executives requesting a Marketing Excellence initiative often do not know precisely what they want. But they made the request based on a strong feeling that the marketing capabilities of the firm have to be upgraded. They know success is not a matter of increasing the size of the marketing budget, but also is investing in people development to improve the effectiveness of the marketing organization. Companies that engage in substantial marketing development programs without having defined what top management needs often go in the wrong direction, waste important resources, and lose crucial time. And the executives responsible for such failures have lost credibility and sometimes careers.

Marketing Excellence Goes Beyond Marketing Skills

Marketing Excellence goes beyond skills: It is about achieving market results in an efficient way. This requires the right attitude and the right actions. Marketing skills are actually the easiest ingredients to develop or to acquire from external suppliers, such as market research firms, advertising agencies, or consultants.

We emphasize this difference between skills and excellence to contrast true marketing excellence with what we encounter most often: a Marketing Excellence initiative is launched by management that is immediately transformed into a series of skill development programs. This happens because this is what marketing and human resources departments are familiar with, and this is what many suppliers recommend.

The development of marketing skills is important for the effectiveness of a marketing department. Many companies have their own "Marketing Academy," offering courses on the essentials of marketing strategy (such as customer orientation, segmentation, positioning, branding, portfolio strategies), elements of the marketing mix, market research, and any other current "hot" topics. Internal marketing academies can offer courses better adapted to the requirements of the firm, in a more convenient fashion, and delivered at a lower cost than if done externally. StratX regularly contributes to the creation and operation of such marketing academies. They play an essential role in the success of a marketing department, but they are only a partial response to a request for a Marketing Excellence initiative. Their primary purpose is the transmission of knowledge, not the creation of new attitudes or new behaviors. And while knowledge is a necessary component of marketing professionalism, it is not enough by itself to guarantee marketing excellence.

If marketing excellence is more than developing skills, how should it be defined? In our experience, we have found it best to help clients define marketing excellence in terms of desired outcomes at two levels: for the marketing organization as a whole and for the individual managers.

The Desired Organizational Outcomes of Marketing Excellence

Marketing is at the interface of the firm and its competitive markets and is, as a result, a special discipline compared to other functions. The impact of marketing is seen primarily in the market and is evaluated through external measures such as market growth, market share, and customer satisfaction. Pragmatically, this means that good marketing departments are those that achieve external results. This is the way they build their reputation, create credibility within the firm, and obtain necessary resources. And good marketers are also those who achieve results. This is the way they build their reputation, create credibility, obtain necessary resources, and are promoted.

The ultimate outcome of Marketing Excellence is thus effectiveness and achievement of results in the market. But this outcome has to be true both for the organization and for a critical mass of individual marketers. One great marketer does not make for marketing excellence. Many firms have for a while achieved short-term results through the drive of a single marketing "whiz kid," yet cannot demonstrate marketing excellence as an organization. The limits of this are shown when the "whiz kid" is promoted or leaves the firm for a more attractive offer.

At the level of the organization, we have identified the two pillars of marketing excellence as being "marketing as a profession" and "marketing as leadership." These two elements drive sustainable results and are the desired outcome of a Marketing Excellence initiative at the organizational level.

Marketing as a Profession In firms that are not blessed with marketing excellence, marketing is perceived as a collection of individuals who do not share the professional standards of other functions of the firm such as accounting, finance, manufacturing, R&D, and IT. Often, executives from other functions have little respect for marketers whom they see as job-hopping mercenaries, spending resources with little justification, and taking credit for successes that are due to favorable external circumstances or the hard work of other departments. Unfortunately, these perceptions are often based on at least some reality. Such a marketing department is rarely effective, and without mutual respect between marketing and the other functions of the firm, it is impossible to develop customer orientation and achieve competitive superiority.

Marketing Excellence must therefore develop marketing as a profession within the company. The components that we recommend to develop marketing as a strong professional group include:

1. Achieving a common language
2. Alignment on a set of rigorous processes and tools
3. Agreement on demanding performance standards and peer pressure to induce compliance
4. An internal network for effective teamwork
5. Pride in belonging to a high performance group

This is the basis of Marketing Excellence as an organizational capability. It cannot be achieved overnight but can certainly be guaranteed within a few years with the proper focus and resources. Building this capacity not only provides sustainable long-term results for the firm, but it is rewarding to witness marketers build a high performance organization, develop their sense of belonging, acquire collective responsibility, and gain the respect of their peers.

Marketing as Leadership The second pillar of Marketing Excellence involves the creation in the marketing department of a sense of leadership, both externally and internally.

External leadership is about gaining superior customer understanding, capturing customer insights, creating new markets, serving new customer segments. Marketers must ensure that the firm discovers new opportunities before competitors, and that it leads customers in new directions that offer new sources of value to all.

Internal leadership is about motivating and enabling the rest of the organization to adapt and contribute to the evolution of the competitive market environment. This involves developing a customer-oriented culture throughout the firm, interacting effectively with other functions, sharing market knowledge, becoming sensitive to the operational requirements of other departments, and becoming involved early in the development of new products. Beyond gaining respect from other functions, marketing must make the organization more competitive and more effective in its markets.

Marketing leadership is more ambitious than developing marketing as a profession. However, both capabilities can be developed in the same initiative, with substantial results achieved within a three-year horizon. The professional aspects of marketing require more emphasis in the early stages, as they are essential to build the self-confidence and credibility required to develop marketing leadership. The efforts to build external and internal marketing leadership take on more importance in later stages of a Marketing Excellence initiative. Once a sufficient professional base has been established, inspirational and action-oriented tasks can be designed to transform competent marketers into motivating leaders.

The Desired Individual Outcomes of Marketing Excellence

The drivers of an upgrade in the marketing effectiveness of a firm will ultimately be individual managers. A successful Marketing Excellence initiative must therefore develop the competences of a critical mass of individual marketers, while delivering and building the proper organizational capabilities.

An in-depth diagnosis of the existing and required marketing competencies is necessary to propose relevant design options to the sponsors of a marketing initiative. Solutions can be widely different depending on many factors involved. Despite these differences, we consider five competences in the design of any Marketing Excellence initiative. In the order in which we usually build them up, these competences are customer focus, marketing professionalism, strategic focus, innovation, and achievement.

1. *Customer Focus.* This involves developing a superior customer understanding, systematically viewing marketing actions from the perspective of the customer, and representing the customer's requirements within the organization. Customer focus is at the heart of marketing excellence. It is often the winning

stroke of entrepreneurs who develop innovative customer solutions, despite having no marketing training; excellence in customer focus can outweigh many other weaknesses. Just as often, it is the weakest marketing competence in more established firms. It is as if the weight of systems and procedures and the use of resources as the easiest way to obtain results progressively eradicate customer focus in big organizations. Regaining customer focus reinvigorates growth in a firm. Developing the competencies for the systematic exploration and use of customer insights is in fact easy and very effective. It should be an early component of a Marketing Excellence initiative.

2. *Marketing Professionalism.* This competence includes the mastery of marketing skills, processes, and tools. In the design of a Marketing Excellence initiative, it is important to identify any significant deficiencies that need to be corrected. However, the development of specific skills is best handled separately in the context of an institutionalized and permanent Marketing Academy. In a Marketing Excellence initiative, marketers have to learn and appreciate the real essence of professionalism: the narrow line between chaos and bureaucracy. Insufficient tools and processes ensure chaotic decision making with unrepeatable success and frequent failure. Misplaced professionalism consists in controlling against such failures by creating a plethora of tools and processes. This leads to bureaucracy, with its heaviness, inefficiencies, and slowness. Real marketing professionalism is about mastering the crucial aspects of marketing strategy and execution so that proper tradeoffs can be made. It is this kind of professionalism that is fundamental to marketing effectiveness.

3. *Strategic Focus.* This is the ability to concentrate minds and resources on the most important elements of a situation in order to achieve results in a highly competitive environment in which time is of the essence. Many marketing professionals know and achieve much. But often they disperse themselves into too many activities and too many products. This strategic focus competence is about learning how to say no to many requests for time and investments, to concentrate on the major opportunities, and to ensure that they become big winners. This is probably one of the greatest challenges for marketers, who are often tempted by exciting proposals or by the latest fads. This is where a higher perspective on marketing and the use of strategic simulations are most essential.

4. *Innovation.* Effective marketing has to be innovative, not only in terms of products but also in ways to learn about customers, in adopting new approaches, and in the use of its resources. In self-assessments, most marketers pride themselves in being innovative. When reviewing marketing activities over time, however, we often find more incremental changes than real innovations. Many changes occur because of new appointments to product management positions

and enticements from suppliers. Real innovations based on a fundamentally new outlook and with a favorable impact on an existing situation—something that would be expected from an entrepreneur—are rare. Developing this competence requires exposure to novel concepts, use of specific innovation frameworks, and most importantly, practice.

5. *Achievement.* When studying the career of great marketers, we find not only successes—which largely outweigh some inevitable failures—but also some major achievements. This can be the launch of a major new concept, a memorable advertising campaign, the creation of a new product category, or the transformation of a marketing department. An excellent exercise for marketers is asking "What is the major contribution I will make over the next three years?" It focuses the mind, forces a longer-term perspective, and creates a healthy ambition. It also demands that the four previous competences—customer focus, professionalism, strategic focus, and innovation—are integrated into a personal vision.

Formulating the Objectives of a Marketing Excellence Initiative

As we have stated earlier, the design of a Marketing Excellence initiative has to be fully adapted to a specific situation and should involve an in-depth diagnostic and insightful interchanges with the sponsors. What we stress here is common and crucial in all situations: the need to understand and concentrate on the strategic objectives. A Marketing Excellence initiative goes beyond the development of skills. Its main purpose is the creation of a high performance marketing organization that can deliver external results in a sustainable way. As a guideline, we have presented the components that in our experience drive the performance of a marketing department, in terms of:

- Two organizational capabilities: marketing as a profession and marketing as leadership
- Five individual competences: customer focus, marketing professionalism, strategic focus, innovation, and achievement.

A successful Marketing Excellence initiative has to effectively develop all these capabilities and competences. The choices made in the design of the initiative—including topics, methodologies, faculty, number and length of modules, location, media, and organization—must be made in the context of the desired priority in the development of these capabilities and competences. The number of options is large, and it is best to illustrate them through a real example.

A Large-Scale Marketing Excellence Initiative

This is the case of a significant program that was deployed over seven years in one of the Global 100 largest firms. The impetus came from its chairman, who decided to create a marketing and sales committee with the mission of significantly upgrading the performance of these functions. This was perceived to be a strategic priority, given the growing challenges of the industry and the pipeline of new products for the coming years.

The Design of a Marketing Excellence Initiative

One of the recommendations of this committee was the creation of a Marketing Excellence initiative that would develop a strong marketing community across the group. This initiative was co-sponsored by the CEO of a major division and the head of Global Human Resources. They asked us to design a proposal for such an initiative. After three months of consultations with key executives, our framework was approved and the first session started six months later.

The main aspects of this Marketing Excellence initiative, soon branded "MEX", were the following:

- A target audience of 120 marketing executives per year organized in three cohorts of forty participants each
- A program organized in three modules, offered three months apart
- Module 1 centered on Marketing Strategy and lasted five days. It covered key aspects of marketing, using examples mainly from outside the industry. A premium was placed on opening minds to novel approaches, developing the sense of belonging to a profession, and forging the ambition of upgrading the performance of marketing in the firm.
- Module 2 centered on Marketing Execution and also lasted five days. It converged on issues specific to the industry and the firm. The emphasis was on linking new ideas to specific actions. During this week, participants organized themselves into teams around selected projects of significance to the firm, and on which they would work during the three months between Modules 2 and 3. These projects concerned opportunities or problems that were not addressed in the normal course of business.
- In the first two days of Module 3, the teams consolidated their projects, using specific methodologies with the help of facilitators. On the third and last day, each team presented their project to a panel of top executives.

- The first two modules were located in "hot spots" coherent with the objectives of the program: on the top of a mountain, in Silicon Valley, in Miami, or in Shanghai. The third module was in the global headquarters to stress the business focus of the presentations and to have access to the panel of top executives.
- The program was staffed by three complementary types of facilitators: professors from leading business schools, top executives from the firm, and senior consultants. This provided a unique blend of leading-edge concepts, internal relevance, and support for change.
- The contents of the initiatives were designed according to the initial objectives and to the current marketing priorities of the firm. While the overall structure remained stable, the contents evolved continuously and were subject to a major reevaluation every two years.
- A wide variety of methodologies were used, including lectures, public cases, specifically designed cases, best-in-class business simulations, videos, inspirational trips, and team projects.

As is often the case, the biggest challenge of this initiative was for the first cohort. In these first sessions, sometimes labeled "pilots", all parties—sponsors, participants, facilitators and support staff—are quite anxious. The rest of the organization is watching and the outcome is crucial for the future of the initiative. Beyond the ratings, the first sign of success is indeed the buzz that spreads after the first session. This is essential to create a demand for the programs that reflects the motivation of managers to actively participate in a process of change.

This initiative lasted for seven years and involved more than one thousand participants. Over time, requests were made to deploy the MEX initiative to broader audiences and to further develop the marketing performance of the firm. A portfolio of other activities was progressively designed and the original program was rebranded "Core MEX" to reflect the fact that it was now the backbone of a broader initiative. Figure 1 illustrates the various parts of this portfolio. Figure 1a represents how the initiative expanded and developed from the initial Core MEX. Figure 1b represents the deployment of the initiative according to the traditional top-down organizational pyramid.

Involving Senior Executives in a Marketing Excellence Initiative

Some MEX requests came from senior executives who had an interest in the topics but not enough time to participate in Core MEX. In response, two different MEX extensions were developed for this audience:

FIGURE 1. A FULL-SCALE MARKETING EXCELLENCE INITIATIVE

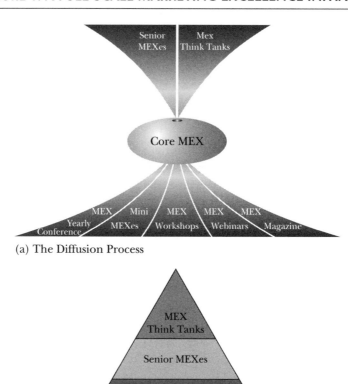

(a) The Diffusion Process

(b) The Deployment Pyramid

- A "Senior MEX" program containing the highlights of the Core MEX as well as sessions to discuss marketing effectiveness. Delivered over three days, it encouraged senior executives to improve marketing practices and allowed them to connect better with members of their staff graduating from the Core MEX.

- "MEX Think Tanks," which used MEX methodologies to discuss specific challenges facing the industry and the firm. Several of these two-day events were organized, and they each involved a dozen executives. The outcome of these Think Tanks was sets of prioritized ideas that were then filtered, evaluated, and followed through by the organization.

Deploying and Nurturing a Marketing Excellence Initiative

Soon after the first sessions of Core MEX, other requests were made to deploy the concepts and methodologies down the organization and to nurture the "MEX spirit."

Over time, five different initiatives were created for that purpose:

- A "MEX Yearly Conference." This two-day event was offered after the managers graduating from Core MEX suggested that a regular event would be valuable to keep up-to-date and maintain the network. It was restricted to alumni from the Core MEX.
- "Mini MEXes." These two-day programs were offered in a decentralized way, at the request of country organizations. Most often, the initiative came from MEX alumni who wanted to deploy their learning locally. The design was based on selected MEX concepts and finalized in cooperation with the local organization and sponsor.
- "MEX Workshops." These were organized at the request of MEX alumni or senior executives on specific issues such as marketing planning, the introduction of a new product, or the repositioning of existing offerings. From one to three days, they involved around a dozen managers for each workshop.
- "MEX Webinars." These "seminars on the web" offered a mechanism to continuously stimulate ideas and keep the global marketing network active. Offered on a quarterly basis, these one-hour events were organized around a specific subject such as branding, marketing for women, or viral marketing, and linked with current company issues. They typically included two short presentations, one by an executive and one by an external expert, followed by questions and answers.
- The "MEX Magazine." To further stimulate ideas for higher marketing performance, a quarterly magazine was created and circulated to all MEX alumni. Most of the contents concerned marketing developments outside of the firm and its industry. Articles were written specifically for this magazine, based on current marketing events or on interviews with leading marketers.

Delivering the Expected Outcomes

This large-scale Marketing Excellence initiative was a great success and used as an example by the firm. Its perceived success was such that other functions developed similar programs labeled HR Excellence, Financial Excellence, or IT Excellence. The individuals involved in its organization received different internal awards. Marketing managers pressed their bosses to be nominated for future sessions. Country operations from Mexico to China requested to have their own local mini-MEXes.

What is most important is that the initiative delivered the expected outcomes, both in terms of organizational capabilities and individual competences. Marketers felt part of a profession with a duty to individually and collectively improve marketing performance. The company initiated a number of marketing and sales innovations in its industry. Individual managers developed their confidence. The development of individual competencies had an enabling impact on customer focus, professionalism, strategic focus, innovation, and achievement.

Another crucial aspect is that this large-scale initiative was supported by other actions. The CEO who sponsored it also drove important changes in the marketing department, including in terms of organization, recruitment, appraisal, remuneration, systems, and planning process. He eventually created the position of "chief marketing officer" at the global level, a first for this industry.

Over the seven years of this initiative, the company's perspective on marketing was transformed. Marketers gained respect internally and interacted more effectively with other functions. From a weak group, the marketing function emerged as one of the leaders in its industry. While the firm initially had to go outside to fill marketing positions, it eventually became a net exporter of marketing talent. The firm now has a solid marketing capability that does not depend on a few individuals and external recruitment. It is robust and has depth.

The Scope of Marketing Excellence Initiatives

The above example is particularly valuable for those interested in creating a Marketing Excellence initiative because it shows the many facets of such a project. Linked to a transformational process of marketing on a global scale, sustained for seven years, and supported with appropriate resources, its impact has been significant. While the Marketing Excellence initiatives we are asked to design and implement often have a more limited scope, the objectives are often of a similar nature, and the design includes subsets of the above example. To complement the above large-scale example, we will now briefly describe three other cases of focused Marketing Excellence initiatives.

Case 1

A business-to-business company found itself trailing the leaders in the key industries where it played. It decided to create a Marketing Excellence initiative aimed at sales and marketing managers and asked StratX to design it and deliver it. The preliminary diagnostic revealed that the initiative should center on the concept of "value creation" for key stakeholders, including employees, customers, and shareholders. This operational definition of marketing was found to best fit the needs of the organization and the political sensitivity of the client's environment. The core of the initiative was a one-week program that involved lectures, case studies, team assignments, and a simulation adapted to the specific requirement of this initiative. Over five years, about forty of these seminars were run, always in the same location, and involving more than eight hundred managers. In addition to having an impact on the personal competences of the participants, this initiative was perceived to have achieved a much stronger cohesion between the sales and marketing organizations.

Case 2

The new CEO of a local subsidiary in a large multinational identified the lack of mutual understanding between functions, and the resulting conflicts, as an important barrier to growth. StratX was asked to investigate the issue and to recommend an initiative. The accepted proposal consisted of a one-week program built around the key strategic concepts of marketing: customer orientation, market segmentation, product positioning, product portfolio, marketing planning, and marketing culture. These concepts were selected because they were relevant and interesting to all functions. The objective was that every manager from every function would have to contribute to the company's efforts to win against competitors in the market place. A business simulation was used to bridge the gap between the concepts and the desired new attitudes and behaviors. For each program, the nomination of participants included a mix of the key functions such as marketing, finance, operations, development, and human resources. Over three years, more than six hundred managers participated in this program. The enthusiasm that resulted and the mutual respect that was created between the functions had a significant impact on the development of this subsidiary. Toward the end of the initiative, in an annual meeting, the country CEO said: "What used to take six months and many memos, now takes one week and just a few phone calls." He was probably carried away by his enthusiasm, but he had felt the move toward higher performance in his organization.

Case 3

In several companies, we have been asked to propose Marketing Excellence solutions to stimulate the marketing community on a global scale while limiting time and travel expenses. One of the most useful solutions is to organize internal "competitions" around a web-based strategic marketing simulation. Managers from around the world are organized in local teams that compete against each other in multiple rounds of a simulation over several months. Online learning modules are offered to complement the simulation with access to both online and local instructors. The design of the simulation and of the learning modules is adapted to the specific objectives of the initiative. In addition to being very efficient, this approach has the benefit of combining local team work, providing a sense of belonging to a global community, and creating a competitive spirit.

Key Success Factors for a Marketing Excellence Initiative

Each Marketing Excellence initiative is different, and our experience gained over the years has continually expanded. We have tried to share this experience by first emphasizing what we believe is specific about Marketing Excellence initiatives compared to other training endeavors. We also have described a number of examples to illustrate the various components of successful Marketing Excellence initiatives. In conclusion, we would like to recapitulate a few key success factors that underlie these examples.

1. *Top Management Support.* This is crucial to deliver on the objectives of a Marketing Excellence initiative. Without it, the risks are numerous and include a misalignment with the CEO's vision; a high-jacking of the initiative by various power groups in the organization; or the project dissolving into a series of training events. But top management support is seldom granted, it has to be deserved. Enlightened top management can see that a successful Marketing Excellence initiative is an opportunity for them to shape the future of the company. They will provide adequate support if they are guided in doing so in the most effective way and with the required guarantees of success.

2. *Strategic Perspective.* Too often a request for a Marketing Excellence initiative is translated into a series of modules that read like the table of contents of a marketing textbook. As we have argued earlier, this will develop skills but will not achieve the more ambitious objectives of Marketing Excellence. The request

reflects a desire to significantly upgrade the performance of marketing and this requires a change strategy agreed with the top management. This has to include the role of the initiative in a broader change program, its objectives in the short and medium term, the targeted management population, the resources available, and the deployment of these resources over key actions. This is the most important and sensitive part of the process. Only when this strategic perspective has been discussed and agreed should the proper design phase start.

3. *Top-Notch Execution.* A Marketing Excellence initiative is an ambitious venture and its execution should reflect that ambition. Not everything will be perfect, and one has to accept that some corrections will have to be made along the way. But the standards have to be placed high in terms of contents, instructors, materials, or facilities. Resources have to be adequate, but imagination has to be mobilized to achieve the highest impact within budget constraints. Beyond the concepts, to drive changes in attitudes and behaviors, participants have to be positively surprised. A successful Marketing Excellence initiative should provide them with memorable experiences.

4. *Constant Monitoring and Alignment.* Despite all the preparation in the design of a successful Marketing Excellence initiative, one should be prepared to continuously improve it from the start. It is crucial to monitor actively the relative impact of its different components and to change or replace the least effective ones. New major developments within the firm, in the industry, or in the world of marketing have to be observed and integrated. While the objectives, structure, and spirit should be protected over its term, its contents should be continuously upgraded. A successful Marketing Excellence initiative has to be alive.

5. *Total Coherence.* A successful Marketing Excellence initiative should be fully integrated in the CEO's vision. At the opposite extreme, too often participants in some corporate programs see an important disconnect between the sessions they attend, the challenges of the firm, and the behavior of top executives. Whatever the objective of these programs, they cannot be successfully attained under these conditions. The four elements described above—top management support, strategic perspective, top-notch execution, constant monitoring and alignment—are essential to achieve a total coherence of the initiative. Every new activity added to the initiative has to be checked against these considerations. New staff brought in to manage various aspects of the initiative has to fully understand these elements. The power of a successful Marketing Excellence initiative is in its total coherence, both internally and in the strategic orientation of the firm.

Marketing Excellence initiatives are important endeavors. They are highly visible, they are long term in nature, and they can mobilize considerable human and financial resources. When they are not properly designed or implemented, they can be the source of expensive disappointments. But when successful, their potential impact on the future of a firm can be significant in terms of organizational capabilities, individual competences, and bottom-line results.

References

Burkitt, H., & Zealley, J. (2006). *Marketing excellence*. Hoboken, NJ: John Wiley & Sons.

Kim, C., & Mauborgne, R. (2005). *Blue ocean strategy*. Boston, MA: Harvard Business School Publishing.

Mazur, L., & Miles, L. (2007). *Conversations with marketing masters*. Hoboken, NJ: John Wiley & Sons.

Mullins, J., Walker, O., Boyd, H., & Larreche, J.C. (2006). *Marketing strategy*. New York: McGraw-Hill/Irwin.

Jean-Claude Larreche is the holder of the Alfred H. Heineken Chair at INSEAD and the chairman of StratX SA, a company that describes its mission as "Challenging people through enabling experiences, so they can drive sustainable and profitable growth." Jean-Claude is a specialist in marketing strategy and has been recognized in a 2007 book as one of the twelve "Marketing Masters" in the world. He is the author of numerous publications and is preparing a new book on "Building Momentum Growth." He has been on the main board of several companies, including Reckitt Benckiser and INSEAD, and a consultant to leading multinational companies. He has an MBA from INSEAD and a Ph.D. from Stanford University.

Mario Castaneda is a director at the StratX Boston office. His areas of expertise include strategic marketing and new product planning and execution. Throughout his twenty-two-year career, he has worked at Fortune 500 firms leading and managing large teams of marketing professionals in the United States and in the international arena. He also has held marketing positions in the retail industry. At StratX, he has assisted and led in the development of marketing excellence solutions and programs for multiple clients in the pharmaceutical, aerospace, and business-to-business industries. He has recently consulted in the development of long-range, five-year strategic business plans jointly with country CEOs of a large pharmaceutical client.

Zohra Jan Mamod is senior consultant at StratX. She is in charge of the customer focus excellence practice and helps her clients reinvent their customer focus strategies to achieve sustainable profitable growth. Her clients have included blue chip companies in the pharmaceutical, financial services, automotive, and consumer goods industries. She is the co-author of a business case that won the 2005 prize from the European Foundation for Management Development and is a member of the research team of Professor Larreche's coming book on "Building Momentum Growth." Before joining StratX, Zohra worked in marketing for two leading pharmaceutical companies. She has a doctorate in pharmacy and a master's degree in marketing.

CHAPTER 11

TIME WARNER CREATIVE LEADERSHIP SUMMIT

Vera Vitels

Executives who oversee employees in creative roles face unique challenges that suggest a modified approach to leadership development. At Time Warner, we have developed an innovative program that harnesses the creativity of a unique group of executives to explore trends impacting our business, look at the creative process itself, and gain insight into the dynamics of managing a creative organization. This article describes the challenge of developing a pilot program for leaders of creative talent, reviews the program as initially presented and concludes with suggestions for future improvements.

Case

Most large, complex organizations spend a significant amount of time developing skilled leaders. For the past several years, business journals and speakers have warned of a leadership crisis in Corporate America, and companies have responded with a renewed focus on assessing the needs of top managers and designing programs to develop and advance their leadership capabilities. Time Warner has been at the forefront of the media industry in these efforts, and the company's focus on leadership development has been critical for what is regarded as one of the entertainment industry's most successful management teams. Over the last several years, Time Warner has developed a set of leadership development programs targeting the needs of different levels of executives in the company. Development programs for senior-most business executives focus on enhancing the leadership skills, building capability around fostering innovation, strategic business discussions with the company's executives, and targeted networking.

Development for executives at the SVP and VP levels enables participants to expand their perspectives on the competitive landscape and enhance their ability to lead strategically, foster innovation, and drive collaboration. Time Warner also provides development opportunities for our high-potential executives, including women and minorities. All of Time Warner's leadership development efforts place a strong and consistent emphasis on a set of common leadership principles and expectations, which are called Foundations of Leadership. Over 1,300 Time Warner executives have participated in these programs in the past several years, and the outcomes have been overwhelmingly positive.

In the past year, we have expanded our leadership development efforts to focus on developing leaders of creative talent, which is a population of critical importance to our company. In fact, one of our divisional senior executives is a former creative and became a key sponsor and advocate for the program. At the time, there was no specialized program within the company to address the particular needs of executives who either led creative groups or were themselves creators of original content. Although Time Warner had exemplary leadership development programs in place, these were all tailored for traditional business leaders. We immediately began developing a development opportunity to fill this gap.

Responding to a Unique Challenge

At the outset of our work, we knew that the structure of our company would itself create complexity. Our businesses include interactive services, cable systems, filmed entertainment, television networks, and publishing. Specifically, Time Warner includes:

- Warner Bros. Entertainment—a worldwide leader in creating, producing, distributing, licensing, and marketing feature films, television shows, home video, animation, and other forms of entertainment
- New Line Cinema—one of the most successful independent film companies, focused on building a branded, diversified library through the development and production of films that have global appeal, with a special emphasis on the creation of valuable franchises

- HBO—America's most successful premium television company, delivering two twenty-four-hour premium television services to nearly forty million U.S. subscribers and selling branded programming into over 150 countries worldwide
- Turner Broadcasting System—operator of worldwide entertainment, animation, and news networks and businesses whose performances lead their respective industry segments
- Time Warner Cable—the second-largest cable company in the United States and an industry leader in matching technological advances to consumer interests in areas of video, high-speed data, and phone offerings, with more innovative products and services coming on-line in the dynamic and growing media
- AOL—the second-largest network of web properties in the United States, attracting 112 million unique visitors a month to some of the best-known brands on the Internet
- Time, Inc.—the leading magazine publisher in the United States and United Kingdom, with over one hundred titles worldwide that lead in nearly all of the most popular consumer categories

It was obvious to us from the outset that the challenges of leading creatives varied considerably across our divisions. The challenges faced by leaders in our filmed entertainment, broadcast, Internet, and print media groups could be expected to be quite different in scope and nuance. Managing the production of a feature film, complete with the panoply of Hollywood stars, famous directors, and substantial investment at risk is a vastly different task than managing editorial content for a print magazine or a CNN news desk. Yet all of the creative content generation activities across our divisions, real-world or online, do share certain conceptual similarities that can be translated into the subject matter of a development program. The key challenge for us was to identify the right series of universal concepts and develop a program to address them.

We began by asking how individuals are creative themselves, how creative styles and leadership styles fit together, and what elements of leading creatives could actually be taught. In order to answer those questions and deepen our understanding of the challenges facing our creative leaders, we conducted interviews with seventy-five senior leaders of creatives and individual contributors, who together represented a cross section of all divisions of Time Warner. We were interested in six key areas:

- Where creative ideas come from;
- Characteristics of successful leaders of creatives;

- Values and behaviors of creative individuals—both within Time Warner and outside the company;
- Conditions fostering creativity, both for individuals and for teams;
- Cultures that enable creative talents to do their best work; and
- How to develop leaders of creative talent.

Our inquiry yielded rich insights into the challenge of leading creatives and as we analyzed it, several important themes emerged. Some of the people we interviewed believed that creative individuals are by definition poor leaders of others. However, many interviewees disagreed with this Hollywood myth, citing many examples of highly creative individuals who were also exceptional leaders of a variety of groups. As one of the interviewees said:

> "There are two kinds of creatives: (1) people who get a thrill out of personally creating something; these people tend to be bad managers, and (2) people who can span the two, who feel best when the creative ship is humming. These people make better managers. You need to develop each of these types differently, in terms of assignments, responsibilities, etc."

As we dug deeper into the interview data, we discovered specific examples of effective leadership of creatives – situations in which the creative shop was indeed "humming." Creatives respond well to a workplace where they can "do their thing." An open, spontaneous environment facilitates their work. The formalized teams that work well for executives in other disciplines are stifling for creatives—an informal environment that encourages collaboration and transparency is far better at fostering ideas, incubating projects, and providing the space and freedom to bring projects to completion. Key leadership attributes in a successful creative division include being able to articulate the vision and logic underlying the content being created (interviewees referred to this many times as "creative vision" or "creative logic") and create appropriate boundaries to keep both the work and creative talent focused. Effective communication skills and a highly developed emotional intelligence are important to effectively leading creatives. Successful managers also have to maintain extensive social networks. This is critical for managing external talent, and given that some of the most powerful people in the industry are involved, requires considerable sophistication and finesse.

The interview data confirmed some of the things we suspected at the outset. We knew, for example, that creatives have enormous personal investment in their work—substantially more than most executives. It came as no surprise that this translates into higher levels of emotional stress, greater sensitivity to criticism, and overall a group harder to manage than most.

The data also gave us a broader understanding of the difficulties in managing creatives. The paradoxical nature of managing creatives—informal yet focused—is one of several ways leading creatives differs from leading traditional executives. Another difference surfaced by the data is in motivation. Since creatives are far more responsive to praise and recognition by peers than other executives, leaders of creatives must be deft at motivating with more than money. Leaders must also carefully calibrate their feedback, so that creatives can hear the information they need without shutting down because they feel their work is being criticized.

Managing creatives entails taking substantial risks, inasmuch as significant capital investment is required to turn concepts into products. The data revealed a pronounced tension between the freedom required to foster a culture of creativity and innovation on the one hand and the urge to cost control, process focus, and standardization inherent in any large, publicly-traded corporation. Interviewees valued leaders of creatives who served as advocates, exhibited courage, were empathetic, and demonstrated ability to be a buffer between talent and the corporate center.

The interview data highlighted the degree to which it is difficult for creatives to stay current with emerging media and technology trends. Interviewees were painfully aware of the impact of these trends on Time Warner and many wanted our help in getting connected and seeing some of the new technology.

Many of the concerns surfaced in the interview data were consistent with other research on the challenges of leading creatives conducted by others. The data we gathered told us that our creative leaders would benefit from development in four areas:

- Focusing on their own leadership;
- Gaining an understanding and exposure to other divisional creative processes;
- Enhancing their understanding of future trends and technologies impacting content and product creation; and
- Developing a strong network across Time Warner divisions and understanding each other's businesses better.

The insights gained from the interview data guided the design and development of a program tailored closely to the needs of this unique group. We were able to refer to some of these insights in the program modules themselves so participants could recognize them.

The act of interviewing a broad series of creative leaders within Time Warner yielded benefits beyond the data gathered. We built relationships with our interviewees as we spoke, and these relationships served us well as we moved forward. We were able to return to interviewees for clarification and advice as we proceeded, and we identified a number of individuals who could easily be speakers or panelists, either in this first program or in subsequent events.

We also looked at assessment tools targeting creativity and leadership as part of our design process. In stark contrast to the numerous leadership assessment tools available for traditional business leaders, there are a limited number of assessment tools specifically targeting creativity and leadership. We conducted a search of the available assessments of what we would term "leading creatives," hoping to find an instrument that would provide executives with insights into creativity. While we found several interesting tools (see Table 1), we concluded that none were an ideal fit for Time Warner's needs.

The Creative Leadership Summit

Our program, entitled *Spark: Creative Leadership Summit*, was held over three days at the Warner Bro's movie studio in Burbank. Twenty-five participants drawn from all the divisions of the company attended. Each of the participants was selected by his or her divisional CEO and HR head. One of the selection criteria was that participants represent thought leaders in the company who could eventually help shape the Summit for the next level in the organization—the top 200 creatives across Time Warner. Many of the participants had already played a role in developing the Summit itself, either as interviewees or through advice on Summit sessions. The four Summit objectives were drawn straight from the development ideas identified in our research above.

The first day of the Summit focused on leadership and management challenges of working with creative talent. Participants began the first day with a quick opening exercise that asked them to talk about their own leadership with their peers. After this activity, the head of one of our operating companies shared his perspectives and personal leadership journey, emphasizing the importance of feedback and coaching in developing his current leadership style. We would return to that point later in the Summit.

Participants spent the majority of the first day examining their personal leadership and motivations. They also discussed parallel concepts such as emotional intelligence, leadership, and self awareness, and looked at how the concept of emotional intelligence plays out in the creative world.

TABLE 1: LEADING CREATIVES ASSESSMENT ANALYSIS

Assessment Name	Assessment Type	Description
4MAT	Personal learning styles	8-box learning approach with four earning types; template for differentiating instruction
ECCI	Personal style/process	Separate versions for assessing either creative competencies or managerial competencies
FARAX	360°	Behavioral and performance feedback on a variety of attributes including innovation and context
FourSight	Process: individual, group, organization	Four phases of thinking process; six stages of CPS process
KEYS	Organizational climate	Management practices; encouragement and support for challenging work; autonomy, etc.
Kirton Adaption-Innovation Indicator	Person thinking style	How people solve problems
LEAF	Personal creativity style	Assess creative cognition and behavior, personality characteristics, cognitive, behavioral preferences, applying creativity at work, stimulating others
SIMPLEX Systems	Individual problem solving	Personal style; personal process; individual problem-solving methods
Situational Outlook Questionnaire	Organizational climate	Assess organizational climate on freedom, trust, openness, idea support, etc.
Whole Brain Creative Indicator	Personal creativity style	Assessment of left brain/right brain application

Before the commencement of the Summit, participants had been asked to fill out 360-degree assessments, which incorporated the concepts of effective leadership for creatives surfaced in the interview data. On the afternoon of the first day, participants working with their 360-degree feedback, engaging in individual coaching sessions to interpret the data and beginning to create action plans.

The second day of the program addressed future trends and creative processes. All media companies today are facing immense challenges in developing creative content for a rapidly changing environment. Younger generations are pioneering new ways to consume media—and these are being rapidly adopted by the mainstream. Vast increases in different platforms (online, mobile, etc.) are resulting in alternative avenues for content creation and distribution. User-generated content is now competing with traditional content. The map for creating content that is relevant, timely, and delivered through an appropriate medium in this environment is still being written. In a world in which our most basic assumptions about what our customers want and how we provide value are changing month by month or even faster, our leaders are hungry for anything that can help them lead through this turbulence.

The second day of the summit gave participants ample opportunity to grapple with these issues. A leading authority on emerging media and technology trends discussed the implications of the move from an information to a media age, outlining potential future states that have the potential to impact content creation and new product development. The futurist was followed by a Technology Lab in which participants saw some emerging technologies and their potential impact on the marketplace. Participants looked at four themed stations:

- The office—which featuring blogging, YouTube, Digg, Wikipedia, and the overall Web 2.0 defining feature of collective decision making.
- The dorm room—which had next-generation video games such as Second Life, World of Warcraft, and Machinimat and served as a mini-focus group around media consumption in today's college dorms.
- The living room—which featured the TV anywhere concept and technologies, such as Slingbox, Sony Locationfree, and video iPod/PSP.
- Mobile station—which provided samples of cutting-edge mobile devices.

The Tech Lab and the guided conversation with a senior Time Warner executive that followed stimulated participants to grapple with the implications of these new technologies—and the ramifications for creating new content. Participants discussed the age gap and the distance between creatives and some of their audiences. A rich and animated conversation ensued, focused on the challenges of bridging these gaps and building an internal capability to monitor and "get ahead" of the trends, as opposed to merely reacting to them.

The second half of the second day focused on the creative process at Time Warner. Participants worked to enhance their knowledge and understanding of other divisions and explored examples of creative processes taking part across the company. First, participants exchanged points of view regarding the creative side of their business and had an in-depth discussion of a creative endeavor that was either a great success or a tremendous failure. In candid discussions, the participants distilled key factors that influenced the outcome the endeavor, learning from each other and sharing similar experiences. The groups also articulated a creative process for their own division (something that often is implicit in how they go about work) and shared key lessons about sustaining and reinvigorating the creative process. The second day concluded with an evening conversation on creativity with David Milch, creator of the hit HBO series, *Deadwood*.

The third day of the Summit was a half-day that focused on: peer consultation and action planning. Participants were able to coach one another on the issues they face managing creative enterprises and leading for sustained creativity. They worked together in small groups to obtain advice and coaching from their peers and then reflected on what they'd covered in the preceding couple of days and discussed how they would integrate key learnings across leadership, the creative process, and emerging trends.

Moving Forward

The overall response to the Summit after its close was very positive. Participants appreciated the program and recognized the value of enhancing their leadership capabilities, sharing best practices around a creative process, gaining exposure to emerging media and technology trends, as well as forging partnerships across divisions. Participants also appreciated learning about themselves as individual leaders and benefited from receiving 360-degree feedback and peer coaching.

As we develop this program further, we will look to incorporate panel discussions featuring external and internal talent discussing their collaborative efforts; almost a behind the scenes look at how a creative collaboration takes place. We will also continue to focus on creative leadership and distilling characteristics and behaviors that differentiate great leaders of creative talent.

The organization is moving forward with our approach and we look forward to a second Creative Leadership Summit this summer.

Vera Vitels joined Time Warner in 2003 and leads a team responsible for leadership and organization development across the enterprise. In partnership with the Time Warner divisions, Vera's team focuses on the design and execution of leadership development strategy, succession and talent planning processes, the employee opinion survey, and executive assessments. Prior to Time Warner, Vera was principal, organization strategy and change at IBM and Pricewaterhouse Coopers. Vera's consulting experience with Fortune 500 organizations includes executive coaching, culture and climate assessments, change management, organization design, and leadership development. She has worked closely in these areas with PepsiCo, Pfizer, Union Bank of Switzerland, Kaiser Permanente, Pacific Gas and Electric Company, and Bell South. Vera earned her Ph.D. in organizational psychology from Columbia University and a B.A. in psychology from the University of California, Berkeley.

CHAPTER 12

BE THE ONE: THE LEADToshiba EXPERIENCE

Anthony V. Codianni and Terry Kristiansen

In October 2005, Toshiba America Business Solutions (TABS) had a major leadership shift. Our new president and CEO, Richard Taylor, charged us with a difficult task: Train our people as well as we train our customers. He didn't set a budget, and he didn't limit our program options. He simply told us to create an education program that was in the best interest of our employees and would meet the goals of retaining talent and developing a top-notch succession pipeline.

Out of that charge came the TABS LEADToshiba (**L**eadership **E**ducation **A**nd **D**evelopment) program—a blended learning approach to educating employees from the top down to fulfill our company mission of creating unbelievable customer passion and irresistible value. The program develops leaders at all levels—from the president to the receptionist in our front office. We began the program in February 2006, and after one year, Toshiba America Business Solutions had trained 98 percent of our management.

Even more exciting was the culture shift and passion for work that grew out of this training investment. One year into the program, TABS employees were aligned and engaged in new ways, and we started to see our people integrate our philosophy and vision in new and exciting ways.

Our Philosophy

To understand why these results are exciting, it's important to first understand our philosophy. The TABS motto is simple: "Be the One." The TABS organization revolves around becoming a principled and customer-focused organization that is so passionate, excited, and engaged that we exceed our customers' expectations in every way. Our goal with the LEADToshiba program was to create leaders—not managers, who could lead the organization today and in the future—not just manage tasks that came across their desks. To that end, we designed the program to be a blended learning approach that integrates a variety of methods and styles to give every leader at every level the tools they need to grow themselves and our company.

Education for the Masses

The LEADToshiba program has four tracks that are designed to meet the needs of four different groups within the company. All four tracks are organized in a way that recognizes and meets different learning styles by incorporating what we call CEM methods—Classroom, Electronic, and Mobile.

We take very seriously our philosophy of training from the top down. Before we could train anyone else, we had to start at the top with our president and his executive team. We couldn't institute a program that encouraged leading from the top until we had trained at the top. After our executive team had gone through training, we launched the program for all employees in February 2006.

Track Three involves training leaders at the senior leader level—vice presidents and directors. They participate in "Leadership at the Top," a program that combines seminars, print learning materials through our monthly *Leadcast* e-newsletter, and virtual learning through our Gigabeats. Every month, participants can download new MP3 material to their Gigabeats and listen to world-renowned consultants and coaches speak on leadership and business topics.

Track Two is targeted to our front-line leaders who are managers and supervisors. They participate in programs designed to provide them with knowledge, skills, and tools appropriate for their leadership positions. One program, FASTrack, includes seminars and the *Leadcast* e-newsletter, and offers a monthly webinar. Webinars are archived each month, so employees have access to them any time or any place that meets their needs.

Track One is aimed at future leaders and is branded the "Be the One" program. Track One brings new hires and individual contributors up-to-speed on our procedures, culture, philosophy, and best practices. They are then enrolled in the FASTrack program.

We also have a special training program for the employees of companies we have acquired. The SWAT (Special Weekly Acquisition Training) program is a ninety-day program to train the employees of our new acquisitions. Since implementing this program, we've seen retention of these employees jump from about 6 percent to 92 percent.

All of our programs are aimed at developing the four pillars we consider our core competencies at TABS: Managing Self, Leading Teams, Managing Projects, and Leading the Business. We also want to encourage understanding and embracing our company values: Focus on the Customer, Integrity, Focus on People, Innovation, Quality, Agility, and Performance. Finally, we tie all of our programs back to our ten strategies of the TABS organization.

Ten Strategies for All TABS Employees

Vision, passion, and values are all vital to the health of any company. However, without the strategies to implement them, vision, passion, and values will fail to create business success. The ten strategies are the TABS way of doing business—of acting out our vision, passion, and values.

1. *Use speed and flexibility:* There's never enough time to make a perfect decision, and with the speed of business today, we can't possibly know everything there is to know before we make a decision. In a world where the amount of information doubles every 266 days, we have to be adaptable, flexible, and ready to think on our feet.
2. *Reinvent the business for the customer:* Not everyone wants the same product. In 2005, there were forty-six different kinds of Tylenol on the market. We have to recognize the uniqueness and individuality of our customers and their needs, and we have to focus on reinventing the business to meet those needs.
3. *Choose your attitude:* We want our people to choose a positive attitude every day. Those who wake up expecting a lousy day will get what they expect! But those who wake up expecting the greatest day ever will still have a good day even if a few things happen to derail that expectation. Our culture is upbeat and positive; people who choose to remain in a negative attitude usually don't last because they don't fit into our culture.
4. *Be Toshiba:* Because we represent Toshiba, we have an obligation to operate with the highest integrity in everything we do.
5. *Develop towering competencies:* We ask everyone: What are you best at? What's your unique towering competency? What can you focus on becoming world class at? These towering competencies are the vertical growth we encourage in everyone.

6. *Communicate frequently and informally:* The inability to communicate effectively will stall a company. We don't have meetings; we have huddles. TABS employees huddle in hallways, over cubicle walls, and in common areas where they can openly exchange ideas and resolve challenges without formal meetings.

7. *Infuse irresistible value:* We call this the "WOW Factor." How can we wow our customers today? How can we make our customers feel exceptional every day?

8. *Develop as a business person/entrepreneur:* While our towering competencies are the vertical growth we want all employees to pursue, developing as a business person is the horizontal growth we also focus on. This area focuses on developing business acumen, understanding the basics of business, and teaching people to strategize and think like a business person. We can be the best in the world at our towering competencies, but without the business skills to go along with those competencies, we'll fail.

9. *Organize around the customer:* If we don't organize around the customer and do everything in the best interests of our customers, we'll ultimately be overtaken by those who do. This is what drives us—being the best in the world at exceeding our customers' expectations.

10. *Be principle-driven:* We are not a process-driven organization; we are principle-driven. For us, everything is about doing the right thing for the customer.

Results

In the first year of the program, we took to the playing field in a big way. We trained nearly every manager in the company, and our senior leaders have been through several leadership programs in this short time. The LEADToshiba program earned accolades from training and learning associations, including the American Society for Training and Development. And we've had sixteen high-potential leaders participate in "The President's Challenge," an action learning program. In post-course evaluations, the participants praised the amount of learning they experienced in such a short time. The action learning program provided legitimacy to the LEADToshiba program as a whole and provided multiple benefits, including:

1. Significant growth in participant knowledge of the business as well as team and project management growth;

2. Exceptional recommendations to the organization that we've already started to implement; and

3. Direct connections between the executive team and some of our organization's most talented and capable people.

We've also measured some tremendous results around the engagement level of our people. One study estimated that only 19 percent of employees are engaged in their companies. That's an unacceptable level of engagement for any company. Comparison studies show that companies with engaged employees have reduced turnover rates and lower absenteeism. At TABS, we have three "Rules of Engagement"—*Enjoy, Believe, and Value*. All TABS employees need to enjoy their work, believe in what they do, and feel they provide value and make a difference in the lives of their customers. After participating in the LEADToshiba program, a majority of employees reported that they were engaged in the company and their work. Our president has commented that he now notices people throughout the organization "speaking the same language" and using terms such as "Customer Passion," "Irresistible Value," and "Be the One."

As we look back on our successful first year, we can say with confidence that our employees are more engaged, excited, and passionate about their work than ever before. When we reflect on the year, we see three key ingredients to the success of any training and development program; we call them the "ABCs":

1. ***A****lways make sure the CEO is the champion of the program*. It's more than just buy-in; the CEO has to be championing your training and development program at every opportunity. Leadership and participation from the top is crucial to success at every level of the organization.
2. ***B****e principle-oriented, not procedure-oriented*. Being a principled organization means doing the right thing all the time, even if the right thing doesn't fit into standard procedures. Let principles drive your education program; the procedures will fall into place. Design the programs around principles that you aspire to as a company and then think about the procedures.
3. ***C****reate consistent language in your communications*. Find the language that people in your organization can rally around—the words and phrases that permeate your organization and describe your principles, mission, and goals. For example, at TABS, the phrase "Be the One" is key to our programs; after a year of consistent communication and rollout from the top down, that phrase has become institutionalized across the organization. When we pat someone on the back for a job well done, it's now very common to hear in response, "I just want to 'Be the One.'"

Are we doing everything perfectly? No. But are we doing the right things? Yes! We're meeting our goals of retaining talent and creating a leadership pipeline brimming with people who are developed to take our company into the future.

People spend an average of 82 percent of their time in work-related activities (at work, commuting to work, and thinking about work, among others). With that much time committed to work, we need engaged, passionate employees to meet our strategic goals. We can't have people just putting in time or coming to work hating their jobs—and to be truthful, those kind of people don't last long at TABS. It's not because we fire them; they simply don't fit in with our culture and the culture drives them away.

It's been said that, without vision, people perish. We agree, but would also say that without passion, companies perish. At TABS, we want to build a passionate, energetic culture that is 100 percent customer-focused and shares a vision to create value and make a difference for the Toshiba organization. With the LEAD-Toshiba program, we are well on our way to meeting that goal.

Anthony V. Codianni has been with the Toshiba Corporation for over twenty-three years. His education and development group has won him numerous world class awards in training. In fact, Mr. Codianni was awarded the Stevie Award for Best Sales Trainer by the American Business Awards in 2005, and in 2006 was awarded an International Stevie Award for Best Sales Trainer in the world by the International Business Association. He was also awarded a Platinum award for CLO (chief learning officer) of the Year in 2006 for Learning Innovation. His programs have been recognized by the ASTD as some of the best in the world, and he continues to garner awards from both inside and out of his industry. Before joining Toshiba, Mr. Codianni was a high school teacher and principal and a professor at various Midwest universities. A former Fulbright Scholar, Mr. Codianni has always had a passion for excellence in education, training, and development.

Terry Kristiansen is the project leader for the recently launched enterprise-wide leadership initiative at Toshiba America Business Systems. The program goal is to become a world-class leadership program and has been identified as a number-one priority by the company president. Ms. Kristiansen is also responsible for a staff of education specialists who deliver leadership and sales training to five different sales channels, internal corporate management, and individual contributors. Prior to joining Toshiba, Ms. Kristiansen was an elementary-level educator and spent ten years in administration at a highly successful national real estate investment company. She holds a master's degree in education from California State University, Fullerton, and a Lifetime California Teaching Credential.

CHAPTER 13

THE QUEST FOR 20:20 VISION: DEVELOPING HR LEADERS AT LUXOTTICA

Ken Meyers

When Mildred Curtis gazes out of the window of her Mason, Ohio, office at Luxottica Retail's North American headquarters these days, she has a lot to reflect on. Over the last three years, she and her team have brought true state-of-the-art human resources practices to this retail giant—practices that were necessary in part because of the company's exponential growth and new dominance of the North American market for eyewear through ownership of LensCrafters, Pearle Vision, Target Optical, Sears Optical, Sunglass Hut, and EyeMed Vision Care. When the company tapped Curtis for the newly created chief HR position, she knew that developing the existing HR department to act as a business partner to line management would be challenging—but also rewarding.

With her long tenure at Luxottica Retail, Curtis was a champion and advocate for the family culture that resulted in Luxottica Retail being named a great place to work year after year. However, with a background in law, Curtis found herself thrust into a world somewhat unfamiliar to her as she stepped into her new role. Suddenly, she had to learn about building organizational capability, creating reward systems that drive selling behavior, and bringing cutting-edge leadership training and development to the fast-growing retail concepts. Curtis readied herself for the new adventure. Now, when she considers all of the chapters of Luxottica Retail's growth in her nearly twenty years with the company, she smiles with

The 2008 Pfeiffer Annual: Leadership Development.
Copyright © 2008 by John Wiley & Sons, Inc. Reproduced by permission of Pfeiffer, an Imprint of Wiley. www.pfeiffer.com

pride at the achievements the HR team has made in creating real and measurable value for the Luxottica Retail organization.

Raising the Bar on HR

Caught in the paradox of the necessary administrative nature of the function and the call from senior executives for tighter alignment and greater partnership with business strategy, human resources professionals often struggle to find the time, focus, and perspective needed to expand beyond traditional roles. Many HR functions have relieved themselves of the administrative burdens through intranet capability or outsourced services. Freed from the shackles of processing paper on benefits and recordkeeping, HR professionals can focus on what CEOs and senior line managers are demanding—building the necessary capability in the organization to deliver the business strategy. Such a move is a big change considering that just a few decades ago, human resources, or then the "personnel" function, largely consisted of payroll and benefits, and was viewed as the place where one was "hired and fired."

In the 1990s, we started to see a shift toward human resources as a business partner—HR professionals working side-by-side with the line to look at issues such as training, people development, and succession planning. Now, in the new millennium, senior leadership recognizes the need for a human resources function as a value creator with the business. In forward-thinking companies, HR is now an integrated arm of the business. Gone are the days of "HR Inc.," where HR acted as its own company within the organization, serving as an enforcer of rules and policies. Progressive HR heads have earned a seat at the business table and speak up and add value in all aspects of running the business. They are developing the function so that it delivers financial results and business value. What a novel concept, given that payroll and workforce expenditures often account for up to 70 percent of a firm's operating costs. Converting that cost into financial return is something any shareholder would cheer.

An important question arises in this discussion around HR—namely, what is "value"? It's easy to use the term as yet another convenient business buzz phrase or cliché. Ulrich and Brockbank (2005) talk about value as the worth to the receiver of the program or service. In the case of the HR professional, if the receiver—say an employee attending a company training program—finds the program to be beneficial to her learning, then value is added. They remark: "Value becomes the bellwether for HR. When others receive value from HR work, HR will become credible, respected, and influential."

Let's take that argument one step further. If the receiver then transforms the service or program into something that delivers financial return to the business, then that is a true "value add." So again, in the case of the employee attending the training program, if she then takes her new learning back to her team and together they create a new innovation that goes to market and delivers profit to the business, that's value! Simply receiving the service and feeling like the service is beneficial is not enough to result in value to the business. Yes, it adds personal value, but not shareholder value.

Luxottica Group: Framed for Success

When it comes to eyewear, Luxottica Group, parent company of the North American Retail division, owns the market. The world's largest eyewear firm, Luxottica Group designs, manufactures, and distributes a range of prescription frames and sunglasses. The company's house brands include Ray-Ban, Revo, Arnette, Persol, Killer Loop, Luxottica, and Vogue, and its designer lines include Chanel, Polo Ralph Lauren, Tiffany, Salvatore Ferragamo, Brooks Brothers, Anne Klein, Bulgari, Versace, Prada, Burberry, and many others. While Luxottica Group had been experiencing top- and bottom-line growth year after year from comp store growth and through acquisitions around the world, including Asia Pacific, it was in 2004 with the acquisition of Cole National (parent of Pearle Vision, Target Optical, and Sears Optical) that Luxottica Retail would come to dominate the North American retail market.

So where did this powerhouse come from? Luxottica Group was founded in 1961 by Leonardo Del Vecchio, referred to in Italy as the "King of Spectacles." The firm's initial business was the production of eyeglass components for Italian frame manufacturers. Del Vecchio quickly vertically integrated the company to command greater profit, and today Luxottica Group continues to own its entire supply chain. The company became the number one eyewear distributor in the United States in the early 1980s, and by 1990, U.S. sales accounted for more than half of the company's revenue. Luxottica Group went public in 1990, the first Italian company to bypass the Milan stock exchange in favor of the NYSE.

A darling on Wall Street, Luxottica Group continuously outperformed analyst expectations. While meeting financial goals, Luxottica Group put social responsibility high on its agenda. With its Gift of Sight program, makeshift clinics are staffed with volunteers, optometrists, and technicians who provide free vision care and eyewear to underprivileged people in North America and developing countries around the world. Since the program's inception in 1988, Gift of Sight has helped more than five million people with a goal of helping seven million by 2008.

Upping the Game for HR at Luxottica Retail

By 2001 Luxottica Group had purchased the Ray-Ban brand from Bausch & Lomb and was closing the deal to acquire U.S. specialty sunglass retailer Sunglass Hut International for about $650 million. With more growth on the way, the business was clamoring for greater focus and expertise in the HR arena. The company had previously never had an executive devoted solely to the HR function. Senior management turned to Mildred Curtis, an insider and proven culture fit with a long tenure of leadership experience with Luxottica, and named her as the newly created Senior Vice President of HR.

Initially Curtis split her time leading both the legal and human resources functions, and then in 2005 dropped the legal piece of her portfolio and focused solely on HR. From the onset Curtis faced her own challenges to taking the top spot. With a background in merger and acquisition law, Curtis identified areas in which she needed to develop in order to both add value to the business and to create a function that effectively served and advocated for employees.

After spending some time developing herself through attending seminars, reading, and working with a coach who specialized in HR transformation, Curtis evaluated the human resources function from a legal and compliance perspective, making sure everything the company was already doing was in line with the law and regulations as applicable. Once the legal and compliance factors were in place, Curtis turned her attention to developing her team and creating an HR department that was a true strategic partner for Luxottica Retail.

Curtis could see potential in all of the senior HR managers for growth and advancement, and she carefully identified improvement plans individually and as a team. There was a very visible turn in expectations when Curtis assumed responsibility for leading the HR function. Valerie Norvell, Assistant Vice President for Training & Development, noted how quickly the world of Luxottica had changed in late 2004. "We essentially went from two brands to six almost overnight," she said. "There was a need to be connected more deeply to the business side of each brand, especially as all of these brands needed HR support."

Curtis and her team established the following HR team developmental needs:

1. *Creating a cohesive and aligned team:* Although the people on Curtis' team had good relationships on a personal level, they functioned largely in silos within the company and did not work as a cohesive team. "The person in compensation and benefits, for example, could spend an entire career doing just that function and never think about training and development," Curtis said. "As a team, they had limited need for interaction and needed greater connectivity."

2. *Focusing and re-allocating HR resources:* From a practical standpoint, the company growth was so rapid that supply of HR resources could not meet the demand required to service the new associates under the Luxottica Retail umbrella. Curtis saw an immediate need for staff to assume some of the process activities and free up her more senior team members to pursue opportunities that would drive business results.

3. *Increasing business acumen:* HR team members were experts in every functional area of HR, including compensation, benefits, employee relations, and training and development. Starting with the senior HR leadership group, the team needed to improve its general business knowledge. Specifically, the team needed grounding in business strategy, financial acumen, levers that drive the Luxottica business, and key metrics—all in order to propel them to a place where they could partner with the other business leaders.

4. *Understanding the impact of globalization on the business:* With the parent company's acquisitions of retail concepts in Australia and China, leaders with primarily U.S. business experience were tasked to think and act globally. Keith Borders, Vice President of Associate Relations and Diversity, said that one of his personal needs was to develop a broader perspective on the implications of operating in a global context. "This need was applicable broadly for our team as well," he said. "We needed to learn more about the global needs of our business and about what our colleagues in other global companies were doing."

HR Accepts the Challenge

Developing leaders comes naturally to HR leaders. It's what we do best. But when it comes to our own development, we often claim to be too busy or prefer to allocate the investment dollars to line managers. As Daryl Hammett, an HR executive whom Curtis moved into a senior line role as Vice President, Store Operations, says, "This is one of the biggest derailers of HR as a whole. It's like how the hairdresser's hair is always the worst—she's busy doing everyone else's hair and neglects her own."

Curtis and team committed to an investment in their own development. They knew that the bar had been raised for them with new requirements set by senior line management; they needed to develop themselves in the areas they identified. All, including Curtis, joined Luxottica Retail when it was a seedling of a retailer—with one brand named LensCrafters. The game had visibly changed in 2004 with the acquisition of Cole National, doubling the employee size to over 38,000. Either the team would accept the challenge and grow with the company, or they would quickly become irrelevant and perish.

The 2008 Pfeiffer Annual: Leadership Development.

So with mission accepted, and with a focus on developing true strategic business leaders for the Luxottica organization, Curtis signed her team up for a high-impact HR development experience (HR Consortium) in early 2005. The team traveled for its first week of learning to Miami where, with teams from Bank of America, Bell Canada, and Time Warner, they were bombarded with new insights in building organizational capability, developing leaders, exploring alternative business models, and most importantly for the Luxottica team, developing financial acumen to influence business outcomes.

Within the framework of a very typical action learning program, the team worked on an issue of strategic importance to the business with Curtis as the sponsor. With a singular and unified focus on the business challenge, the senior HR team accelerated their development as a high-execution team. Coupled with individual leadership assessments, first reviewed privately with a coach and then shared to understand each individual's impact on the team, this group of competent team members quickly developed the trust and the ability to constructively conflict and debate with one another to elevate them to a results-driven team.

Two months later, the team flew to Lisbon for the final week of their program. With their team challenge near completion, the team was exposed to thought leadership on globalization and its impact on them as leaders within Luxottica. What better place to discuss cross-cultural leadership than in historic Lisbon—far away from Cincinnati and the Ohio River Valley, home of five-way chili! When Curtis arrived on the final day for the team's delivery of its presentation of the business challenge she posed to them, Curtis found her own "dream team!"

"It was a little surreal," said Curtis of the final presentation stage in Lisbon. "When I went to Lisbon to participate as the team's sponsor, I could see the difference even then. These people who had had such a siloed approach before were solving problems together. Their empowerment meters were running—it was amazing to watch!" Feedback from the team reinforced Curtis' observations. "They felt they had really gelled as a team," Curtis observed.

Innovate and Create Value

Following their participation in the Human Resources Consortium and with a new sense of empowerment, Luxottica Retail's human resources senior leaders began to push down or reprioritize many of the daily tasks that had distracted them from pursuing more strategic initiatives. Together, with their newly found team spirit, the senior team explored ways to actively grow its involvement in the business. The team embarked on a new path to creating value through innovation. Here's what they did:

1. *Elevated people development as a top priority:* Senior management listed employee development as a critical priority given the rapid growth in the business. Opportunities for internal movement required that employees be equipped to assume additional levels of responsibility rapidly in their career. Valerie Norvell, newly minted Assistant Vice President of Training & Development, said there was a very clear need to invest in technology as it related to training. "Training had remained basically stagnant in the organization, even though we went from 12,000 to 38,000 employees almost overnight," she said. In 2007, her department led the push to implement innovative training and development processes through web-based and intranet technology.

In addition, employee feedback indicated dissatisfaction with visibility to job opportunities. Through a partnership with Monster.com, the company now advertises all job openings online, giving employees greater access to opportunities across the globe.

2. *Transferred accountability for diversity initiatives to line management:* Fresh from the HR Consortium, Keith Borders, VP of Associate Relations and Diversity, worked closely with senior line managers to redefine how to incorporate diversity efforts as a part of a line manager's role. In days past, diversity had been a "program" pushed down the organization by HR. Now, instead, having a diverse workforce is a value and priority for the entire organization. As a result of transferring responsibility and holding line managers accountable to inclusion and diversity, "We're focused on diversity," said Frank Baynham, Executive Vice President of Stores. "We're not just letting it happen."

3. *Developed "new and improved" communication links to employees:* With the exponential growth of size of the employee population, the team explored innovative approaches to extending the company's reach and creating just-in-time communication. An investment in online capability gives employees greater access to employee benefits information, company news, training opportunities, and internal job openings. Line managers and employees are noticing the greater connections. Executive VP Frank Baynham is encouraged by the company's progress in communicating with employees more frequently and interactively, and he acknowledged the leadership role that HR has played in transforming internal communication. "We've made a commitment to keeping people informed," he stated. "Line managers are now better equipped to communicate internal matters directly with their teams."

4. *Established an employer brand to create an emotional connection with employees:* Having learned the benefits of employment branding, the Luxottica Retail team moved quickly to develop a plan that supported company values and culture. A fresh approach to human resources at Luxottica Retail is exemplified in its own innovation: be!LUX. The be!LUX brand creates a new image that transcends

all aspects of training and development. For example, Norvell and team created stunning artwork and snappy communication designed to fully engage Luxottica Retail employees. The be!LUX mission statement reads, in part, "The binders are gone, boring manuals are a thing of the past, and training is delivered in a multi-dimensional, multi-media fashion." Creating an emotional connection with Luxottica Retail employees increases employee engagement, which, in turn, results in higher levels of customer satisfaction, which in retail, leads directly to increased sales. That's value—value that not only feels good for the receiver, the employee, but also the shareholder.

How You, Too, Can Get to 20:20 Vision

Now, over two years after the HR Consortium, the HR senior team's impact is felt throughout the business. With both individual and team development objectives met, Curtis promoted several of the team leaders, and all have assumed greater responsibility. The team has stepped up to a new level of leadership, not only partnering with the line leaders, but converting plans and actions into tangible value for the business. The proof in the pudding came when Curtis charged the team to develop an integrated HR strategy that supported the 2007 business plan. Mission accomplished!

What should you keep in mind as you up your game? Here are three key lessons for other HR leaders as they step up to create 20:20 vision in their businesses:

1. Re-examine everything you do and ensure that you are adding value for the receiver AND creating value for the shareholder. You need to do both. Your company's HR practices are a key lever for strategy execution and for delivery of financial results. "Firms that survive and prosper over the long run develop internally consistent systems of HR policies and practices that are specifically designed to execute strategy" (Huselid, Becker, & Beatty, 2005).
2. Join at the hip your line leaders and empower them with tools and information to enable their employees. Break down the knowledge barriers between HR and the line. "HR must learn more about the business, and the line managers must become more proficient at managing their human resources" (Lawler & Mohrman, 2003).
3. Create an emotional connection with your employees to up their level of engagement. You will see their energy ignite your customers and, in turn, you create shareholder value through increased financial performance. Your employer brand translates to "what it means to your employees to be a part

of what you are trying to accomplish. Why they will want to choose to work and commit. How it can feel at the end of the day to go home and say, 'I did my job.'" (Sartain & Schumann, 2006).

As in many of today's global companies, growth happens quickly. It happens organically. It happens through acquisition. It can catch you off-guard. The new HR function in this new millennium is fully integrated with the business and the days of being "caught off-guard" are days of the past. Building the organizational capability and enabling the organization to capitalize on the growth are where all HR executives' eyes are focused. Put on your glasses. Learn from the Luxottica Retail story and fulfill your quest for 20:20 vision.

References

Huselid, M.A., Becker, B.E., & Beatty, R.W. (2005). *The workforce scorecard*. Boston, MA: Harvard Business School Press.

Lawler, E., & Mohrman, S. (2003, September). HR as a strategic partner: What does it take to make it happen? *HR Planning*.

Sartain, L., & Schumann, M. (2006). *Brand from the inside*. San Francisco, CA: Jossey-Bass.

Ulrich, D., & Brockbank, W. (2005). The HR value proposition. Boston, MA: Harvard Business School Press.

Ken Meyers is a partner with Oliver Wyman Delta Executive Learning Center. Meyers' interest in leadership development stems from his twenty years' experience in global human resources and senior line management at top global corporations, most recently as senior vice president of human resources at Starbucks and senior vice president of human resources and operations at Gymboree. Meyers has extensive experience working with senior teams in their acceleration to high performance. He has served as principal consultant and coach to numerous senior executives and teams at companies such as Unilever, Sara Lee, Amgen, Disney, Nike, Luxottica, Thomson, Time Warner, and L'Oréal. Meyers earned his bachelor's degree in international business and human resources management from the Wharton School of the University of Pennsylvania and his MBA from the Harvard Business School.

CHAPTER 14

WHAT WOMEN EXECUTIVES NEED FROM LEADERSHIP DEVELOPMENT PROGRAMS

Marijo Bos

Despite the advances women have made in business in the last few decades, their representation at senior levels is still very low. Is it possible that we are overlooking opportunities in the leadership development field to propel women into senior positions?

Of Fortune 500 companies, only eleven CEOs are women; only 15 percent of directors and 16 percent of senior officer positions in the same group of companies are women. Indra Nooyi, CEO of PepsiCo, sees "a lot of hope," as she told the *Financial Times* in March 2007. "The next five to ten years I think are very promising. . . . I am meeting more and more fantastic women at what I call almost-CEO levels." However, Ms. Nooyi also says that companies have a responsibility to set up programs that will help women rise to the top (Babcock & Laschever, 2003).

Ms. Nooyi's call for companies to start making a concerted effort to help women rise to the top is one that more women need to make. On-ramps and off-ramps and opting out aside, there's a need to address the gender differences in leadership development and to begin tailoring mixed-gender programs to more readily engage, enhance, and appreciate female-specific leadership characteristics and opportunities for growth.

The 2008 Pfeiffer Annual: Leadership Development.

In their 2003 study "Women in U.S. Corporate Leadership," the non-profit organization Catalyst surveyed women executives from Fortune 1000 companies to learn what keeps women from the top and what strategies they employ to succeed. Barriers to success were identified as:

- Lack of significant general management or line experience—47 percent
- Exclusion from informal networks—41 percent
- Stereotyping and preconceptions of women's roles and abilities—33 percent
- Failure of senior leadership to assume accountability for women's advancement—29 percent
- Commitment to personal or family responsibilities—26 percent

The top strategies for success were:

- Consistently exceeding performance expectations—69 percent
- Successfully managing others—49 percent
- Developing a style with which male managers are comfortable—47 percent
- Having recognized expertise in a specific content area—46 percent
- Seeking out difficult or highly visible assignments—40 percent

In work I've done in leadership training programs around the world, I've observed women executives who struggle with these and other challenges as female leaders in business. In my observations, the barriers these women face and the strategies they use are not being consistently addressed through leadership development programs, and I wanted to find out what is missing and desired according to women who have gone through formal development programs. I conducted specific interviews around leadership development programs with over a dozen women at the senior-vice-president level and up in global Fortune 1000 companies across a variety of industries, including pharmaceutical, consumer goods, financial services, and technology. I also interviewed consultants with backgrounds in training and coaching both men and women in a variety of environments.

Consistently, the people I interviewed identified the same barriers and strategies as the women in the Catalyst study. Most of the issues really come down to two basic and fundamental challenges facing women in leadership roles today: gender stereotyping and leadership neutralizing. Women still face gender stereotypes and perceptions that must be dispelled; on the other hand, leadership programs today assume that women have the same development needs that men have.

Many traditional programs are geared to a typically male-dominated group and often have men playing the dominant roles, either as facilitators or "expert" speakers. By not embracing the specific styles, needs, gifts, and perspectives of women, are we missing opportunities to fully develop half of our leadership pipeline and at the same time leverage female leadership skills across the entire group?

Back to Basics

Let's start with a basic assumption. There are many core leadership skills that are imperative, regardless of gender. All business leaders benefit from honing skills such as business acumen; the ability to strategize and set a vision; an understanding of how complex business works; the ability to negotiate, resolve conflict, and make tough choices; the ability to relate to people; and an ability to coach others, build effective teams, and foster communication. Likewise, men and women have similar transitions on the path to becoming fully developed leaders. The book *The Leadership Pipeline: How to Build the Leadership Powered Company*, by Ram Charan, Stephen Drotter, and James Noel (2001), outlines the passages that leaders must navigate as they gain responsibility in an organization, and how these passages translate to new skill requirements, new time horizons and applications, and new work values. Clearly, all leaders must go through these transitions as they move up in an organization or they'll slow or halt their progress.

A problem with current leadership development programs is that men and women are at different starting points and levels of perception in both *what* skills need to be developed and *how* we develop them in women as opposed to men, and these differences are not taken into account. Let's say, for example, that men are yellow and women are blue, and both need to get to red—in other words, a fully developed, whole leader. By the same token, within each group, you have different shades of yellow and different shades of blue. Getting to red will require the addition of different amounts of different colors to each starting place; no one formula will work for the entire group.

Likewise, no one leadership development formula works for an entire group, whether it's a group organized by gender, culture, or function. And while leadership development programs must reflect the CEO's agenda and strategy, there may be a need and opportunity to encourage the programs of today and tomorrow to have a stronger aspect of individuality for participants beyond the individual coaching that is often part of development programs. Many of the women I spoke with noted the need for more individuality related to practical situational leadership scenarios that are tied to real-time challenges they face. They would like more knowledge sharing from participants who have faced similar challenges in order to get into the state of their current business and the leadership skills needed. There was a clear request for less theory and more practical applications or more situational leadership examples and experiences shared within the group.

I hope to encourage a different way of thinking about development programs and provoke women leaders to ask for these subtle differences to be addressed in order to more effectively support their professional development.

Dispelling the Stereotypes

Time and again in surveys, women are given credit for certain skills that often set them apart as good managers in the eyes of subordinates. But in psychological studies, little difference appears between women and men. According to Catalyst (2005), both women and men fall for the same stereotypes about women as leaders; both women and men consider women better at "take care" behaviors such as supporting and rewarding, and both consider men better at "take charge" behaviors such as delegating and influencing upward. If behavioral analyses and psychological studies show little appreciable difference between the sexes, then what do we do with these perceptions?

From a practical perspective, whether the differences are there is really not the issue. Instead, the issue is one of perceptions and how we reinforce these perceptions in everyday business. Many programs often refer to the Pygmalion effect and its power over behavior and performance. Men and women come from different starting places, so we have to address the perceptions and begin to dispel the stereotypes from both directions. To do that, let's look first at some of the "taking care" behaviors that women and men both point to as being strong areas of leadership for women.

First, women are often given credit for notable competencies that are important to lateral thinking and management—gathering information from a variety of sources, considering a variety of opinions, multi-tasking across a numerous boundaries at the same time, exhibiting a collaborative style in building relationships and a natural ability for empathy, and taking the perspective of others. Dr. Helen Fisher, an anthropologist at Rutgers University, calls this ability "web thinking." Fisher says that "Women gather more data from their environment and construct more intricate relationships between the information. By contrast, men tend to compartmentalize— to get rid of ancillary data and focus only on what they regard as important." She notes that some attributes related to web thinking are intuition, imagination, and a tolerance of ambiguity—attributes that will become more necessary in the global business environment of the future (Griffin, 1999).

Lateral thinking is important in the fast-paced, global environment of today and tomorrow. Increasingly, business leaders who can operate effectively across an ambiguous lateral business system that requires building bridges across geographic areas and within often highly matrixed organizations are the ones who will create the best results. Leadership development programs need to include modules, scenarios, or opportunities that provide more in-depth lateral challenges and find ways to engage women's perceived skills in this area. These kinds of opportunities would engage the women in the group to more fully participate and offer feedback within the group.

Second, women are given credit for being talented communicators and relaters or collaborators, as noted earlier. This relational nature allows women to communicate well across gender, cultural, generational, and other boundaries; they tend to focus on building consensus through sharing ideas and by bringing others into the discussion. With an increased focus on retention, motivation, and a workplace that puts people first, in part because of the growing war for talent, this relational nature could be a real plus in a growing a diverse workforce in a business setting that needs to attract talent and foster a sense of belonging.

The generation of up-and-coming executives—Generations X and Y or what in combination are the "We" generation—appears to be placing a lot of emphasis on relationships, and while many companies are reviewing and altering their environments and messages on quality of life and work/life balance, the real adjustment to corporate lifestyle needed in order to retain and motivate this generation remains to be seen. This generation is always connected to something—technology, blogs, or other forms of sharing and socializing through online communities such as MySpace and Facebook. This group is less willing to totally sacrifice their "free or we" time in support of a career. In a recent article from the *Harvard Business Review*, authors Sylvia Ann Hewlett and Carolyn Buck Luce (2006) discuss "extreme jobs"—jobs where employees work seventy or more hours per week—and mention that "the next generations of management—the so-called Gen X and Gen Y cohorts—seem less enamored with their careers than baby boomers." They are asking what companies can do for them, rather than what they can do for companies. In their survey, 65 percent of people ages twenty-five to forty-four said they would decline a promotion that required more energy from them.

If we also consider the war for talent that is on the minds of many executives and the Generation X and Y employees, there are opportunities to harness the ability of women to build strong connections across generations and attract the top talent in the next generation, who are looking for supportive, relationship-oriented work environments. As an example, a female executive who is married with three young children told me that because she puts her family at the top of her priorities, she shuts down her computer by 6:30 P.M. when she's in town and encourages those around her—both male and female—to do the same. She defies the norm of the country, which is to work until 9 P.M., to make relationship-building a priority.

Closely tied to this ability to build relationships is the inherent nature to express empathy—to put themselves in other people's shoes. The irony of this gift is that, while it gives women the ability to relate well to their subordinates and to have a customer service orientation, it can also put them at a disadvantage. In a presentation to the Professional Women's Association of Milan, Cristina Bombelli, professor at SDA Bocconi and Bicocca University in Milan, Italy, pointed out that women's natural empathy "makes them particularly susceptible to how they perceive themselves to be judged and, at the extreme, results in losing sight of their own agenda." Women should not, as Ms. Bombelli cautions, put themselves so much into the other person's shoes that they forget to occupy their own!

While they are naturally skilled at communicating, relating, and empathizing, women do need to develop the abilities to communicate, relate, and empathize effectively in business. This is where leadership development can help—if it would focus on those areas as it relates to a women's point of view. Formal programs should include teaching about how to communicate, relate, and empathize in ways that make sense in a business environment still largely run by men, but they should also include teaching for men about how to temper some of their linear connections and sometimes clumsy communications with the finesse that women often have in those areas.

"Taking Charge": Developing Self-Assessment, Negotiating, and Networking Skills in Women

Now we turn our attention to some areas that are commonly cited as significant areas of development for women. Again, these are areas that are typically noted by women as natural strengths for men, but areas of development and barriers to advancement for themselves.

The first area is self-assessment. Leadership development programs are often built around 360 degree assessments and other leadership assessment tools. In the programs when I've coached participants, I see that women often take the feedback of others much more personally than men do. I've found myself reassuring women more than men about feedback reports and also encouraging women to lead team or table discussions and initiate dialogue when reporting back to the group at large on business leadership topics. They often don't naturally gravitate to being the spokespersons in leadership programs.

Such critical self-assessment is often seen as a lack of confidence in women, and a big part of challenging that perception is learning to *act* with confidence. In a 2006 panel interview in *The Wall Street Journal*, Carol Bartz, Executive Chairman of Autodesk, suggested that a woman in business should "learn to be an actor.

You have to learn to be confident when you are not. You have to learn to be calm when you are not and brave when you are not. Learn to be a cobra and act until you really have that confidence" (Hymowitz, 2006). From my experience in coaching women leaders, there is a clear need for rehearsing ways to bury the hesitation and often apologetic style of communicating messages around their vision, strategies, and team leadership and replace this with a take-charge style of certainty.

Second, it's noted that women often have a tougher time initiating "the ask," negotiating, and delegating than men do. The ability to negotiate is a required skill for any senior leader in all aspects of business. Often the most tangible area of negotiation is compensation. In their book *Women Don't Ask: Negotiation and the Gender Divide,* Linda Babcock and Sara Laschever (2003) say that by not negotiating a first salary, a person may lose more than $500,000 by age sixty—and men are more than four times as likely as women to negotiate the important first salary. When offered a new job at a higher salary, women will often simply take the new offer rather than use it as a negotiating point, whereas men will often use the new offer as leverage in a negotiation (Nardella, undated). How can we incorporate this difference into professional development training programs so women learn to negotiate more effectively in relation to day-to-day business?

When it comes to delegating, many women say that they had to consciously develop the ability to delegate readily and effectively, and that this skill has been critical to their success. In addition, they have had to consistently coach female reports on how to delegate—often without success. Why this is the case is debatable; I've heard a variety of reasons from these women. There's often a need to volunteer to take on extra projects in order to demonstrate capabilities, and other times, it's the "It's just faster to do it myself" reason, the tendency to want to be in control. Whatever the reason, their lack of delegation skills can make women miserable, unhappy, and hard to work with. They are overloaded by the amount of things to do and unwilling or unable to ask for help, and they become tired, burned out, and frustrated. Of critical importance, the reluctance to delegate may be seen by senior managers as a sign that these women aren't ready for promotions; delegating is a necessary skill for anyone in a senior position, and when women can't demonstrate the ability to delegate tasks, they are often overlooked for bigger roles or stretch assignments, a catalyst for many to the top.

Finally, the ability to build the right networks is a skill that many women do not have, and it's one that is critical to reaching senior management levels. Women have extensive networks, just as men do, but they are far less likely to have the *right* networks than men are in high-profile organizations. Women may hold back when it comes to building networks with the right people in an organization, possibly due to a lack of confidence to initiate relationship-building opportunities with the most influential or visible executives, fear of appearing improper, or a concern that they don't have enough to offer such high-level relationships.

Also, women are often more purpose-driven networkers. They have an objective in mind, whereas men will jump in and build the broader networks they need. This is an area of development in which women can learn a lot from men, and perhaps with some specific coaching, encouragement, and advice on how to best nurture those contacts, men could provide insight on "how to." Knowing that this is one of the most impermeable career obstacles for women, professional development programs should more clearly address and develop this important skill in women.

Some companies are beginning to see the value in encouraging the development of networking skills in women through structured programs and events. There are a number of creative initiatives focusing on women-only networking events at a variety of companies, including Ernst & Young, Merrill Lynch, General Electric, and Mercer Human Resources Consulting. From spa retreats to resort conferences to art gallery events—even events with a fashion theme and cooking demonstrations—women who want to network and socialize with clients in their own way are organizing events that recognize the preferred environments and styles of women. Certainly, these events enhance and strengthen the comfort level of women with networking, but it should not be overlooked that the most influential people with whom to build relationships and network are the men who may not be at these events. Leadership programs can support women in mapping out these necessary relationships and how best to engage in this process.

What All of Us Need: Tailoring Development Programs to Meet the Needs of Both Genders

The trend in leadership development at the moment is to have leadership programs just for women to address female-specific issues and opportunities. While there are benefits and advantages to these programs, many women I spoke with were concerned about this type of environment since it's not at all representative of the real business world (a mixed-gender environment) and the chance to learn with men and from men may be underemphasized. Of note, the style, environment, and exercises in these types of programs are many times unique to this setting and very different from the structure and framework of programs for a male-dominated audience. This difference itself is a reminder that, for the core leadership programs, we still create an environment and exchange of information and learnings that cater to a male mindset and comfort level.

Going back to our color metaphor, I'll discuss now how we can help those in the blue camp (women) help those in the yellow camp (men) get to red, and vice versa. Now we have to ask: How do we tailor current development programs to meet the needs of both genders? It's not our desire to alienate men and swing the pendulum too far to one side; rather, we need to recognize that both genders have unique talents and gifts, and within those genders, each person has talents and gifts that can benefit everyone if given the opportunity. The question is, how?

Here are some ideas to consider when designing leadership programs for the future that will meet the needs of both genders:

1. *Have modules specifically for women taught by men that focus on areas of development for women.* Many women I interviewed for this article commented on how helpful it would be to have a "communications gap module" in leadership development programs where specific interactions and responses to possibly difficult circumstances are reviewed and rehearsed. It was suggested that men take a more active role within leadership development programs to teach women how to network with them in appropriate, constructive ways that do both genders justice. In any leadership development program, break-out sessions designed to address the issues women face in dealing with men would be welcome—especially if taught by men. Some deliberate, pre-defined situations would go a long way toward helping women in the areas of communication and business networks they need to advance.

2. *Ensure user-friendly environments for both genders, where all participants can learn.* There are many team-building oriented programs that gravitate toward sports-related environments or hard-core, outdoor competition. Are these types of environments promoting a leadership learning experience for most women? While many women enjoy sports and competition, most women I spoke with get nothing out of this in a learning environment. Likewise, we don't necessarily want to encourage meeting in a place where men would feel shut out or uncomfortable either. There may be no perfect solution, but the idea is to at least try to avoid the environments that only cater to one gender.

3. *Provide scenarios for in-the-moment feedback and coaching across genders.* The women I spoke with discussed how helpful it would be to run through scenarios with men to find out how to respond to them in assertive, healthy ways that don't offend them or sabotage their own growth. If a man says something to a woman that perpetuates a stereotype, how should she respond? For example, at a recent meeting of a global household product company, twelve male executives and one female executive were discussing the launch of a new bathroom

cleanser. One of the male executives turned to the others and suggested they give the product to this female executive to try out and give her feedback. This woman didn't know how to respond; to her, the suggestion implied that she would have more experience using this product than the men in the room because women naturally would clean bathrooms more than men would. Even a gently assertive response could come across as sarcastic, mean, irritable—and she didn't want to appear that way. Laughing it off might make her male colleagues feel insecure, and ignoring it might indicate that she wasn't bothered by it at all. How could she assertively say no to the suggestion, but not sabotage her relationships with these men? Maybe scenarios such as these within formal programs would help foster communication between the genders that would transfer to the everyday environment.

4. *Establish new assessment criteria for leadership development programs.* Once we begin to include more training across genders, cultures, and generations, we will have to redefine the assessment criteria that we use to say our leadership development programs are successful. Are we assessing sensitivity to and support of diversity? Many experts say that diversity as part of an overall discipline leads to innovation; perhaps programs should more regularly have an assessment on an executive's ability to appreciate and embrace diversity—gender or otherwise.

5. *Use a "buddy" or in-program mentoring system.* All of the women I interviewed said they would like to have more opportunities to learn from others within formal programs. One potential method for developing skills across genders that I've used is matching up executives at the beginning of a program in a "buddy system." In programs, I often match up a female executive who needs to develop certain skills like networking with a male executive who may be more comfortable expressing and initiating communication across levels within an organization. They can learn from each other during and possibly after a program. The idea is to take people who score high in opposing areas and pair them up to learn from each other, the way company mentoring programs often operate. The possible scenarios are endless across complementary learning areas. By pairing up strengths as well as areas for development, both parties benefit.

It's exciting to see that more and more companies are initiating male to female mentoring programs in response to the real need and opportunity they see for cross-gender knowledge and skills sharing. Microsoft, Siemens, IBM, Schlumberger, and Novartis are just a few companies that are sponsoring and mentoring young women to enter the fields of technology and science. Other companies, such as Ernst & Young, have programs in place to support high-potential female leaders. Many past Catalyst award winners, such as BP, Goldman Sachs, and Safeway, have active mentoring programs to support women in their rise to the top. These programs are a great start, and we can hope that with time, these innovations and philosophies will spread to other companies so that they can begin propelling more women to the top as well.

6. *Steer clear of programs that are too generic or off the shelf.* A failing of leadership development efforts in general—for men as well as women—is the tendency to follow the trend or product of the day—the productization of leadership development. Women I interviewed for this article all decried the design of leadership development programs toward a focus on theory rather than situational, daily challenges. Women say that they would like more time for shared experiences and increased dialogue—they would like to hear from colleagues, both male and female, about how they handled or are managing certain situations. Such dialogue would make leadership development programs far more relevant to the state of their own business and the daily leadership challenges they are facing. Of course, programs must stay current and address the gender-neutral leadership challenges from a big-picture perspective, but the need to get into more practical day-to-day applications for participants in these programs should not be ignored as a result.

Where Do We Go from Here?

Let's return to our color metaphor one more time. Pretend that after some time, trial, and effort, you've been able to turn most of the yellow shades red and most of the blue shades red. Do you have a dozen of the same red? No. Rather, you have everything from magenta to a fire-engine red to a brick red. That's the way leadership is—a lot of diverse shades and styles that meet the same requirements, but in their own unique ways.

As we look for ways to really engage women in the process of developing senior leaders and keeping the leadership pipeline full, it's critical to remember that our goal is not to create a glut of uniform, automated leaders who think, feel, act, and interact in exactly the same ways. Instead, we want to create male and female leaders who are all well-developed and competent to lead the global companies of the future by finding new ways to learn from each other and better understand one another's perspectives and points of view, encouraging diversity of styles and learning environments, and fostering communication between the genders. The setting of a leadership program in which talented male and female minds come together to discuss business and leadership challenges seems like a natural place to begin having these discussions.

References

Babcock, L., & Laschever, S. (2003). *Women don't ask: Negotiation and the gender divide.* Princeton, NJ: Princeton University Press.

Catalyst. (2003). *Women in U.S. corporate leadership.* San Jose, CA: Catalyst.

Catalyst. (2005). *Women "take care," men "take charge": Stereotyping of U.S. business leaders exposed.* San Jose, CA: Catalyst..

Charan, R., Drotter, S., & Noel, J. (2001). *The leadership pipeline: How to build the leadership-powered company.* San Francisco, CA: Jossey-Bass.

Griffin, C.E. (1999, November). Vive la difference! *Entrepreneur.* Entrepreneur.com

Guerrera, F., & Ward, A. (2007, March). Women on march to top of U.S. companies. *Financial Times.*

Hewlett, S.A., & Luce, C.B. (2006, December). Extreme jobs: The dangerous allure of the 70-hour workweek. *Harvard Business Review,* p. 8.

Hymowitz, C. (2006, November 20). Women to watch (a special report): View from the top. *The Wall Street Journal,* p. R6.

Nardella, A. (n.d.) Female negotiation. European Professional Women's Network. www.europeanpwn.net/tht_career/articles_indiv_career/female_negociation.html

Marijo Bos leads Bos Advisory and has experience in executive talent management and leadership development across industries with global organizations and international business schools. She spends her time between the United States and Europe and is a founding member and president of European Professional Women's Network in Spain. She consults on the topics of talent management and development across genders and cultures. Earlier in her career she was a partner with Russell Reynolds Associates, as well as a founding executive of a start-up new media organization. She is currently affiliated with Oliver Wyman Delta Executive Learning Center in the delivery of leadership programs around the world.

CHAPTER 15

CREATING REAL EMPLOYEE ENGAGEMENT

Alaric Mostyn

In a recent speech, NASA leader Michael Griffin made the point that business and political leaders have become wholly focused on persuading people with what he called "acceptable reasons"—the rational arguments of a business case, measurable economic gain, and other eminently logical benefits. As he says, these reasons are neither intuitive nor emotionally compelling. For real success, Griffin argues the need for "real reasons—reasons that involve curiosity, competitiveness, a desire to do good, or stand out, or make a difference." Over recent decades, businesses have attempted to build their relationships with employees around these "acceptable reasons." The recent rise in interest in engagement is a recognition that this will no longer deliver everything we need.

Instead, organizations need to start being much smarter at creating a real and emotional connection to employees if they want to improve performance and achieve their business goals. This is the focus of successful engagement: employees making a practical difference to a big emotionally-driven purpose.

So why this increased interest in engagement? We live in interesting times. The world that corporations operate in has become more global, more complex, more pressurized, and more competitive. Differentials are diminishing and customer loyalty is eroding. Against all this, a company's reputation is becoming increasingly important as the best way to put clear blue water between themselves and competitors—both in driving growth and in managing risk. However, reputation is increasingly difficult to manage given wide scale increases in information availability, and the way increasingly assertive constituencies—internal and external—connect with each other.

So no surprise that a study from Accenture shows "engaging and aligning multiple stakeholders" in the top three requirements of senior executives looking at what it takes to compete in the marketplace. Many consultancies have offerings on "engagement" and how to measure it. While there is a common-sense consensus on what engagement means in general, there is much less so on what it means in practical terms, how to achieve it, and what its business value is. So is it just motherhood and apple pie, is it just another buzzword, or is it a way to build long-lasting business value that all leaders should feel equipped to deliver and improve?

Let's agree on a meaning first: We achieve engagement when employees identify strongly with the and its purpose in the world, are passionate advocates for what it does, and volunteer significant extra effort to help it achieve its goals. Those with quick, intuitive, ability to lead will engage their employees naturally. The ability to do this is perhaps the core test of leadership. Those seeking to build their leadership capabilities can learn the skills and techniques to engage. If approached with the right combination of rational rigor, but above all emotional intelligence and a visible belief in what they are doing, leaders will deliver real employee engagement.

Why Engagement Is Increasingly Important

In the past few decades, as the remaining "jobs for life" disappeared from the corporate world, leaders have had to think differently about how to expect more from their "most valuable asset." What is the new contract of mutual loyalty and how do you build it? This has also driven a range of recent research into what engagement means and why it makes a difference:

- *Engagement is essential to turning new strategy into execution:* Analysis by Mercer Delta of client employee surveys shows that engaged employees are more likely to
  - Align with strategic intent of organization
  - Be customer-centric
  - Go the extra mile to deliver
  - Recommend their company's products and services to friends
- *Engagement is a fundamental driver of performance (or lack of it):* Studies by Gallup, Watson Wyatt, and others have demonstrated a strong relationship between

engagement and overall business performance—growth, margins, share price, and long-term return.

New Challenges to Leadership

There are also much newer factors driving leaders to pay more attention to engagement. Socioeconomic and technology driven changes mean, yet again, our emotional contract with employees has to change. Only this time, it is the employees and not companies that are driving the changes:

- Organizations and their leaders are held in less esteem than in the past:
    - As Edelman's annual survey tells us, trust in CEOs is falling. They are now only trusted by 20 percent of people in general. Only 40 percent of employees trust their own CEO. This falling trust is true of all leaders and figures of authority. Having the right strategy, the right plan, having integrity, experience, and skills will no longer mean that a leader will succeed in engaging employees. The role and job title provide an automatically negative start. Today, employees trust other ordinary employees and other "people like us."
    - This move from "deference" (for major institutions and their leaders), to "reference" (to peer group, friends, and colleagues as the key point of influence) requires radical changes in the methods of engagement, as the traditional best practice "top down" ones don't work so well any more.
- Organizations have to manage increasingly powerful internal and external constituencies—who are influencing each other more than ever:
    - The influence the organization has over each of them is decreasing, while these internal and external groups are increasingly seeking to be influenced by each other (accelerated by the Internet and social media).
    - Barriers between internal and external constituencies are now porous and transparent.
    - This means it is no longer possible to manage employee engagement in isolation from a wider 360-degree approach to all constituencies.

Look at the news. The employees of an investment bank overthrow senior leadership, with help from a public relations company, a website, and the media. A PC manufacturer finally confronts its problems when subjected to relentless criticism on a customer and employee blog. Today, by the time a listed company actively reaches its employees about its quarterly results, many will have read about them online, as well as the comments of financial analysts, journalists, and customer activists and made up their minds about how they feel.

- It is less clear what the definition of an "employee" is:
  - Increasing use of significant outsourcing, long-term contractors, and temporary workforces, as well as joint ventures, raise questions about who a company's "employees" are.
  - Manpower suggests that around 20 percent of the workforce in large organizations are now part of the growing "contingent" employees.
  - The established HR and communication practices ignore this growing group of employee stakeholders and yet companies need their engagement.

Measuring Engagement

How do we define engagement precisely enough to allow us to develop plans and measure it? And how is this different from other related employee concepts such as satisfaction and motivation? Based on Mercer Delta's analysis of employee survey and business performance data across a range of clients, the degree of employee engagement can usefully be measured as the number of employees who are satisfied, *and* motivated, *and* committed, *and* recommend their company's products and services. It is the last of these in particular—being an active advocate of the company and what it does—that really leads to direct relationship with the financial performance of the business. (See Figure 1.)

FIGURE 1. MEASURING ENGAGEMENT AND ITS BUSINESS IMPACT

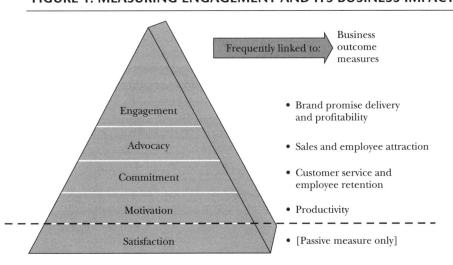

What Is a Leader's Core Engagement Role?

Engagement is the responsibility of leaders at all levels. A leader's willingness and ability to engage will be a key driver of success. Today, it may have become the single most important aspect of a leader's role. Recent research into what drives early CEO failure these days revealed a common pattern. Leaders more focused on "content" (the substance of the business) are more likely to fail. Content leaders believe in analysis and the power of the right answer. Their interests focus on corporate strategy, financial structure and performance, and the portfolio of the business. Those leaders focused on "context" (the environment) were less likely to fail. Context leaders believe in the importance of values and culture, in engaging people across the organization and are more team-focused. These are the ones more suited to succeed today. So this suggests a shift in what leaders should focus on to successfully engage employees, as shown in Table 1.

Aside from this shift, leaders seeking to engage employees should tend to the following:

- Seek for and articulate the wider emotional motivational purpose for the organization—beyond the essential business numbers. This is the core context for engagement—What are the real underlying reasons why people come and work in your organization? Ensure clarity and credibility of the "engagement promise."

TABLE 1. FOCUS FOR ENGAGING LEADERS

Engaging Leaders Do Less of This	Engaging Leaders Do More of This
Content Focus	*Context Focus*
• Focus on what you are saying	• Focus on who you are talking with
• Decide—then tell	• Listen—then decide
• Inside out	• Outside in
• Talk the talk	• Walk the talk
• Write the rules	• Be a role model
• Be seen to know all the answers	• Be seen to know the key questions
• Make sure the CEO communicates	• Make sure all leaders communicate, aligned with CEO
• Continually improve and update messages	• Continually improve and update stakeholder plan

- Own an engagement plan—especially at times of significant change—to mobilise your employees to ensure execution of strategy and business performance improvement.
- Create clarity in the organization about what engagement means, and why it matters. Define the benefit you are trying to gain: Is it improved performance or customer service? Define who you are trying to engage. Is it some employee groups, all employees, contingent employees, partners, retailers, franchisees?
- Be a key visible player in building engagement—not just by what you do, but by ensuring that the managers who work for you all understand what is expected of them.

Engagement for Aligned Performance

So what does a full engagement plan look like? How do we engage employees in a world in which their trust in leaders is slipping and they are most influenced by their peer group? The most powerful route is to find ways for employees to experience the chance, with their colleagues, to really make a practical difference to the way the company succeeds in its marketplace. A favorite engagement framework is the one shown in Figure 2, used most often with organizations that need a significant change in strategy or improvement in the way they perform. It has four key phases, but these will often overlap, be run in some parallel, and also as a continuous and virtuous circle.

FIGURE 2. PROCESS FOR ENGAGEMENT

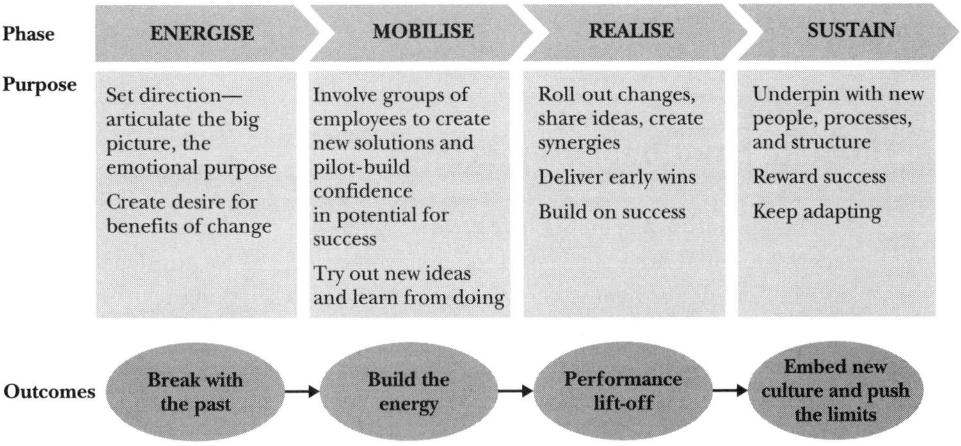

Phase	ENERGISE	MOBILISE	REALISE	SUSTAIN
Purpose	Set direction—articulate the big picture, the emotional purpose Create desire for benefits of change	Involve groups of employees to create new solutions and pilot-build confidence in potential for success Try out new ideas and learn from doing	Roll out changes, share ideas, create synergies Deliver early wins Build on success	Underpin with new people, processes, and structure Reward success Keep adapting
Outcomes	Break with the past	Build the energy	Performance lift-off	Embed new culture and push the limits

The essential point in this framework is the "mobilisation" phase early on. It assumes that, instead of imposing detailed changes on employees or waiting until we have developed all the aspects of a plan, we set the new direction and expectations and actively involve employees in working out how to make a difference, through practical, intensive, and well-planned experiences such as simulations and workshops. The focus of this early work is to enable employees to understand the business imperative and to connect emotionally to a big purpose, and know they are making a practical difference in achieving it. This is not, as some may think, a form of bottom-up, consensus-building way of working. Indeed it relies on a clear and strong sense of direction and intended outcome. It recognizes that people do not engage, or change their behavior, by being told something—however compelling it may be. Instead they need to have a chance to take control, try things out, and use the full resource of their brains, experience, capabilities, and imaginations to deliver a plan.

This is also a way of speeding-up progress—of turning strategy into execution. A technology client was returning to profit after a downturn. The rapidly changing market offered fast-changing new opportunities, which it was not taking. The CEO spent a month on the road, raising everyone's eyes to new horizons, encouraging discussions about what could happen if they tried for the impossible. He shared marketplace and industry data widely. He raised impossible-sounding goals. He soon had people demanding he raise the company's profit target fourfold. Having created the energy, he then launched a campaign to enable people to take personal responsibility for growing the company through new markets, new service levels, and new ways of working in their own teams. His leadership colleagues were very sceptical about going out so publicly with a strong set of goals and with so much open about how to bring them about. They changed their minds when they say how passionate everyone was becoming, very quickly, in working out the practical steps.

Creating Full Engagement—
The Ultimate Emotional Connection

The change across all our societies from "deference" to "reference" requires deeper emotional drivers to build full engagement. So as we construct the key platforms for engagement we now have to assume two key things.

First, as NASA's Griffin pointed out, we have become far too addicted to "acceptable" reasons for doing things. Profit, sales, bonuses, and recognition tied to financial business results alone, will only go so far. It is rational; it is true; it is essential. Indeed it is a required foundation for engagement in terms of building credibility (many organizations fail to ensure full clarity on business models and sources of growth). But the business plan, on its own, is not what really engages. People need to feel the deep personal accomplishment of making a difference to a purpose that goes beyond the numbers. (See Table 2.)

This emotional purpose that goes beyond the business numbers requires a new approach to communication and engagement. The textbook approach used to be known as "AIDA"—first you raised Awareness, and then this would lead to Interest, which you then developed into Desire, and eventually Action. This used to work well and is based on well-researched success. But today, awareness does not inevitably lead to interest and desire—especially if the awareness comes from a senior leader and is immediately out-influenced by alternative, respected, sources.

To engage, we need to involve people directly, as soon as possible, and create desire driven by real reasons. Figure 3 presents a new framework for developing content for engagement and communication plans. Instead of going through the AIDA sequence, this needs to be planned in parallel, and especially focus on the second two.

TABLE 2. MAKING A PERSONAL DIFFERENCE TO SOMETHING THAT MATTERS—THREE LEVELS

1. MAKING A DIFFERENCE TO THE LIVES OF CONSUMERS

You work in Barnes and Noble and have just helped an aunt find the perfect book for her nephew; or you work on the Toyota plant in Indiana and have just stopped production to sort out a seat-belt installation that looks like it might cause a future problem; or you work for the Dove personal care range and feel you are helping build women's self-esteem. This, of course, is the employee experience of a strong consumer brand.

2. MAKING A DIFFERENCE TO THE COMPANY AND THE MARKET

Beating competition, leading the market, being faster than anyone else. In a turnaround, having an opportunity to recapture market leadership and change the industry by offering customers services that had never existed before. People like to be in a winning team.

3. MAKING A DIFFERENCE TO THE WORLD

You work for a logistics company that is reducing its carbon footprint, or a technology company that is helping accelerate the economic growth of remote communities in Brazil and India. In a post-Enron world, you might feel the need to know you are helping make a profit in ways that cause good not harm— perhaps you work for a clothing retailer that has done more than any other to source from manufacturers in Southeast Asia that pay above-average wages. This is one reason why CSR has become a more powerful business tool.

FIGURE 3. DEVELOPING ENGAGEMENT AND COMMUNICATION STORY

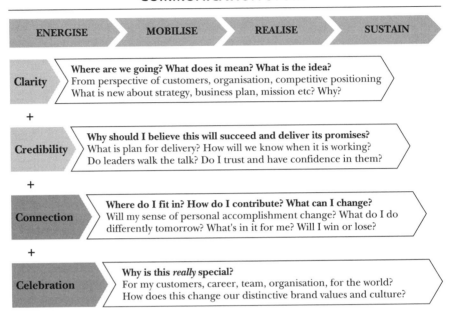

What does this mean in practice? It means finding the Connection and Celebration points fast—finding ways to get straight to what it means for employees and what will drive their emotional commitment. A few years ago a large consumer goods company was introducing a completely new mission. It was essential that this not be seen as just a few sentences on a plaque on the wall. It was to help shape strategy, guide behaviour, and capture what was special about the company with ideas that could act as a focal point for engagement. Instead of a big launch, with all the communication paraphernalia that people expect—it was started in a simple, fast, low-key way. The CEO emailed all employees around the world (to get to everyone at the same time) with the new mission, and a couple of paragraphs about why this meant so much to him, as a long-term employee of the organization. It did not have any detailed rationale, or the business case, or the underpinning arguments. It was just one (senior) employee being genuinely and personally passionate about the best things about the company. He asked people to respond with their thoughts about what the new mission meant to them. He was flooded with personal stories, arguments, suggestions, examples from the past, present, and future. These were then used to influence the content of a six-month program of practical workshops, road shows, events, and online interactions as groups of employees built out the full story—complete with business case, strategic intent, looking at new product ideas, and new ways of working. During this same period, the mission was announced externally. Again, there was no "launch." Instead, a series of seminars was held with a range of key influencers, partners, and members of other external constituencies. After laying out the new mission, discussion and suggestions were invited about how it could best be made to succeed and whether it mattered. The company was quite clear about the direction it was going, but was very keen to engage people who mattered in what that actually should mean in practice. This was a much more grown-up approach than the classic top–down, inside-out "tell and sell." Needless to say, engagement scores stopped declining and started turning back up.

What Is the Intended Business Outcome?

Engagement is best built around four key types of business outcome. What balance and combination of these is right will depend on where the strengths and weaknesses of the current business is and where the greatest changes are required:

1. *Customer experience and advocacy:* Possibly the strongest long-term test of engagement is the extent to which employees are active advocates of the company's products and services and provide the desired experience for customers. This is not about being a great salesperson; it is about being passionate and knowledgeable and genuinely wanting customers to benefit from the great things the company does. For the customer it should be like having a best friend who happens to work there. You trust him, you know him, and you listen to him. What drives this kind of employee engagement are often the culture and team climate, supervisor and local leader behavior, communication, and the recognition systems. The main business benefits come out in increased sales, profitability (lower cost of sales, less need to discount), and customer retention.
2. *Employee advocacy and loyalty:* Some HR people talk about engagement as if it is mainly about the employee experience. Although important in general, this does not provide full business benefits on its own. Employees who enjoy working somewhere enough that they will actively recommend it are a sign of a very well-run company. And this is not often about pay rates or clever reward strategy. It is more likely to be about excellent goal alignment and recognition, a sense of personal achievement, and chances for development, along with culture, leadership behavior, and communication. Not only will these employees stay longer and attract other like-minded friends (reducing recruitment costs), but more importantly they will be much more likely to go the extra mile, working harder than they need. Again, the outcomes will be increased sales and profit.

3. *Brand building and risk management:* This is a broader, longer-term benefit than just customer advocacy. Key to the initial growth and success of companies like Starbucks, Virgin Atlantic, or Nike was a widespread, deep, and emotionally driven understanding of the attitude, behavior, and style that made up the brand they worked for. These brands were built by leaders who were great at recruiting employees who "got" it, and did it, with an instinctive passion. As some of these brands have since shown, once the company is large and successful and the pressure of investors focuses hard on maintaining sales and profit growth, the original brand behavior can be lost or sidelined. Those engaged employees are also those in the best position (next to customers) to warn you when you lose direction or go off track. They will feel the growing risk well before it hits the financial numbers. So keep it touch and manage your risk.

4. *Business turnaround:* Of course, all three aspects of engagement above will deliver better business performance. But there are times, especially during turnaround or a rapid change in the marketplace or the economic cycle, when the straight-forward need to improve sales and profit in the short term is paramount. And it is in these circumstances that leaders most often abandon any plan to engage employees. After all, if there are jobs to be cut, or we want everyone to work that much harder and more flexibly, and it is going to be tough with some bad news on the way—how can we engage? In fact, the reverse is true. Some of the most positive outcomes can be achieved in tough times, when leaders reach out with integrity and engage employees in being at the center of the solutions. Employees are not stupid. They do not want to work in a company that is failing. They are looking to leaders to lead the company into battle—with real intent to win back in the market. Engaging employees to find the better ways to do that, even when some of them will lose their jobs or find themselves in less comfortable roles, is the best chance of rapid success. Among the drivers here will be leadership, culture, communication, and the performance management system.

How Do You Know It Is Working?

Needless to say, something this important is worth measuring. It is worth basing engagement planning on rigorous insight and analysis. Almost by definition, engagement is something you can't just sit behind your desk and understand. There are three ways in which we can keep track and improve engagement success and performance outcomes.

1. *Employee insight:* Start planning for improved employee engagement with good data. Use existing employee survey data or adapt or create new tools as well as

qualitative input. Existing data may not be enough unless it is based on the right questions. Questions about job satisfaction or pride in the company, on their own, will not be enough. Do employees actively recommend products and services? What drives the emotional commitment to the company (or lack of it)? Ask the research team to use regression analysis to find the answers. If you want new data fast, try a sample survey or pulse check with a few hundred employees.

2. *Tracking engagement:* Once you have started, repeat the analysis regularly. Large organizations with major engagement programs will often use survey samples quarterly. This allows them to spot good and bad trends early and learn from them, accelerating and changing plans. Benchmarking like this with yourself over time is a much more fruitful exercise than benchmarking with other organizations. Nothing keeps momentum up more than early proof of progress— or finding out that progress is much slower than it should be.

3. *Integrated approach to metrics:* Finally, it is always worth tracking and demonstrating the overall business impact with an integrated approach to metrics. Ask research colleagues to analyze the employee survey data, together with existing employee and customer data (such as staff turnover, sickness levels, customer churn, net promoter scores), as well as financial data such as sales and margin. See whether improved engagement scores lead to improved sales, profit, or even ultimately brand strength and long-term share price. Ever since the well-known publication of the Sears service-sales-profit chain analysis, companies have shown employee engagement to be a powerful leading indicator of these key business outcomes. A recent hospitality and travel client used integrated metrics to look at data hotel by hotel around the world, measuring exactly how employee engagement was driving customer loyalty and, in turn, margins. The key drivers of engagement were recognition, the living of values by line managers, and effective communication.

Summary: The Practical Leadership Questions

The following questions can help you determine whether your approach is working or not:

- Can you articulate a big emotionally driven purpose for the organization or your team that goes beyond the numbers?
- Is there an engagement plan, process, and content? Is it clear who is responsible and what everyone's role is? Are your role and accountability clear?
- Does the engagement plan involve things you do *with* employees? Are you asking them to take practical steps to influence and improve? Or is it only about something to do *to* employees?

- Are you clear what employee engagement means to you? Do you articulate this to your team and those who work with you?
- Are you gathering insight and data and using analysis to know where you are, what is working, and what the return on investment is for engagement?

In the end, can you draw a clear line of sight between the key business imperatives, a strong, emotionally driven purpose for the organization, and the potential for employees to make practical contributions to accelerating or improving the route to success?

References

Brakeley, H., Cheese, P., & Clinton, D. (2004). *High performance workforce study*. New York: Accenture.

Conger, J.A., & Nadler, D.A. (2004, Spring). When CEOs step up to fail. *MIT Sloan Management Review*.

Deloitte. (2006). *Flying high: 2006 global survey of CEOs in the Deloitte technology fast 500*. New York: Author.

Economist Intelligent Unit. (2006). CEO briefing: Corporate priorities for 2007 and beyond. *The Economist*.

Edelman. (2007). *Annual Edelman trust barometer*. New York: Edelman.

Griffin, M. (2007, January 19). Real reasons and acceptable reasons. Quasar Award Dinner, Bay Area/Houston Economic Partnership, Houston, Texas.

Manpower. (2006). *Engaging the total workforce*. Milwaukee, WI: Manpower Inc.

Melcrum. (2005). *Employee engagement*. Chicago, IL: Melcrum.

Mercer HR. (2006). *Human capital agenda forum: Employee engagement inside Britain's most-admired companies*. New York: Author.

Watson Wyatt. (2006). WorkUSA 2006/2007: Debunking the myths of employee engagement. Watsonwyatt.com.

Alaric Mostyn is a partner at Oliver Wyman Delta Organization and Leadership, leading their expertise in communication, engagement and culture. He brings over twenty-five years of experience helping leaders and organizations in North America and Europe deliver change, performance, and brand promise. Previously, Alaric has held senior roles at PricewaterhouseCoopers Consulting (as global director of communication), Young & Rubicam (leading the European change communication practice), Wolff Olins (leading communication consulting), and the BBC (as head of internal communication). Past clients have included Accenture, AOL, British Airways, BP, Citibank, General Motors, UK Inland Revenue, Johnson & Johnson, McDonald's, Metropolitan Police (London), HSBC, and Unilever—helping these organizations and their key external and internal stakeholders through the challenges of changing marketplaces, M&A transactions, regulatory pressure, new ways of operating, new strategy, and new structure. Alaric has a BSc (Econ) from University College, London, and an MSc (Econ) from the London School of Economics.

CHAPTER 16

LEADING ACROSS BOUNDARIES: ADVENTURES IN THE "WHITE SPACES" AT GENERAL MILLS

Kevin D. Wilde

Some would say it was a match made in heaven. She was America's sweetheart; he was a steady, trusted partner of families around the world. Betty Crocker and the Dough Boy seemed like the perfect pair, and when General Mills merged with Pillsbury in 2001, everyone welcomed the merger. However, bringing together two companies of equal size in this way presented some unique leadership and integration challenges. What could Pillsbury teach General Mills about marketing Cheerios, for example? Or how could a company that's a staple on the cereal and baking aisles make a transition to marketing the Progresso Soup brand?

That first post-merger year was a lot like a first year of marriage. The collective leadership focused on bringing together these two equal partners by thorough restructuring and other typical integration efforts. At the one-year anniversary of the merger, in 2002, the company conducted the first all-employee survey to assess progress. In creating the survey, a senior leadership team identified nine critical capabilities and cultural areas as indicators of success of the new enterprise. When the results were in, both external benchmarking metrics and historical General Mills data were used to compare results.

While results showed that the new company was performing at well above benchmark/external norms in eight of the critical areas, when it came to cross-boundary teamwork, the results were low (see Table 1). Further, the

TABLE 1. MANDATE FOR CROSS-BOUNDARY TEAMWORK: 2002 ORGANIZATION CLIMATE vs. BENCHMARKS

Above 5% to 30%	Below
• Goal Clarity • Diversity • Commitment • Development • Empowerment • Performance Management • Leadership • Innovation	• Cross-Boundary Teamwork

FIGURE 1. CROSS-DIVISIONAL TEAMWORK GIVEN RECOGNITION, YEAR ONE

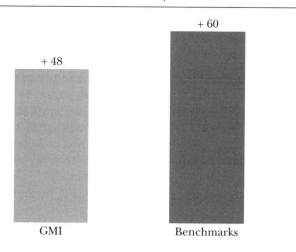

cross-boundary items faired poorly when compared to external benchmarks and historical General Mills scores.

The survey posed questions such as, "Is cross-divisional teamwork given recognition?" Fewer than half of employees responded positively. In fact, compared to the external benchmark of 60 percent, the company fell far below average (see Figure 1); internal historic scores were also much higher. The leadership team considered these results as a clear message to address this critical area and began consideration on how to make connections stronger throughout the organization.

There was a temptation at that point to conclude that scoring well on eight out of nine cultural dimensions isn't bad. However, the leadership team recognized that General Mills didn't just merge with the Pillsbury brands—it also brought into the new organization the Pillsbury employees and their sense of consumers, their ability to innovate, and their understanding of their brands. Much of the value of the merger was in getting the people who understood refrigerated dough working our refrigerated yogurt business, or the people who understood the Progresso Brand and the adult consumer dealing with the adult brands in cereal. It was important for leaders to connect those people to those businesses and brands.

Another early indication of misconnections surfaced as part of a meeting. A few months prior to the all-employee survey, a small pre-conference survey was administered to the combined sales teams of heritage Pillsbury and heritage General Mills employees. One survey item asked, "Do you know how to get your job done?" The Pillsbury employees and General Mills sales employees gave dramatically different responses to that question. These results were the first clue to realize that, in the sales world, connections were not happening. If these cross-boundary connections couldn't be made, the company would not only get reduced value out of the merger, but down the road, the high scores in the other dimensions such as commitment and performance capabilities would most likely decline. Thus began our leadership adventures in the white spaces.

White Spaces: The GE Perspective

I'd learned about the importance of strong, informal organization connections during my earlier days at another General—General Electric. I served as program manager for executive courses at GE's training center, Crotonville. The CEO at the time, Jack Welch, would visit the center to participate in training the GE executives. I had the good fortune to hear him speak to each class and often found a few minutes to chat one-on-one as we would debrief class sessions.

On one particular day, Jack talked about the notion that organizations are imperfect—no matter how you draw the charts. As much as you try to get roles and responsibilities correct, and as much as you try to do everything to make the functions and the units work well, there's still white space. The white space is the gap between organization chart drawings of formal responsibilities. Leadership authority and actions inside the lines and boxes are clear, but we all know much of organization dynamics play out with informal space when authority isn't clear. Welch had coined a somewhat awkward term, "boundarylessness," and he promoted the notion that if you're going to be a good leader, you have to lead in the white space.

At that point, I realized that, through my career at GE, I was doing a lot of good work in the box that I saw as my job, but I wasn't doing as much outside my formal role. In other words, if you're just doing your job, you're probably not doing the *full job*. In my case, by only paying attention to my learning champion charter, I missed adding value as I witnessed parts of the organization that weren't working well together.

This perspective was helpful as the challenge to build greater cross-boundary teamwork at the new General Mills organization became clear. The vastness between the Pillsbury brands and employees and the General Mills brands and employees was the white space the leadership of the new organization needed to address.

Connecting the Dots: Traversing the White Spaces

Coming back to the General Mills story, it was the fall of 2002, and the senior leadership team was reviewing the climate survey results. The group immediately understood the significance of the cross-boundary score and saw the potential impact to the organization of a lack of cross-boundary teamwork. Senior leadership commissioned a team to identify meaningful ways to address this challenge. The team returned a few weeks later with recommendations in four areas to better "connect the dots" in the white spaces of the new company. These four keys were:

1. Engaging and enabling leaders;
2. Communicating with and reaching employees;
3. Aligning the human resources systems; and
4. Enabling cross-boundary learning.

Engaging and Enabling Leaders

Actions toward improving cross-boundary teamwork began at the very next all-employee meeting. As the chairman shared his views of the progress so far in creating the new General Mills, he segued into the recently completed employee survey. The many positive results of the survey, such as goal clarity, employee commitment, and innovation, were highlighted first. He went on to say, "However, I'm concerned about cross-boundary teamwork and I'm asking for all of you to help us to improve." This CEO call-to-action let the company know that he valued this area and expected improvement.

Soon after the employee meeting, the CEO repeated his message for the top-level officers as we launched a leadership training program of the merged cultures. Top of the agenda was cross-boundary teamwork. As each class engaged the topic, a candid dialogue would ensue. In one session, one leader said, "*The term cross-boundary doesn't mean anything. It doesn't stand alone. If we're going to do something about this, we've got to connect it with a real business situation, a business result, or a performance goal. If we can marry the two concepts, we think we can move forward.*" That insight triggered a reframing of the cross-boundary teamwork mission to deliver specific business objectives.

As part of the leadership training, all participants received a 360-degree survey with specific behavior items to profile their own cross-boundary behavior and impact. Through this personal feedback and one-on-one executive coaching, leaders began to embrace the challenge of better teamwork. Momentum built as we cascaded the leadership program to all officers, directors, and high-potential managers in the company, and we used ensuing programs to reinforce ownership.

One of the other GE lessons I brought to General Mills was the importance of leveraging internal talent for teaching. This powerful concept of "leaders teaching leaders" was applied to the cross-boundary section of each program. The strongest cross-boundary officers became core faculty for the director training; the best directors taught the managers. At each session, the inside faculty provided credibility and commitment to the topic of cross-boundary leadership, and the two-way conversations deepened our insight on what had to be done.

In addition to the new leadership program, a cross-boundary module was added to the standard manager training curriculum of the General Mills Institute. The Institute offers a series of training programs based on career stages. The new module ensured that the message of cross-boundary leadership was heard in all new manager programs, experienced manager classes, and high-potential training events. The entire approach was aimed at connecting leaders to the cause, keeping it ongoing, and digging deeper to find out what leaders needed to do to build the connections in this new company. All these development events served as a platform to engage all the leaders, but the work would be incomplete without reaching the whole company.

Communicating with and Reaching Employees

The leadership training also pointed out the need for new tools to reach the broader employee population. The response was a series of communications projects to connect employees. Stories of cross-boundary efforts were highlighted through a new internal website and e-mail offering called "Champions Daily." For example, one story highlighted how the yogurt team connected with Pillsbury groups to share best practices and common areas of interest to improve business results.

Another effort at increased communication was to address the inconsistency of regular employee meetings. All of our officers and directors were asked to start holding quarterly meetings within their divisions, and in those meetings, always to bring a cross-boundary guest. When sales had a quarterly sales meeting, for example, in addition to the sales topic, they might have someone there from the supply chain to talk about the connection of sales to the supply chain. This process helped to knit the company together. Finally, at the annual employee meetings, the CEO would bring this topic up again to reinforce his view of the importance of improvement.

Aligning the Human Resources Systems

If you've been in the development field for some time, you know it's possible to drive an improvement initiative, but stall out because of an existing HR system that is a barrier to your initiative. At General Mills, the leadership team took a hard look at performance management and talent management to evaluate whether these things were friendly to the cross-boundary cause or getting in the way. The first action for better HR system alignment happened in the following year as leaders set annual performance objectives together. They were asked to identify their critical internal cross-boundary partners and compare and coordinate objectives before finalizing them. This process had never been done before, and it became an important link to creating a performance management system that would work well across boundaries.

The second action involved rewards and recognition. New categories of cross-business teamwork were created and applied at the division and corporate levels. Numerous examples were highlighted as teamwork resulted in unique accomplishments. Leaders were reinforcing the new behaviors and the organization responded.

The third action involved career pathing. A team was commissioned to create more systematic human resource plans to move people across functional boundaries. For example, great sales leaders were moved into high-profile marketing roles, and great engineering executives were placed into operations positions. While this practice may be common for other companies, it was not common at General Mills. Traditional career movement only happened within the bounds of a function, which subtly reinforced narrow-minded perspectives. By moving the best talent around, leaders in all functions could build important new connections. Over time, the HR systems of talent management and performance management became facilitators of cross-boundary teamwork.

Enabling Cross-Boundary Learning

Finally, in training and development, a new learning program was launched—titled Brand Champions—which helped connect the dots in a critical "white space" area.

It became clear over time that there were two ways of building brands in the new company divisions: the old General Mills way or the old Pillsbury way. Very little was blended or shared. The new development program would encourage a common platform and extend beyond two ways of marketing to add the best external thinking. Over one thousand leaders around the world were trained. In addition to presenting a blended approach to the content, we consciously mingled the divisions together in the classroom. Rather than training intact marketing teams, we created classes in which people from across the groups would learn together and establish ongoing relationships across the divisional boundaries. The Brand Champions learning became a great place to connect the white spaces by connecting individuals.

The efforts continued to leverage all four change levers: leadership development, communication, HR system alignment, and learning. So how did the business respond to these efforts?

Business Impact

A visit to the grocery store reveals the payoff of the General Mills cross-boundary efforts. Consumers began to notice a promotion called "Dinner Made Easy," where three different General Mills product divisions would promote each other's products. Consumers don't fill their shopping carts based on our division organization structure. They think about hungry families and putting dinner on the table. The new promotion of "Dinner Made Easy" combined efforts of multiple internal divisions to reflect the consumer task of putting a meal together. So Betty Crocker suggested a pasta salad with Green Giant vegetables and Pillsbury dinner rolls. As a result of these three divisions combining forces, the promotion resulted in a significant increase in sales, with over two million cross-purchases. Beyond the impressive business results, Dinner Made Easy taught lessons about cross-boundary work. Its success continued with similar efforts throughout the company.

In another grocery store aisle, a cross-boundary team from the cereal business and the yogurt business promoted each other's products using the Trix rabbit. While both divisions shared the rabbit icon, this was the first time they collaborated with an innovative on-air, multi-product promotion. When a Trix cereal and yogurt commercial aired in conjunction with in-store promotions, both divisions saw significant increase in sales. Just as importantly, household penetration—that metric of how many households have General Mills products in their refrigerators or on their shelves—increased. In other words, the Trix rabbit was invited into more American households as a result of this cross-boundary teamwork.

The final example of cross-boundary teamwork involves a different boundary—a national one. The Canadian division reexamined the Hamburger Helper brand

and realized much of their marketing efforts missed their core consumer. Through the Brand Champion class in Canada, the division redesigned their brand architecture. The resulting promotion was called "In the Heartland"; through it, the Canadian team reached out to consumers in places where they spend leisure and volunteer time. The sales results were impressive. After seeing the success of the Canadian promotion, the corresponding U.S. team adopted a similar promotional strategy and saw significant increase in sales with key retailers. The most interesting part of this story is that the U.S. team had the humility to adapt the breakthrough work of another group rather than creating their own solution. The In the Heartland promotion bridged the white space of geographic boundaries.

Improving Trends in Cross-Boundary Teamwork

One year after launching the cross-boundary teamwork initiatives, the leadership team approached the next employee survey with apprehension. Would employees see the cross-boundary building efforts as meaningful? Were the dots starting to connect? Responses to this category were encouraging, increasing from 48 percent to 65 percent positive (see Figure 2). In other words, about two-thirds of employees recognized the progress on cross-boundary teamwork.

FIGURE 2. CROSS-DIVISIONAL TEAMWORK GIVEN RECOGNITION, YEAR TWO

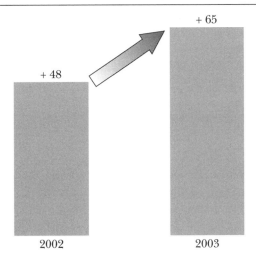

+ 65

+ 48

2002   2003

The survey probed deeper into different aspects of cross-boundary teamwork. We found it valuable to compare the results of groups with greater rates of improvement to others with lower rates of improvement. We followed up with a case-study approach to provide best-practice ideas. The case-study findings were broadly shared to keep the momentum going and demonstrate the best-practice learning dimension of cross-boundary improvement. The senior leadership team was pleased to see the progress in employee perception, the impact on business results, and the positive momentum that was taking hold in the new company.

Key Principles

Stepping back, seven themes emerged as the lessons learned. I offer these to anyone considering leadership improvement in the white spaces:

1. *Listen to what your employees are telling you.* After that first employee climate survey, it would have been easy to rest on our laurels. We could have decided that eight of nine integration items done well was fine. Instead, through listening to our employees, we understood the importance of cross-boundary teamwork for business success.

2. *Don't ignore the white spaces.* It's so tempting to just stay within comfort zones, silos, borders, and organization chart boxes. But even though the white space dynamics are a little uncomfortable, there is huge value in tackling this area. Don't ignore or be afraid of the uncharted territory.

3. *Use multiple levers.* Change interventions have a better chance of succeeding when multiple levers are used. We used four levers to approach the cross-boundary issues. If we'd only approached this issue through HR systems, we would have profoundly limited our success. With four levers, we addressed the entire organization in multiple ways for a single mission—to improve cross-boundary teamwork.

4. *Issues don't stand alone.* Cross-boundary misconnections are linked to other business issues. These issues don't exist in a vacuum. Allowing weakness in this leadership and cultural capability area would affect other performance attributes over time and cried out for improvement.

5. *Think from a customer's point of view.* When we started thinking about hungry families or wholesome, heartland meals, we were able to see how improving our internal issue could benefit the customer. Internal resources rally well when aligned with external missions, such as serving the customer better.

6. *Encourage a culture of humility.* When a company has a real culture of humility in which people are willing to openly exchange ideas, change is much easier

than when people are possessive and siloed. Leadership and learning happens best when there is a hunger for a better way.

7. *Don't declare success too soon.* Just when we thought we were well on our way, we ran into a minor snag. Year three brought a climate resurvey with mixed results as we saw cross-boundary scores below the prior year improvements. What happened? We concluded that the level of employee expectations of great cross-boundary leadership went up; in fact, they needed to see more cross-boundary teamwork. After reaffirming the value of continued effort with our senior management team, we revisited the four change levers and added new energy and initiatives. The work paid off in year four's survey results as the scores rebounded and, in fact, set record highs (see Figure 3). The lesson is to be ever-vigilant in your improvement efforts. There is a need for continual attention and innovation to make long-term culture gains.

In the end, Betty and the Dough Boy have come through those first couple of years a more mature, more integrated team. They've learned to work together—sharing ideas, best practices, and talent across both organizations. It didn't happen overnight. It took senior leadership commitment, disciplined attention, and a great deal of energy over a period of time. Today, the new General Mills organization has a clear path toward a future of increasing cross-boundary teamwork and

FIGURE 3. CROSS-DIVISIONAL TEAMWORK GIVEN RECOGNITION, YEAR FOUR

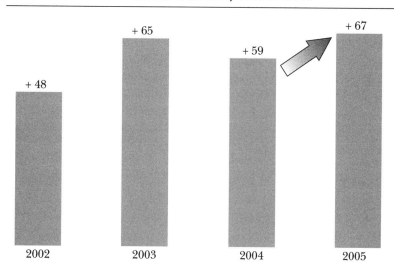

improved business results—and a greater willingness to take further adventures in the white spaces.

Kevin D. Wilde is vice president, organization effectiveness, and chief learning officer at General Mills, Inc. As VP-CLO, his major responsibilities center around stewardship of core people and organization development systems, the General Mills Leadership Institute, and business consulting. His work has been recognized by *Training* magazine's Top Five Companies for Training award, *Chief Executive* magazine's Top 20 for leadership development and *Chief Learning Officer* magazine's Gold Award for leading business change. Kevin is also a columnist for *Talent Management* magazine. Prior to joining General Mills, Kevin was a seventeen-year veteran of General Electric. He served in two high-growth divisions and also in two corporate roles managing global leadership development at the Crotonville Education Center and corporate WorkOut consulting.

CHAPTER 17

BANK OF AMERICA: WINNING THE GROWTH CHALLENGE

Brian Fishel

When Hugh McColl retired from his tenure at Bank of America in 2001, the appointment of Ken Lewis as chairman and CEO ushered in a new era in Bank of America's rich history. McColl's goal was to grow through acquisitions to create the biggest coast-to-coast bank in America. Lewis has continued to build on that growth, organically and through acquisitions under his leadership. In this era of rapid growth and massive globalization, Bank of America has remained one of the most successful companies in the world. In 2006, it was the world's fifth most profitable company, with a net profit of more than $21 billion.

Key to that profitability has been Bank of America's ability to both efficiently and effectively integrate acquired businesses and talent into the company's culture and leadership expectations while still aggressively developing existing talent from within the organization. Under Lewis' leadership over the last six years, the priorities, focus, and goals of the bank have evolved. The company has simultaneously looked for even more organic growth production, strategic joint ventures and partnerships (e.g., Santander-Serfin, China Construction Bank, etc.), international expansion and globalization, and strategic acquisitions (e.g., Fleet, MBNA, U.S. Trust). As a result, there is a renewed emphasis on developing the bank's current leaders and filling the pipeline with leaders who can help Bank of America succeed in the short run while enabling it to continue growing into the future.

Our Development Mission

The development mission of Bank of America is simple. We are striving to be the "world's most admired" company. To that end, we need to develop a cadre of senior leaders who have the skills and competencies to take us there. As we evaluate our organization's ability to create these leaders, we ask ourselves:

1. Is the current pipeline of leaders deep and broad enough to shape and execute the bank's current and future strategy?
2. Are we growing the pipeline of leaders fast enough to stay ahead of growth projections, business mix, and customer demographics requirements?
3. Do we have the rigor and discipline to manage our best people proactively and deliberately as "enterprise assets"?
4. Do we have sufficient processes, programs, and resources to prepare our best leaders for the future in a sustainable manner?

The Business Challenges

Through this era of rapid growth and expansion, Bank of America continues to face new challenges in both the business and leadership development. The bank has roughly doubled in size in the last five years and is poised to double again in the future; in this environment, innovation becomes a differentiator, both in our overall business and for individual leaders within the company. Increasing complexity is also a challenge. The roles of our leaders are ever-growing in size and scope and leading across the matrix is more critical and demanding than ever. External regulatory and socio-economic pressures are having a deeper impact. We are faced with greater and greater integration challenges as we acquire and partner with more businesses, and in the process, more cultures. And finally, new partnerships and alliances across the globe increasingly mean new challenges in building an international platform, brand, and employee proposition.

In turn, these business challenges have significant implications for the growth of the bank's leaders. First, as the size and scale of the business increase, leadership accountability and complexity intensify. Today's senior leaders' roles are in many ways the roles of their bosses from just a year or so ago. Second, as leaders are promoted, they have to expand their "enterprise perspective," requiring intentional focus on "resetting" their expectations for what it takes to succeed. We need a new breed of leader to accelerate and sustain business growth in this new environment—a breed of leader who can face these business challenges head on and deal with operating a global business while managing the complexity and ambiguity that go along with it. Identifying and intensely developing high-potentials deeper in the organization is fundamental to sustaining business success, and identifying potential "stars" earlier in their careers is crucial to sustaining a leadership pipeline that will be equipped to provide the future leaders the bank will need.

Building a Strong Bench: The Core Development Principles That Drive Our Actions

The Bank of America leadership development system is based on several guiding principles. Our major core principle is that leaders really do matter in managing and driving accountability, results, and culture within the company. From the top down, our leadership development practices are absolutely grounded in this fundamental principle as well as clearly aligned to the company's growth priorities and initiatives. Our CEO and his direct reports are more than just traditional sponsors; they are actively and deeply engaged in the development of leaders who matter to the bank's strategy and growth.

The second core principle is recognizing the transitions and development stages that leaders pass through. We recognize five key transitions:

1. Individual contributor (approximately 155,000 people)
2. Supervisor (approximately 50,000 people)
3. Senior leaders (approximately 3,000 people)
4. Executives (approximately 650 people)
5. Enterprise senior executive (10 people)

Leaders pass through these transitions and common developmental stages as they progress in their career and "up the chain of command," as Ram Charan, Stephen Drotter, and James Noel outline in their book, *The Leadership Pipeline: How to Build the Leadership Powered Company*. This progression requires new capabilities, time perspectives, and operating values with each transition and new stage. Our goal is to target talent management to identify the leaders who are ready for new stretch assignments on their way to the next transition. We also want to target leaders for on-boarding activities and targeted development programs right after each transition.

The third principle is that a broad set of experiences and assignments is the best classroom, yet a balanced approach is still necessary for development. We look at it as an equation we've adapted from the Center for Creative Leadership: raw material (intellect, character, ability to relate, and motivation to achieve and lead) PLUS experiences (variety, intensity, adversity) MULTIPLIED BY an ability and willingness to learn from experience (responsiveness to feedback, self-awareness, etc.) EQUALS a fully developing leader.

Fourth, today's top-performing leaders aren't necessarily tomorrow's; even our best leaders can fall behind or derail. Along with that principle is the idea that it's incumbent on today's top-100 leaders to leave a legacy of future talent. Our current leaders must teach, mentor, and role model others on what it takes to succeed. Likewise, we must continue to develop those top performers to keep them moving forward in their own development processes and avoid the derailers that can occur as leaders progress to the top.

Finally, while we encourage all associates across the bank to participate in any and all training available to them, at the higher executive ranks, we want to make sure that our investments are pinpointed at developing leaders for the largest and longest-term impact for the company. When identifying the best approach to developing leaders as they transition through stages of development, we look at two key areas: the "what" and the "how." The "what" refers to our deliverables and goals—in essence, whether the leader we're evaluating is able to meet and exceed expectations. The "how" refers to the behaviors we want to see in leaders at Bank of America and whether the leader we're evaluating is living the values of the company as he or she delivers the "what." Identifying the top executives for focused leadership development programs does not preclude others from participating in the broader set of development programs. Leaders who do not meet performance expectations are given action plans for improvement, and those who don't exhibit leadership behaviors that are in line with the bank's values are given immediate coaching and improvement plans. In this highly data-driven, Six Sigma culture, people are evaluated frequently and given feedback often so that areas for improvement are identified continuously and the opportunity to develop is given.

Building a Strong Bench: Simple Integrated Programs/Processes Set the Agenda

As we evaluate where we are and where we're going and tie that evaluation back to the overall strategy of Bank of America for the next generation, we want to develop the right integrated programs and processes for talent planning— ones that will put the right people in critical roles; manage their performance; continually upgrade, grow, and develop them; and reward them by paying for performance.

For the coming years, we've identified four areas of focus around talent planning—a multi-pronged approach to filling the leadership pipeline (see Figure 1).

FIGURE 1. LEADERSHIP DEVELOPMENT AT BANK OF AMERICA

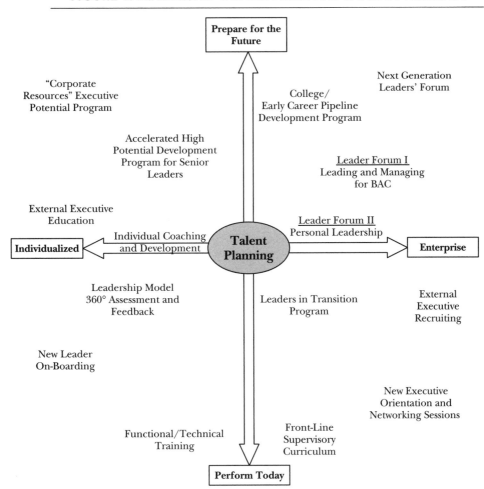

1. *Prepare for the future:* Preparing for the future at Bank of America involves more than just training our current high-potential people. We need to also look at recruiting at the college/early career level and bringing in people who show promise early in their careers to encourage the development of high-performing leaders at all levels of the organization. In fact, at Bank of America, recruiting and talent acquisition is directly aligned with overall executive development and talent management activity.

2. *Establish a strong enterprise leadership bench:* While we want to develop and encourage high performers within our current leadership pipeline, we also recognize that sometimes we need to recruit externally for executive-level assignments. However, we also want to encourage our current leaders to attend leader forums appropriate to their level within the organization to continue to develop to their full potential.

3. *Ensure high performance today:* Thinking about and preparing for the future is only one piece of the puzzle. We also have to make sure our people are performing at the highest level possible today. We use a combination of front-line supervisory training, 360-degree feedback, new leader on-boarding, and internal or external development programs as appropriate.

4. *Encourage an individualized approach:* We don't expect to develop a cadre of leaders who are all exactly the same, nor do we believe that every leader needs the same kind of development opportunities. Rather, we recognize that leaders within our current pipeline need different forms and levels of development. We offer a combination of external executive development, individual coaching and development, and participation in our "Senior Leaders in Transition" program, among other activities, to aid in this quest.

Leadership development at Bank of America doesn't exist in a vacuum, nor does it look in only one direction to develop or find the leaders of tomorrow. Our approach to developing the leaders we need for the future is holistic, integrated, and balanced. Without any one piece of this puzzle, we'd fall short of our leadership development goals.

As we look toward the future, we recognize that if leadership development doesn't permeate every part of the bank's operations, we'll be leaving the puzzle unfinished—and Bank of America unprepared to meet its goals.

Talent Management Process: What Executives Should Expect from Us

As we approach this new environment and the challenges and needs of the bank going forward, we recognize that senior management has several expectations for the talent management and executive development function of Bank of America:

1. *Relevance:* It's absolutely crucial to the success of both the bank and the talent management and executive development function that we connect

talent management and development to the overall business rhythm of Bank of America. That means integrating training and development with strategy (where the business must go), financial planning (what the business must deliver), performance management (what people must do to contribute to success), and talent planning (leveraging our talent to execute today and build for the future). Without alignment of those key elements, talent management will fail to remain relevant to the bank's overall business and vision.

2. *Simplicity:* Simplicity is the key to creating a talent management program that can be facilitated centrally and still executed successfully in the business units. Keeping it simple at Bank of America involves two main areas: assessment and analysis and review. For assessments, we use common performance/potential rating scales and guidelines such as individual profiles and development plans and our leadership model. This leadership model represents the leadership expectations and standards of Bank of America. For analysis and review, we use an organization overview template, which is our executive summary and calibration tool, and a talent planning playbook, which allows us to analyze and summarize our organizational health on an ongoing basis. One overarching principle governs our goal of keeping things simple: Be flexible! We have to ensure that the line owns this process, and we try to encourage that ownership through less paper and better dialogue. This approach results in greater action and better execution of the talent management process.

3. *Flawless Execution:* As we strive to institutionalize the talent management process at Bank of America, we always look for ways to improve our execution. To that end, Ken Lewis holds separate, periodic three-hour meetings with key executives to review their organization and talent, focusing on the top one thousand leaders in the company. These are candid, action-oriented meetings that focus on candor and dialogue instead of presentation binders; result in rigorous, action-oriented, real-time decision making; and create accountability for follow-through.

4. *Value Added:* Of course, all talent management and executive development functions need to add value to the organization. Everything we do has to connect to driving change and decisions that push the business forward. In the interests of specific measures, we track a host of metrics, but at the end of the day it all comes down to getting the right leaders in the right roles with the right skills at the right time. When our leaders and future leaders have a true grasp and understanding of leadership requirements, when the organization has the bench strength to fill any open position at a moment's notice, and when we are able to track and make sure people are taking actions they have committed to taking—that's value added.

Practices That Work: Lessons Learned

For talent management and leadership development to truly make a difference in a company, there are several lessons we've learned at Bank of America that are applicable in virtually any organization:

- *Work must be relevant.* There has to be a compelling BUSINESS reason for the work. In other words, the leadership development efforts must be relevant to the business leaders you are trying to impact on issues that matter to them and their businesses. You cannot push product and processes if the business leaders don't see or understand the value to their business goals and challenges inherent in the work.
- *There is no substitute for sponsorship.* Without true sponsorship, the work can't have deep and lasting impact. And despite all the notions of building sponsorship from grass-roots, bottom–up efforts, direct endorsement from the top down is absolutely the key to making it all work in a sustainable fashion. Without CEO, executive, and senior leader championship of any development program or process, there's little hope of sustaining it.
- *Engagement of senior leaders in the development and delivery of programs, processes, and practices is essential.* At times, engaging and leveraging leaders in this capacity may feel like it is slowing you down. Resist the desire to work around them, because having them engaged throughout actually speeds up the adoption faster and stronger in the long run.
- *Keep things simple.* Use the language of the business—not HR or technical jargon. Be a practitioner when applying work in your businesses. Don't be too wedded to the theory or technical research, because those things don't matter to the businesses leaders you are trying to influence and impact.
- *Don't create something separate.* Leadership development should never be just another HR push, stand-alone activity, or annual event. It must become a continuous mindset across the company. It's important to link your leadership development practices to other already firmly established business or human resources' processes, weaving them into the natural fabric and rhythm of company's core processes, systems, and cycles.
- *Don't try to do everything.* Be focused and planful in how and what you implement and when. Timing is critical. It's far better to take a methodical, measured approach to leadership development as it ties into the readiness of the business to accept it than to make an all-out push and fail because the business wasn't ready. But once a leadership development program is underway, it's also important to stay the course. Results may not be immediate, but they will come.

In the end, the growth challenges faced by Bank of America are really not much different than those faced by most other growing companies—if perhaps on a different scale. Any company poised to grow must have the right leaders in place at all levels of the leadership pipeline, ready to step into the gap at a moment's notice. These same companies also must have a plan to keep that pipeline full—to continually develop and improve that leadership pipeline to meet the new challenges that arise—and arise they will! The global environment we all operate in changes daily. Whether a company operates on a local, regional, national, or global level, the speed of business, war for talent, and strong focus on business results all require leaders who are equipped to meet every challenge.

Bank of America continues to face new and exciting business challenges every day. As we face this new environment and pursue new opportunities, we know that new challenges are around every corner. If we want to achieve our goal of being the "world's most admired" company, it's more critical than ever before in our history to have the right leaders in place to take us to that position.

It's impossible for any one company to do everything right when it comes to leadership development. However, by continuing down the road we're on and pursuing the same focused, integrated, and holistic approach to development, we're confident that Bank of America can win the growth challenge before us.

Brian Fishel is senior vice president of learning and leadership development at Bank of America. He currently heads up Bank of America's Executive and Leadership Pipeline Development group. In his current role, he and his team serve as the enterprise's center of excellence, responsible for advancing the development, deployment, and overall effectiveness of the bank's senior leaders' performance and their teams' performance. The group also has responsibility for driving common enterprise processes, programs, and services that accelerate the assessment, identification, acquisition, management and deployment, and overall growth of a pipeline of senior leaders capable of shaping and executing the bank's future growth strategy.

SECTION 5

METHODOLOGIES

Leadership development would fall flat without the methodologies that go along with the theories. The authors in this section provide an overview of coaching, assessment, competencies, and action learning that help put theory and practice together to develop leaders for the future.

Coaching Leadership Transitions, by Jim Sutton

Executive Assessment for Succession Planning and Development: A Sequenced Process and a Few Helpful Hints, by Adam Ortiz

Do Leadership Competencies Define Effective Leadership? by Jill Conner

Transition Support: Best Practices from the Field, by Stacey E. Philpot

Action Learning: Creating Leaders Through Work, by Jim Noel and David Dotlich

CHAPTER 18

COACHING LEADERSHIP TRANSITIONS

Jim Sutton

David Dotlich and Peter Cairo propose that one of the most troubling transitions is a job change. Job and role changes and the consequential challenges associated with transitions are not new. It has been a part of organizational life since its inception. What is new is the context in which those job transitions occur in today's business environment. Because of the speed of change and the need to respond to a constantly changing competitive landscape, there is an organizational expectation to complete the transition quickly and to produce immediate results. In addition to the challenge of adjusting to their job transition, the new-to-role leader faces an environment in which they must simultaneously cope with immediate and rapid changes in the market place, competitors, innovation, technology, customer expectations, and the complexity of globalization, to name only a few.

Research recently completed by the Learning and Development Roundtable concludes that 46 percent of transitioning leaders under-perform in their new roles, primarily because of these demands. The Roundtable report states that, in any given year, nearly half of an organization's workforce feels the direct effects of leaders undergoing transitions by affecting their direct reports in three important ways—performance, retention, and level of engagement.

Organizations are beginning to become more aware of the impact of transitions on the business and the employees, as well as the transitioning leader.

They are beginning to examine how to effectively support transitioning leaders. Considering these facts—the significant numbers of under-performing transitioning leaders, the negative impact they have on an organization's employees, and the impact on business results—professional coaching for leadership transitions is a key element for supporting transitioning leaders.

Job/level transition coaching shares the same goals and basic process of traditional coaching (creating self-awareness that leads to a change plan that generates results that benefit the individual) with an added goal—benefiting the business. Coaches with the knowledge and skill set to coach job transitions add value by helping the manager minimize (or eliminate) the impact of the performance plateau on the business and by accelerating their timeline to optimum leadership effectiveness and delivering business results.

Timing the Employment of Coaching

Research and transition literature indicate that transitions impact performance and effectiveness at some point during the transition. Transitioning leaders and their managers should anticipate and expect a performance plateau or decline during the transition process as the leader learns how to manage the complexities of the new role and adjust to the organizational dynamics of the new level.

Timing the employment of the coaching process is an important consideration. The Learning and Development Roundtable's research revealed that performance plateaus occur at different phases for different leadership levels. For example, the first-time manager's plateau occurs almost immediately, within the first ninety days of the new role, while middle managers and senior managers experience the plateau after the first ninety days. This information suggests that the timing of coaching support provided to the first-time manager is important just prior to beginning the new role or at the beginning of the new role, while middle and senior managers may require the most support just after their first ninety days.

The Role of the Coach in Support of Leadership Transitions

Coaching for successful leadership transitions is more than supporting leadership development (growing in the role). The value of transition coaching is to accelerate the process by collapsing the time needed to learn the new job, to build trust and credibility, and to speed up the time to delivering high performance. The professional executive coach plays a key role by helping the transitioning leader in six crucial areas:

1. Realizing the business and organization realities they face
2. Understanding the new skills and behavioral requirements
3. Creating a new level of self-awareness—*strengths, weaknesses and blind spots relative to the requirements of the new role*
4. Navigating transition challenges and building transition capability by accelerating the rate at which trust is created and open communication is established
5. Establishing goals and creating an action plan
6. Providing support to the client

Realizing the Business and Organization Realities

Given the strong impact of the external environment on companies today, it is important for any coach attempting to help a transitioning leader begin with the context and demands in which the leader's success must occur. Transitions do not occur in a vacuum where the transitioning leader's issues are the only dynamics in play. It is important for the coach and the client to be aware of the complexity and business drivers in which their client is making their transition—complexity made up of organizational issues, strategies, plans, organization structure, and expectations of the new leader. These factors dictate the leadership expectations and requirements for the new role. Other factors are also an important part of the context in which transitions occur. In addition to the individual's specific goals, aspirations, expectations, and personal issues, there are peers, direct reports, and other key stakeholders in the mix. An additional, significant factor is establishing a trusting, credible relationship with the leader's boss. This cocktail of issues makes for a complex coaching situation. To be effective, the coach must consider the readiness of the transitioning leader, while at the same time considering the organization's goals and the organizational environment in which the leader works.

Common sense recognizes that one coaching approach does not fit all situations. In his recent book, *The First 90 Days,* Michael Watkins says: "The challenges of transition acceleration vary depending on situational factors. It matters a great deal whether you are making a key career 'passage' in terms of level in the organization, whether you are an insider or and outsider, whether you have formal authority, and whether you a taking over a successful or troubled group." Watkins continues by providing the following advice to the reader: "Practical advice has to be tailored to the situation, the level of the new leader, his or her experience with the organization and the conditions of the business." Substitute "practical coaching" in the preceding sentence and the advice is the same for the executive coach. Guiding the clients to identify, diagnose, and evaluate the organizational factors that will impact their performance is a key process for the coach to employ. Watkins's "STARS" model (an acronym for Start-Up, Turnaround, Realignment, and Sustaining) is a useful model for diagnosing the business situation.

Understanding New Skills and Behavioral Requirements

Ram Charan, Stephen Drotter, and James Noel, in their book *The Leadership Pipeline: How to Build the Leadership-Powered Company,* wrote that transitioning leaders must acquire three new ways of managing and leading—new skills, new time applications, and new work values—and that each of these is different at each level of the pipeline. They point out that most leaders attempt to succeed in a new role by employing those skills and behaviors that have worked in their previous positions.

Their model is useful to the coach in helping the client identify the difference between the new level and the previous one. The new *skill requirements* are the new

TABLE 1. FROM MANAGING OTHERS TO MANAGING MANAGERS

From Managing Others	To Managing Managers
Skills	Skills
• Planning work	• Selecting and training first-line managers
• Filling jobs	• Holding first-line managers accountable for managerial work
• Assigning work	
• Measuring work of others	• Allocating resources
• Motivating others	• Managing boundaries between other work units to facilitate work flow
Time Application	Time Application
• Communicating priorities	• Communicating vertically and horizontally
• Managing performance	
• Providing feedback	• Team development
	• Coaching
Values (focus of effort)	Values (focus of effort)
• Getting work done through others	• Strategic thinking and planning

capabilities required to execute the new responsibilities. *Time applications* are about the new time frames that govern how one works. New *work values* are what people believe are important and are therefore the focus of their efforts. To illustrate the change requirements for a new leadership level, Table 1 contrasts a few of the differences in skills, time applications, and values that the new-to-role manager must consider as he or she transitions from managing others to managing mangers.

Creating a New Level of Self-Awareness

In their *Harvard Business Review* article, "Primal Leadership: The Hidden Driver of Great Performance," Daniel Goleman, Richard Boytzis, and Annie McKee write: "Our research . . . showed an incontrovertible link between an executive's emotional maturity, exemplified by such capabilities as self-awareness and empathy, and his or her financial performance." Self awareness constitutes one's understanding of him- or herself—personality, strengths, weaknesses, and impact on others. Goleman, Boytzis, and McKee go on to say: "Leadership demands more than putting on a game face every day. It requires an executive to determine, through reflective analysis, how his emotional leadership drives the moods and actions of the organization, and then with equal discipline, to adjust his behavior accordingly."

Ergo, the third element of the executive coach's role for helping leaders accelerate their transition is creating a safe environment for obtaining insightful information and a process for meaningful reflection and confrontation with the data. A key contribution is to help clients identify and address their blind spots. I suggest using four sources to provide clients with insights:

1. Multi-rater instruments and/or interviews with the clients' direct reports and peers (and can include customers)
2. Personality and style instruments (e.g., Myers-Briggs Type Indicator, FIRO-B)
3. Assimilation with the new team (e.g., New Leader Assimilation)
4. Clear and direct feedback based on the coach's observation and interpretation of the various sources of data

The coach needs to weigh when to introduce providing feedback from the other sources. It should occur when the client-coach relationship is established and trust exists. The coach must be skilled at obtaining the feedback, delivering it, and dealing with resistance and comfortable with challenge and confrontation. Last, a crucial role of the coach is to help the client interpret the data and choose the critical few things on which to focus the change efforts that will provide the greatest impact for improving personal and business performance, as well as leadership effectiveness.

Navigating Transition Challenges and Building Transition Capability

The Learning and Development Roundtable names three distinct phases of leader transitions: acclimation, adjustment, and acceleration. According to their definitions, *Acclimation* is the period in which leaders familiarize themselves with their new roles. *Adjustment* is the period in which leaders fine-tune their approach to their jobs, and *Acceleration* is the period in which the leaders hit their stride and contribute at a high performance level.

A change to a higher job level is normally the result of a promotion and is generally viewed as positive. However, the client is likely to experience many of the emotions of other life transitions. William Bridges, in his book, *Transitions: Making Sense of Life's Changes*, proposes three passages of personal transition: endings, the neutral zone, and new beginnings. He states: "Divorces, deaths, **job changes** [emphasis added], moves, illness . . . disengage us from the contexts in which we have known ourselves. They break up the old cue-system which served to reinforce our roles and to pattern our behavior."

Transitions begin with endings. To be successful at the next level, managers must learn to think, manage, lead, and behave differently from how they performed in their previous roles. This is asking a lot. The new level is asking the manager to let go of many of the things that made him or her successful in the past and to learn the new skills that will make him or her successful at the new level. Leaders must grasp the magnitude of the shift in skills required, how they apply their time, and what the higher level requires them to value in their work. For example, the transition from a middle manager (managing managers, functional manager) to a senior manager responsible for managing a business is significant. As business managers, they must shift from thinking about functional strategy to business strategy. They are responsible for P&L versus a cost center. They must shift from valuing their previous functions to valuing all functions. Time is allocated to communicating internally and externally and fulfilling the ceremonial aspects that come with this level (e.g., representing the company in the country, with governmental agencies, etc.).

Equally as important as helping the client navigate the transition is building transition capability. The old adage, "Give a man a fish; you have fed him today. Teach a man to fish, and he will eat for a lifetime" applies to building transition capability. Coaches can help clients build transition skills that will serve them in future leadership transitions. John J. Gabarro, through his study of managerial transitions, discovered three common success factors: (1) create mutual expectations for performance and roles, (2) establish trust through integrity and openness, and (3) use personal influence rather than positional authority to accomplish things.

In my experience of working with managers in job transition, the traits that I observe in those who successfully navigate the change include high emotional intelligence, the ability to manage their egos, demonstrate good interpersonal skills, and use personal influence versus positional influence. They are effective at creating strong relationships, build an expansive supporting network, focus on building their teams, and they are trustworthy and credible.

The point of this discussion about transition capability is that the coach can add additional value by helping the clients develop transition capability by facilitating their learning about key transition competencies specific to their organizational environments, to evaluate their effectiveness in the use of them, to create a change plan to close the gaps, and to practice their use. The saying "success breeds success" applies to transitions. If the transitioning leader masters the fundamentals of transition capability at one level, that learning and competence can be successfully applied with each successive leadership level change.

Establishing Goals and Creating an Action Plan

To this point in the process, the fundamental work is complete. The clients know the requirements of the new level. They have assessed the organizational realities and are aware of the organization's expectation of them. Through feedback, self-assessment, and reflection, they are aware of their behavioral and skill gaps. It is time for the clients to establish their goals and create the action plans that will deliver the desired results. A model for helping the clients set and achieve their goals is the SMART model—specific, measurable, attainable, relevant, and time-bound. Below are questions that will help clients focus on the most important goals and create action plans.

- What business results must you achieve?
- What is the business situation?
- What strategies should you employ for the situation?
- What kind of leader do you want to be?
- What are the behavioral changes you need to make?
- What new skills do you require for the new role?
- How should you allocate and apply your time?
- What are your biggest challenges and how will you surmount them?
- Who do you need in your network to support you?

- What resources do you need?
- What support from your boss and direct reports do you need?
- What is the "low hanging fruit" that will provide for early wins and provide opportunities to establish your credibility in the new role?
- How will you ensure balance and build in recovery time from the demands of the new role and its consequential learning curve?
- What support do you need from me, your coach, to implement your plan and sustain the change?

Providing Support

When the change plan creation is complete and the client is acting on it, the job of the coach is still not complete. Supporting the client during the implementation phase is crucial. As David Dotlich and Peter Cairo point out: "To change long-held attitudes and behaviors, managers need different types of support . . . the coach's support can mean the difference between achieving a bit of self-awareness and making a performance breakthrough."

What things can the coach do to facilitate a performance breakthrough? Examples of supporting activities include:

- Be available to listen with an objective ear.
- Make periodic contact (telephone and/or email) to monitor progress.
- Schedule periodic check-in meetings.
- Challenge the client when he or she is not acting with integrity relative to the plan.
- Provide advice appropriate to helping the client with an action step with which he or she is struggling.
- Role play to prepare the client for crucial interactions.
- Provide references to other resources.
- Connect the client with others who can provide help with an particular issue.

Tips for the Coach

Job transitions are intense and challenging for the transitioning manager. Coaching the manager can be equally intense and challenging for the coach when the coaching is for the dual purposes of coaching for individual performance and for company performance. David Dotlich and Peter Cairo offer tips to stay on track.

1. Take "breaks" during the coaching process that allows you and your client to reflect on the issues involved; don't problem solve yourself to death and lose sight of the larger business issues.
2. Keep your own coaching journal that documents what you have talked about with the person you're coaching; have a column for business requirements discussed and one for behaviors and development issues. Is there a balance between the two?
3. Avoid jumping to simplistic conclusions.
4. Think holistically; consider all the factors that may affect individual behaviors and organizational requirements, including the problematic behaviors of others (boss, customers, direct reports), the competitive environment (resulting in tremendous pressure for performance), or the career aspirations of the individual and personal crisis (for example, a divorce, illness, death of a loved one, etc.).

References

Bridges, W. (1980). *Transitions: Making sense of life's changes.* Reading, MA: Addison-Wesley.

Charan, R., Drotter, D., & Noel, J. (2001). *The leadership pipeline: How to build the leadership-powered company.* San Francisco, CA: Jossey-Bass.

Dotlich, D.L., & Cairo, P.C. (1999). *Action coaching: How to leverage individual performance for company success.* San Francisco, CA: Jossey-Bass.

Gabarro, J. (1987). *The dynamics of taking charge.* Cambridge, MA: Harvard University Press.

Goleman, D., Boyatizis, R., & McKee, A. (2001). Primal leadership: The hidden driver of great performance. *Harvard Business Review.*

Learning and Development Roundtable. (2005). *Navigating leaders across critical upward transitions: A quantitative analysis of the drivers of transitioning-leader success.* Washington, DC: Corporate Executive Board.

Watkins, M. (2003). *The first 90 days: Critical Success strategies for new leaders at all levels.* Boston, MA: Harvard Business School Press.

Jim Sutton, senior director of Global Organization and Leadership Development, leads Nike's talent development practices and programs for the company's world-wide businesses that include the Nike brand and five subsidiary brands—Cole Haan, Hurley International, Converse, Nike-Bauer Hockey, and Exeter Brands Group. In Jim's thirty-plus years of working in recognized global brands like Nike, Inc., and Levi Strauss & Company, he has held senior leadership roles responsible for performance management systems, learning curriculums, succession planning, organization effectiveness, and leadership development. He serves as an advisor and coach to senior executives who are responsible for leading organization change and managing organization performance.

CHAPTER 19

EXECUTIVE ASSESSMENT FOR SUCCESSION PLANNING AND DEVELOPMENT: A SEQUENCED PROCESS AND A FEW HELPFUL HINTS

Adam Ortiz

Assessment is a big commitment for an organization. It can be complex and laden with hidden challenges. My goal is to offer a sequenced assessment process and to highlight several potential challenges to look out for along the way. I do this in the hope of providing a benchmarked structure to make your assessment experience as smooth and productive as possible.

There are many questions to answer when considering an executive assessment engagement for your organization:

- What exactly is executive assessment?
- When should it be leveraged?
- How do you know if you're assessing the right things?
- Will it help the organization manage executive talent?
- Will it aid the executive in targeting high-priority and meaningful development opportunities?

These questions and many more are regularly raised in discussions that I have with my clients.

Executive assessment is a big investment for organizations. It is expensive, but more importantly it requires the commitment of the time and energy of the executives who will participate in the assessment process and of the human resource staff. Thus, it's critical that organizations be clear about how to effectively execute the assessment process and about when and how to use the assessment data within their organization. All organizations differ with regard to the answers to these questions, but there are some constants.

Defining Executive Assessment

Before we consider those constants, let's first establish a basic definition of executive assessment. Simply put, executive assessment is a process that establishes criteria for an executive's success, measures those criteria on an individual-by-individual basis, and then provides input to help executives and their managers make decisions and form plans to enhance individual and organizational performance. Executive assessment can be used as a decision-making tool as well as an executive development tool.

In one capacity or another it has been used throughout the 20th Century by government institutions and corporations to help them make better decisions about their people. A great deal of research has been done on assessment techniques and on approaches to assessment. Nevertheless, organizations continue to wrestle with introducing assessment, with determining the best method for executing it, and with making use of the information once they have it. If the process isn't well-managed and information isn't appropriately used, it can quickly become a waste of time and money and, worse, undermine the credibility of the sponsors of the process.

When I talk to people about assessment, I receive a pretty broad range of reactions—some positive and some not so positive, but often polarized. These reactions are in part due to the fact that we call a lot of different activities "assessment." They range from MBTI profiling to "360-degree feedback" all the way to very complex and sophisticated assessment centers that make use of behavioral interviews, simulations, as well as personality and cognitive ability tests. This broad range of reference to "assessment" has created a bit of confusion for both those who want to adopt it and those who are subjected to it. So let me first say that to give somebody an MBTI is not to put him or her through an executive assessment. An MBTI is a test accompanied by some feedback and nothing more. To give somebody 360-degree feedback is not what I mean by assessment. In short, when I refer to assessment, what I mean is a process that uses multiple sources of input in combination. The sources typically include behavioral interviews, personality and cognitive ability testing, and business simulations or systematically gathered feedback from people with whom the person being assessed has worked. All this information is then brought together and the themes are identified. This is what I mean when I refer to executive assessment.

The "Constants" of the Executive Assessment Process

As I said, executive assessment can be a great asset when done well. It can also be useless or, worse, create considerable unintended problems and be quite destructive if poorly thought out, executed, and inappropriately used. Now, I have found that there is a set of more or less universal constants that if attended to will smooth the path and will likely increase the success of the assessment engagement by ensuring that critical stages happen when they should. (See Figure 1.)

Clarify—Defining What Is to Be Measured Through the Assessment

The first step in any well-designed assessment process is understanding organizational and individual success factors for today as well as for tomorrow. Where do we want to go as an organization? What stands in the way of that? What do we need from our people to get there? These queries lead ultimately to the question: What specific behaviors do we need our executives to demonstrate? Clarity on this question must be achieved before the assessments commence, so that the assessment can be tailored to measure these behaviors. This is typically achieved through a competency modeling process or a process that establishes a set of characteristics that are important for the individual to possess in order to be

FIGURE 1. THE "CONSTANTS" OF THE EXECUTIVE ASSESSMENT PROCESS

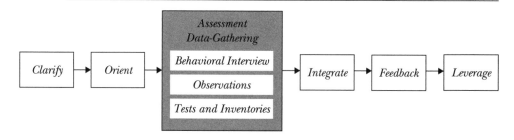

successful in the role that he or she is taking on. There are generic competency models and there are highly customized competency models. My experience is that most competency models fall under seven broad headings: (1) leadership; (2) management skills; (3) judgment and decision making; (4) communication; (5) self-management; (6) relationship management; and (7) motivation. Again, it is important to determine what the assessment will measure because only then can the assessment be assembled, remembering that the assessment itself is only as valuable as the importance of what is measured.

It is also crucial to be very clear about why you're conducting the assessment, what's driving the process, and how you'll be using the information. These questions are absolutely imperative because this will help you to communicate the process to the participants, and it will be extremely valuable for your assessors—giving them a context in which to design and conduct the assessments. Not establishing this clarity and direction is the equivalent of climbing into your car and driving in circles. It will be a profound waste of energy, time, and other valuable resources. Note where you want to go, understand how assessment can help you get there, and use it to help you get to that end.

Interestingly, most organizations have some idea of why they want assessment information and what they think they are going to derive from it. However, some parties may want the assessments done for one reason and other parties may want them done for another. This, of course, presents a problem. The challenge is to ensure that whoever is doing the communicating is fully aware of all reasons for putting people through an assessment process and ensure that they're all taken into consideration as the assessment process is being designed, communicated, and conducted. For example, the purpose for the executive assessment may very well result in different types of assessment tools being deployed, so it's important that all of the reasons for leveraging executive assessment be clarified, if for no other reason than to ensure that you're designing the assessment properly and including tools and procedures appropriate for that type of assessment.

Orientation—Ensuring That People Know What to Expect

For participants, the assessment process often creates anxiety and raises questions. Therefore, it is critical that they be provided as much information as possible when they enter into the process. Thoroughly communicating the process is absolutely essential to ensuring a successful assessment engagement. When I say communicating the process, I don't mean simply communicating when a task needs to be done or communicating the results at the end of the process. I mean communicating in detail with the assessees and anybody else who might be involved before the process begins. They must be given a clear understanding of how the output will be used, who will have access to the data, and what the roles are of the various parties—even if they don't like that use. This is also referred to as establishing informed consent. The notion is that assessees will know what to expect and are entering into the process on a consensual basis. When an individual knows what to expect in advance of the assessment, he or she is going to be more likely to engage more fully in the process. Often we don't like what's being asked of us, but as long as we know what's coming, and it feels up-front and honest, we tend to accept it. We have problems when we feel that we've been deceived or that we haven't been given the whole truth. That's when people have issues and become disgruntled. So in any assessment process, it's absolutely imperative that the organization partner with the vendor or whoever it is who is administering the process to find out what to communicate to the assessees, to management, to feedback givers, and to anyone else involved in the process.

Next comes knowing who should do the communicating and when they should do it. For example, management—not HR—should communicate to the assessees if management is sponsoring the assessment. If there are feedback givers, they should be communicated to by the assesses, not by management, because it's the assessees who are asking for the feedback. I recall a time when the information was not provided up-front to people. In this particular example, the assessees were told that the sole purpose of the process they were going to be participating in was to help them be better leaders and to give them a little more insight into themselves. They all went through the process, and in the end management took the results and stack ranked the people—which was actually okay from a psycho-metric standpoint because it was a well-designed process—and then presented the results in the form of a succession plan to the board. Some of the assess-ees found out about that. They had not been told that the information would be presented to the board, and they came unglued. They were very distraught, not because it was a bad process, and not because the assessment was not use-ful to them, but because they felt deceived. Since then, assessment has never been used in that organization. It is a question of trust. The unannounced use of the assessment data undermined its future use and in addition undermined the credibility of management. We all know what happens when credibility is damaged; it becomes a trust issue, and trust issues are not quickly resolved. The takeaway here is that you should tell people in an up-front and open way how the information will be used. Executive assessment is a practice designed to help the business get a better handle on where people are with respect to competencies and criteria critical for the success of the business. It's perfectly legitimate to want to do what you can as an organization to gain that kind of insight into people. It is important to be up-front about the assessment and let people know how it will be used. If not, it will create more harm than good.

Data-Gathering—Using the Right Tools to Obtain the Right Information

Results from only one source of data don't adequately achieve the goal of accurately assessing and in turn describing an individual. Three of the most accurate sources of assessment information are behavioral interviews, well-validated tests, and feedback from people who work with the assessee or from trained role players. When combined (versus when used alone), the results of these data sources offer even greater predictive power regarding how an executive will deal with issues in day-to-day conditions, as well as in highly stressful situations. Importantly, by using methods that look at core beliefs, values, and motives, as well as at how aspects of an individual's personality play out in the work setting, the assessment is able to offer a foundation for understanding the sources of behavior and for predicting future behavior.

Critical to the process of data gathering are consistency and standardization. This is a psychometric issue—you can't establish validity without establishing an acceptable level of reliability. It is critically important to make sure that you're comparing apples to apples and that your raters are using the same criteria to make the ratings and to evaluate those who are being assessed. In order to realize this level of consistency, you need to have everybody who is being assessed go through the same process. By putting everyone through the same process and ensuring that your raters are on the same page, you will make great strides toward achieving requisite levels of consistency, such that when you start looking at how one person did relative to the criteria compared to another person, you can have an apples to apples conversation about people, not as they compare to one another, but as they compare to the criteria. Thus, having defined criteria, such as behaviorally anchored rating scales, is absolutely imperative, as is making sure that your raters are calibrated in the way they view behaviors when they're making their evaluations of people.

So what would undermine this process? It sounds pretty simple after all. Here is an example. There was a situation when an organization felt they would significantly benefit by being involved in the assessment process. Management felt that they knew their organization better than any outside firm, so they decided to take a hands-on role in modifying the assessment to ensure that it would "optimally" fit their organization. Consequently, they ended up with an assessment that couldn't easily be replicated (a standardization issue) from one person to the next because of some of the unique characteristics that the organization decided to include in the assessment process. The advice that I give people is that it's great for organizations to be involved because that's what will ultimately yield information that will be most beneficial to that organization. Indeed, you need information from the organization about the climate of the company, the needs of the company, why the assessments are being conducted, and other types of information that have led to or contributed to commissioning the assessments. This is the appropriate level of involvement for the organization. Sometimes however, the organization wants to be involved in designing the "wing." The metaphor goes like this: The client shows up at the plane manufacturer and the designer shows them swatches of fabric and tells them how the plane can be detailed. They even talk about the passenger cabin layout. However, if they try to re-engineer the wing, they run a risk. If that wing isn't built properly, the plane may very well not fly. There are certain properties that need to be managed carefully in the assessment process to make sure that everybody is assessed the same way—not so that the assessees feel good, although that's important too—because if they aren't, at the end of the day, the process can't be validated. Then you will have baskets filled with all different kinds of fruit—a basket of oranges, a basket of apples, a basket of pears, or maybe a basket with some kind of fruit that you've conceived of. That's not helpful. Everyone needs to have the same experience. The process has to be designed to ensure that everyone has the same experience and that it leverages proven assessment methods. If it doesn't, you can't leverage the results.

Integration—Bringing It All Together

Integrating the information and deriving key messages is at the core of the assessment process. Research demonstrates that a key factor in predicting how an executive will behave and be perceived by others is to combine the judgment of a seasoned assessor with objective information data about the person. In essence, this suggests that assessment is both a science and an art. It's a process that makes the most of psychometric rigor and of the strong analytical abilities of a well-trained and experienced assessor. A well-designed, psychometrically rigorous process coupled with a talented assessor who is able to apply a deep internal norm set will produce a highly predictive and illustrative depiction of the executives being assessed, revealing how they're likely to respond in complex, highly stressful environments when they don't have a lot of time or the opportunity to leisurely reason through the situation.

What assessment is *not* is fortune-telling. I think I can best illustrate this point through an experience I had myself. I mentioned earlier that what we're looking at in an assessment is typically tied to a senior leader's judgment, leadership, management abilities, communication, self-awareness, motivation, and relationship management.Quite some time ago, I was supervising a psychologist who was conducting an assessment of an individual who was a public school system administrator. At the time, he was a principal and was being considered for an assistant superintendent position. When the data gathering for the assessment had been completed, the psychologist integrated the results and prepared to give the principal feedback on the results. The assessee came in and the psychologist reminded him of how the assessment worked. Then the psychologist began reviewing the results with him. They went over the assessee's cognitive ability testing and compared that to some of the behavioral observations that come from some of the other components of the assessment. Then the psychologist began telling him that he was going to achieve great things and perhaps be the author of book and a major contributor to his field. After all, he'd done very well on his assessment. After going on like this for a while, the psychologist paused and the assessee asked him how he knew all of that and the psychologist responded, "That's a good question." The psychologist developed at that point a keen awareness of the crystal ball syndrome that assessors all too often fall prey to. The moral of the story is that you can only assess what your process is designed to measure. If you try to go beyond that, you will lose credibility. If you are on the side of the organization, the way to leverage the information from your assessment process is to take the new information and add it to other information you may have from other sources and try to fill out the picture—to look for the themes to see what's happening. Don't, however, take the assessment data and stretch it too far because what you'll end up with is a faulty set of predictions about whoever it is that you're looking at through the assessment.

Feedback—Sharing the Results

Feedback for the executive being assessed aims to bring to life the results of the assessment. The dialogue during the feedback session is centered on the needs of the executive and of the organization, in light of the perspectives gleaned through the assessment. Themes are brought to the forefront of the discussion and implications are discussed. In the end, the goal is to get to "so what" and "now what."

Feedback to the organization is given in accordance with the stated purpose of the assessment. This approach enables the organization to use the assessment information to support the organization's needs, whether those are to make a hiring decision, help a high-potential executive develop a critical skill set, or support succession planning.

In both instances, it is critical that you talk with your assessors. Obtain their feedback and their opinions on the results. Finding out from your assessors what they think will likely bring added value. If you've done a good job setting up your process, they will understand your needs and be able to contribute a valuable perspective. Leverage their expertise—don't expect them to be experts in your business and don't pretend in to be full experts in their business (if you were you wouldn't need them).

Let me give you an example. I was working with an organization not too long ago and the organization decided that they wanted to actually participate as co-assessors in the process. The assessment firm reluctantly allowed it. The effect was one of draining the focus away from the primary goal of the process. The organization's internal assessors didn't really get as much as the organization thought they would, as they were too busy to fully engage and only had a two-day orientation to assessment so that they really did not know what was going on. The assessees were extra-cautious, and that minimized their ability to focus on the assessment. The assessors were preoccupied with what was going to be reported back to the organization, so they too had a bit of a drain on their concentration. At the end of the day, everybody had a less than optimal experience. It's analogous to taking your car to the garage and sitting with the mechanic the entire time that he is working on your car. I think that most would agree that it is best to go off to do your job while he does his job. When you come back, have a conversation to learn about what you can do to keep your car running well and then drive away—keeping records and trying to do some of what the mechanic said to do because that's his job, and he's the expert. In that same vein, you hire your financial advisor to advise you. Every time your financial advisor wants to make a change to your portfolio you don't typically sit down with her throughout that process. You may talk to her about your goals in advance, but then you let her do her work and you take her advice. Your assessors are professionals who have spent many years perfecting their craft. When they're through, have a very detailed conversation with them about what they came to know through the process. Use that information in conjunction with all the other things that you know about the individual. Don't micromanage the process, and don't insert yourself into the process, because it's not likely to bring additional value. In fact, I would argue that it's going to detract from the investment that you're making in your assessment process.

Leverage—Making the Most of the Assessment Investment

There are many ways to use the information gained through executive assessment. While there is usually a primary reason for conducting an assessment, other applications may also prove valuable for the executive and the organization, such as:

- Establishing clarity regarding the most critical characteristics needed in executives.
- Predicting the behavior of individuals under stress.

- Understanding differentiating assets and vulnerabilities.
- Gaining objective opinions and insight.
- Making key placements, and aligning teams based on objective information.
- Reducing the number of people hired who are not a good fit.
- Understanding the resources a new hire would benefit from to increase the likelihood of success.
- Targeting group and organizational development opportunities and prioritization of investments.

In light of and supporting the above, the next profound and I mean *profoundly*, profound insight is "don't use the information in isolation." Using the information in isolation will result in one thing—poorly drawn, inaccurate, or inappropriate conclusions. In contrast, the opportunity is to take the assessment data and use it in conjunction with other information (e.g., performance reviews, business performance data, and other general observations of management and others who have interacted with the assessee). Bring all the information together and have a dialogue about the person or group of people. When organizations use assessment data as the end-all and be-all body of information for making decisions about a person, they will likely be taking too narrow a perspective. It's a snapshot. It's the performance of the person that day when he or she went through the process, but it doesn't say exactly what his or her capability is going to be down the road. Again, it's a snapshot that should be blended in with a lot of other information about the person so that you can ultimately gain as full and vivid a picture of the person as possible.

Getting Started

If at this point you're asking yourself, "Where should I start?" I would suggest you "start at the top." Starting at the top has a number of benefits. First, it gives your senior leaders first-hand knowledge of what they're subjecting the others in the organization to. The second thing it does is, when people start asking the senior leaders whether they've gone through the process, they can quickly answer yes. And when that answer is followed up with "and I found it to be a valuable and insightful process" gaining buy-in by people deeper in the organization becomes much easier. A third reason it is particularly critical for the senior leaders to go through the process, particularly when it's used for succession planning and development, is that they then understand what the process comprises and what it will reveal about people, making it easier for them to blend that information with other information that they may already know or have access to. Again these are examples of why you should have your senior leaders go through the process.

I remember a time when I was working with an organization that had a very staid culture. They had not used assessment broadly in the past. People weren't accustomed to having this level of rigor in the measurement of their effectiveness as leaders and executives. Nonetheless, the CEO thought it would be a good idea. Frankly, he was also getting a little encouragement from his board. On the upside, the CEO had actually gone through an assessment many years prior and it had been a very good experience for him. So when the board brought up the notion of having the executive and his staff go through an assessment process for talent planning purposes, he actually called on his previous experience with assessment and thought "You know, I think it's a good idea." Consequently, when he went to talk to his senior management team, he found it significantly easier to espouse its values and benefits. Some time later, after the senior management team had gone through their assessments, they found the same to be true. At the end of the day, assessment has become common practice in that company. Having the senior leadership go through and receive first-hand knowledge of the process and increasing their understanding of what others would go through provides a valuable platform to bring assessment into the organization.

Summary

In summary, I want to leave you with the notion that there are a number of constants that apply to conducting an executive assessment process. If attended to, they will help you to execute the process with less difficulty and greater ease. There will always be some modicum of difficulty because there will be challenges no matter how much planning you do. No matter how thoroughly you communicate, someone will not be listening. People will always have questions. They will always wonder what's really going on—at least some of them will. You'll never be 100 percent clear about exactly what it's going to take to be successful in the future, but if you're disciplined about it, you can reach a much higher level of clarity. By using multiple tools to measure what's critical for your executives to be capable of, your ability to gain insight will be significantly enhanced. However, it's not a crystal ball and it's not perfect, and because we're dealing with the most complex of subjects, the human being, there will be uncontrollable and unexplained variance. So as a great leader once said, "Be thoughtful and you will have great success with your endeavor."

Adam Ortiz, Psy.D., is the managing partner of Executive Development Consulting. He provides executive assessment, coaching, and leadership development consultation services aimed at creating sustainable improvements in individual and organizational performance. By leveraging assessment techniques to define and objectively measure the leadership skills that impact key business drivers, he helps senior executives and organizations to establish targeted plans for increased effectiveness. Adam has held executive leadership positions at Time Warner and Bank of America. In addition, he spent several years with an internationally recognized consulting firm, where he designed and managed large-scale talent solutions and provided executive assessment and coaching services. He began his career with the United States Air Force. Adam graduated summa cum laude with a degree in social psychology from Park College in Parkville, Missouri, and received his doctorate in counseling psychology from the University of St. Thomas in St. Paul, Minnesota. He is a licensed psychologist in the State of Minnesota.

CHAPTER 20

DO LEADERSHIP COMPETENCIES DEFINE EFFECTIVE LEADERSHIP?

Jill Conner

When I first joined Colgate Palmolive, I was advised not to use the word "leadership." The word was considered jargon by the CEO; he preferred the word "executive." It's an important distinction—and reflective of a corporate philosophy that considers everyone a leader.

In fact, today, Colgate Palmolive has a model called Personal Leadership. Like many other companies operating in today's competitive business climate, Colgate Palmolive believes that it must practice personal leadership every day, everywhere, at every level of the organization to take it forward into the future. Leadership is no longer a jargon term reserved for senior management; with the pressures and demands on business performance today, the word "leadership" represents a set of skills required of everyone within the organization.

In order to develop the leadership qualities and skills required today, companies are turning in ever-increasing numbers to leadership competencies for help. Competency models are nothing new; the practice has been around for decades and has been gaining in popularity since the early 1990s. What is new, however, is an emphasis on the individual as leader and the role that competencies can play in developing the skills needed by the individual—whether that individual is in upper-level management or further down the leadership pipeline.

Although most companies do now recognize that leadership competencies are valuable for everyone within the company, creating effective models that help develop those competencies can be challenging. In my work with global companies across a wide spectrum of industries, I see similar mistakes made over and over—models that don't align to strategy and values, models that are not specific enough, and models that are so detailed that communications and ease of use in HR practices become issues later on. In this article, I'll illustrate some of the innovative and useful methods companies can use to create leadership competency models that work to develop the leadership needed to grow the business.

Defining Leadership Competencies

As I've worked with companies over the years to develop leadership competency models, I've seen many valiant attempts at developing models that fail in the implementation. The biggest issue facing companies when defining competencies is making them specific without being too detailed. There's a fine balance to achieve when developing a competency model. While the model has to be simple enough to be useful, it needs to be specific enough to be relevant. There's also a danger in going to an extreme of too detailed to be practical.

Early on, it's important to consider how much detail should be in the model—specifically, the number of competencies and behaviors. This impacts communications, ease of understanding, relevance to job level, and ease of use in HR practices. Important questions to consider are: Do we want one set of behavioral standards that apply to everyone? Do we want to level the competencies and have separate behaviors based on the different job levels? Or do we want to level the competencies on the basis on proficiency, identifying behaviors associated with different levels of effectiveness from low to high?

The best way to illustrate this principle of simplicity and practicality is by comparing different real-world examples. I once worked with NASA, and at the time, the organization was using five different competency models, one for each manager and executive level in the organization. Within each model, there were six clusters of competencies, and then within each cluster, six individual competencies. Under each of those competencies were a series of specific behaviors that demonstrated the competencies, and the number of behaviors averaged something like 142 per model. Not only were there multiple models, but they were overly detailed. In addition, there were redundancies and overlap between the models. When it came time to create a 360-degree feedback tool, multiple versions were needed. Feedback reports were voluminous to read and difficult to use for targeting development opportunities.

Contrast this approach with a competency model from a Fortune 500 company. This company had one model with nineteen competencies organized into six roles and seventy-five behavior standards. When a new CEO took over, he led the charge to redefine the model and streamline the approach. The simplified model included four roles with forty-three behavioral standards. Streamlined? Yes. Effective? Perhaps not. In streamlining the number of behaviors and eliminating the competency layer, the behavioral standards tended to be so general that they lacked the specificity and clarity needed to observe behaviors and to have meaningful discussions about performance management, career development, and talent planning. Eventually, I was asked to develop three to four specific, observable examples of successful and unsuccessful performance for all forty-three behavior standards.

I use these two examples to illustrate the paradox faced when trying to develop an effective competency model. While it might be easier to see that NASA's model was too detailed to be practical, what isn't quite so obvious is how the simpler model is too vague to provide the clarity needed in defining leadership.

A competency model that does a great job of walking that fine line between simplicity and clarity is the one used at Time Warner. The model includes four competency clusters—all worded in clear language that the corporate culture understands—with seventeen competencies and seventy-seven behavior standards. This single model is used for everyone (as opposed to NASA's five separate models) and the number of competencies and behavior standards within the model give enough clarity and guidance to be useful and practical.

For a model to be effective and user-friendly, it must be both simple *and* relevant. Several additional examples illustrate the issue of differentiating behaviors by job level or proficiency level. Another Fortune 500 company used a model similar to NASA's that defined behavior standards for five different job levels. While there were specific behaviors tailored to each job level, there was no simple way of communicating the critical leadership competencies needed by the company. We ended up creating two versions of the model. The first one was a list of the twelve competencies with one set of observable behaviors that differentiated outstanding leadership regardless of job level. The behaviors were presented as examples of the competencies needed collectively by the company, not a comprehensive listing. The second version included specific examples of behaviors to help people know which competencies and behaviors to focus on at their job levels.

Another approach is to have one model for everyone and to identify behaviors for different levels of proficiency, usually three or five levels. In the course of watching companies put competency models to use, I've noticed how this becomes problematic later on when integrating into feedback and interviewing tools. A competency model that is both simple and practical is the one used by

Colgate Palmolive. I created one model with two categories of competence—strengths and development needs—and a sampling of behaviors in each category. To make them relevant to specific job levels, job profiles are created for key jobs and behaviors from the model are adapted and included in the job profiles. In the end, there is one model for everyone that is easy to communicate, understand, and use in HR practices. Moreover, the job profiles create the relevance that people are looking for at their job levels.

The bottom line: Remember that people will use these models. They have to be simple, practical, and easy to remember—yet relevant to the company, culture, and job.

Other Principles for Defining Competencies

I've analyzed competency models at companies across various industries for well over a decade. I've seen models that work well and models that are problematic. This experience has helped me identify some additional principles to consider when defining competencies:

1. *Competencies must speak the language of the company.* As companies look at creating leadership competency models, it's important to keep in mind that even the best model is only effective if it's relevant and supportive of the culture. Leadership competency models must support the culture and speak the language of a company. Especially in a global company, speaking the same language in these competencies helps create a unified standard, but it can also help create a common language. As managers discuss and develop the talent in the organization, they can speak in the same terms.

2. *Competencies must use the relevant, everyday language that people within the company use.* When I work with a company to develop competency models, I interview people within the company to hear the language they use and get a sense of the words and behaviors that they find relevant. I find that often HR people use jargon when developing competency models, but these words rarely find their way into the everyday conversation of the business people outside of HR. Finding the simple words that business people use every day is critical to creating relevant and effective competency models.

3. *Competencies must be integrated with the values of the company.* Many times, the values of a company exist before the competencies, and those in charge of creating the competency model try to create competencies as a separate framework from the values. Unfortunately, this approach results in two separate models, and the question becomes: Do we measure on values or on these separate

leadership competencies? In truth, both should be measured. Creating a model that integrates the values of the company but doesn't create a redundant model is essential.

4. *Competencies must be aligned with the business strategy.* If the business strategy of a company includes an emphasis on innovation, but the leadership competency model doesn't include behaviors associated with innovation, the model will not help create the capability to drive innovation. Competency models must align to specific business strategies in order to develop the leadership competencies required for business success.

5. *Competency models must emphasize business results as well as leadership competencies.* It's not sufficient to emphasize leadership competencies and values in a leadership model. People need to understand that there are three areas required to demonstrate effective leadership: demonstrating leadership competencies, driving values, and delivering results. Colgate Palmolive and other companies I've worked with communicate the importance of all three components and effectively integrate these into their leadership model and leadership development practices.

Challenges to Defining Leadership Competencies

As I've worked with a variety of companies over the last nine years, I've seen the same challenges to defining leadership competencies presented over and over again. Some of the biggest challenges include:

1. *Not identifying observable behaviors within the competencies.* All behaviors identified within the competencies need to be specific and observable. For example, the boss of an executive I was coaching told me, "She needs to have more presence." This particular executive has a quiet manner and style of interaction, but simply saying "She needs more presence" doesn't give her a specific behavior to target for improvement. In response to that comment, I asked, "What does her lack of presence look like?" At that point, this executive's boss was able to identify specific behaviors that we could target: "She usually stands away from people as if she's intimidated, and she doesn't participate actively in discussions." Once we narrowed down those observable behaviors, I was able to coach the executive on how to improve them.

Pick up most competency models for any company, and you will see a number of behaviors that use the word "understands" as a lead-in to the behavior standard. The problem with the word is that figuring out whether someone understands something almost requires being a mind reader! When

I interview people as I'm helping to create a competency model, I ask them to describe what they observe others do to demonstrate their understanding. For example, if you "speak knowledgeably" about a topic, you are likely to have a good understanding of that topic. "Speaking knowledgeably" about something is an observable behavior, and something that can be evaluated when identifying strengths and development opportunities.

2. *Using job responsibilities versus behaviors to differentiate people.* Some companies focus in on job responsibilities in their competency models rather than specific behaviors that differentiate leadership capability. However, several problems arise with this approach. When people have similar job responsibilities and are performing their jobs well, it becomes difficult to differentiate people for career development and talent planning. As new positions open up, managers have a tougher time selecting people for promotions when people are rated similarly. In addition, it's tough to find ways to stretch people and develop them when the behavior standards are more descriptive of what they are expected to do to fulfill their job responsibilities.

For example, say that one of the job responsibilities is "creates teams to work on projects." To translate into a behavior for the competency model, it could be phrased as "creates high-performing teams for projects." Whereas one is just a job responsibility, the other creates an opportunity to differentiate leadership capability.

3. *Not engaging the organization in the competency development process and roll-out.* Too often, executives charge the HR department with creating a competency model and rolling it out across the organization—almost as if HR will just create a model from brainstorming or a database—like opening a dictionary and picking and choosing words. Unfortunately, this process leaves out the vital input of line managers—and often results in a lack of buy-in. A process that creates much better results includes interviewing those people who are currently high-performers—those who are operating at a level desired for the entire company.

A pharmaceutical company designed a competency development process that would create buy-in from the entire organization. The company interviewed high-performers and created a draft competency model, then created a team to fine-tune the model. Within the team, each person was assigned a single competency and asked to review the behaviors within the competency to make sure they were relevant and aligned with the company's strategies. Although the process was time-consuming, it created a great spirit of buy-in and engagement.

4. *Confronting a perception of inflexibility.* One company I worked with didn't want to consider a competency model because it would be "too inflexible."

A competency model is not an inflexible straight-jacket; as I relayed to my client, it is a practical tool that gives direction to the company and its leadership development practices. In this company, the culture is oriented toward entrepreneurship and innovation, and the fear was that a competency "checklist" would stifle those qualities. As I pointed out to my client, if those qualities are important to the culture and strategy of the company, they should be included in the competency model.

5. *Running into HR as a roadblock.* I say this as a former HR professional—HR is often a roadblock in the process of creating a competency model. HR managers who work in isolation make assumptions about what line managers need, and they often don't use the language that line managers use. I've seen models that are too detailed and impractical based on inaccurate assumptions of what line managers need. Also, creating a competency model takes hard work. I find that some HR professionals resist improving an existing competency model because it will require extensive time to communicate and educate line managers about the changes, and practices and existing materials will need updating. This additional work adds to the pressures and priorities HR already faces with its day-to-day responsibilities.

6. *Creating too complex a model.* I always argue for more simplicity in the creation of an effective competency model. Models that break down competencies and behaviors into too much detail quickly become more complicated and impractical when integrating into leadership development practices. In my experience there should never be more than sixty to eighty behaviors organized into ten to twelve competencies. Although the models I create typically don't have the clusters that earlier examples have, I would use them to communicate important messages about the company culture. Keep in mind that more than three clusters become difficult to remember.

It's also important to create concise definitions for each competency. Using brief, one-line definitions for each competency versus a paragraph of three or four run-on sentences that look almost like behaviors is one more step toward creating practical competency models.

The Core Question: Does It Work?

The big question as you begin to design a competency model is does it work? If you go through the time and effort of defining competencies and behaviors, will the effort be worthwhile? Will you get more effective leadership out of the process?

To get the most out of your competency model development and implementation process, consider the following:

Remember That Competency Models Are Not Stand-Alone Tools

The truth is that competency models by themselves don't really develop leaders. Instead, competency models are a tool—a very useful tool when properly designed and executed—that can be one piece of an overall leadership development process. I consider competency models the glue that holds the other pieces of succession planning, career development, performance management, training, and recruiting together. By incorporating the competencies into these HR practices, there will be consistency and alignment for developing effective leadership. As a stand-alone tool, competency models will fall flat.

Use 360-Degree Feedback to Its Full Potential

As common as 360-degree feedback is becoming, it's still amazing to me how many companies implement the process, but don't use it to its full potential. When used appropriately, 360-degree feedback is a valuable tool for initiating dialogue. However, if it's just a report with numbers, and people are left to figure out what those numbers mean on their own, 360-degree feedback can cause more harm than good. People can be confused, even upset, by a report; they go to a meeting and receive a report, and then have to try to understand why they have a certain impact.

A big part of using 360-degree feedback is to use the process to identify strengths, development opportunities, and development priorities. A low score on a report doesn't always tell someone what he or she should be doing or not doing unless a credible and competent professional (internal or external) helps analyze the data. The tool is not enough on its own; it must be used to translate development opportunities into action.

Another aspect of 360-degree feedback that is often overlooked is including the appropriate data; in addition to the average rating and range of results, the report is most helpful when it provides frequency of ratings as well. Often, in the name of confidentiality or anonymity, companies don't want to give frequency of ratings because they don't want people to figure out who gave what ratings; instead, they'll opt to include only the average rating, and highest and lowest ratings for each question. The problem is that averages can enable people to overlook issues. If just one person gives a low rating that brings down an average, for example, that's a much different scenario than if four of six people give a so-so rating on a competency that results in a similar average.

Use Coaching Creatively

In the past, coaching was often viewed as one last effort to help someone improve before exiting the company. In my experience, coaching continues to grow in popularity as a leadership development practice. Companies are increasingly using coaching more effectively to help people who have increased responsibilities achieve success in new roles and by investing in people so that they will be promoted. I am working with a company that is proactively using coaching deeper in the organization. Instead of relying on the six days of coaching that is common to executive coaching engagements, they are providing three days of coaching to a broader group of people identified as the next generation of leaders. The company's leadership competencies are essential to the coaching process since we begin by doing a comprehensive analysis of their 360-degree feedback results.

Convince HR to Think Like Marketing

I've said for some time that one of the big opportunities facing HR is that HR professionals should think like marketers. Look at what marketers do—they think about prospective consumers, think about the language they use, consider what speaks to that audience and what doesn't, interview people, conduct focus groups, and test market products. They look at distribution channels—how to get products to consumers—and they look at ways to generate awareness and demand. They also look at creative ways to package the product.

When HR approaches competency modeling, it needs to act like the marketing department. HR professionals need to engage their consumers and create products that are easy to understand and use—in this case, competency models. They also need to create awareness through multiple distribution channels, including printed materials and the Internet. If it's not easy to use and people are not aware of it, then the company will not be able to develop people's full leadership potential.

A good example is my work with a large consumer products company. As I started to look at their leadership competency model, I was given a twenty-five-page document with lots of detail. It was not visually appealing or user-friendly and it contained no information that gave people a common and clear understanding of why the competencies are critical for business success. Through the process of developing the new model, we also revised the packaging. We created an attractive twenty-page booklet with professional graphics. The line managers loved it—and more importantly, found it very useful in selecting and developing people.

Do Leadership Competencies Develop Leadership?

Of course, the whole approach of developing competency models raises an important question—and really, it's a core question to the whole process. Do these leadership competency models develop leaders? Can leaders, in fact, be developed—or are they born? Dick Parsons, CEO of Time Warner, answers this question by saying that anyone can become a better leader.

I agree with Parsons that leadership competency models do develop better leaders. Keep in mind what I've said: Competency models are just a tool—one of many that can be used for strengthening leadership. A strong competency model creates alignment across the leadership development tools and practices that are pieces of creating the leadership a company needs to produce business results. With the glue of a competency model holding the other pieces together, a healthy leadership pipeline is a goal that can be realized by any company.

Dr. Jill Conner is recognized as an accomplished practitioner in leadership and organizational development. Consulting with business executives and HR organizations worldwide, she helps companies enhance their competitiveness by taking actions to strengthen organizational capacity and performance. She publishes frequently and presents at conferences worldwide.

CHAPTER 21

TRANSITION SUPPORT:
BEST PRACTICES FROM THE FIELD

Stacey E. Philpot

Faced with the reality that growth has become more challenging in today's global market, businesses realize that in order to meet their objectives they will need leaders with high levels of technical expertise, the skills to motivate and develop others, and the ability to adapt to fast-changing market and industry conditions. This link between business growth and leadership has become clearer, yet the number of executives who possess the required skills or who "have what it takes" is decreasing. Unfortunately, this problem will only worsen as a significant percentage of senior executive talent retires in the next five to seven years.

Today's businesses face a true talent crunch—the reality is that they will have to work harder than ever before to adequately fill their leadership pipelines. For talent management, this predicament is made more difficult by the demands of CEOs and boards of directors for human resources to demonstrate a significant return on their investment in leadership development. The question faced by business leaders and human resources has undoubtedly become: What is the best and most cost-effective way to ensure that the next generation of leadership talent is in place to grow and build our business?

Along these lines, the dilemma of "building versus buying" talent has received much attention. Should companies develop the talent they need, and if so how? Or is it better to simply recruit the best outside talent available? At the heart of

The 2008 Pfeiffer Annual: Leadership Development.

this debate is the question of how much to invest in outside talent for the executive ranks. Newspaper articles and the business press have devoted much time to describing recent fads and techniques for "onboarding" executives. But despite this attention, many companies are still unable to distinguish strategic transition support from things like orientation. Likewise, few organizations are examining how transition support for *internal hires* can provide a strategic advantage in a competitive market for talent.

This article will explore both types of transition support: (1) preparing executives for their entrance into a new organization and (2) assisting high-potentials with their upward moves into new leadership roles within the same company. The article will also discuss the reasons why both types of transition support are strategic investments and provide recommendations for what can be done by individuals, managers, and talent management to best prepare new leaders.

Transition into a New Organization: Preparing Outside Hires

The case for effectively investing in onboarding processes for outside hires has been consistently made over the past decade. Few in the leadership development field are unaware of the increasing pressure on executives to perform quickly in new roles. Nor are they unaware of the often quite public examples of failure. A recent *BusinessWeek* article lamented the number of executives hired in 2006 who "did not even make it to their first annual review" (CEOs, 2007). Research by Don Ciampa and Michael Watkins (1999) and others have cited as high as a 60 percent failure rate for outside hires at the executive level.

Such failures are costly to organizations. Direct costs such as recruitment, relocation, severance, and bonuses are typically in the hundreds of thousands of dollars. And for those at the very top of the organization, the costs can be equivalent to as much as ten times the executive's salary. Indirect costs such as lost time implementing a strategy, weakened customer relationships, or damage to the company image/brand are harder to quantify but similarly high. With the rate and corresponding costs of failure being so high, transition processes are an ever-important component to ensuring a beneficial return on investment. For example, a $400,000 annual investment to help external hires assimilate into the organization would pay for itself if it prevented only *two* departures.

If preparing external hires for their new roles makes such economic sense, the next obvious question is: What is the most effective way to do so? The answer to this question requires a fundamental shift in the way most organizations and people view transitions.

Viewing Transition as an Organizational Process

In general, transitions are too often incorrectly viewed as an individual process rather than an organizational one. This view results in companies placing most of their resources (financial, human, and otherwise) on selecting the "right" person, rather than ensuring that once that person is hired that he or she will be able to perform quickly and effectively. The individual perspective is incorrect simply because it underestimates the complexity of entering any organization. For example, this way of thinking ignores the fact that different people will view the new executive from different perspectives—peers, direct reports, and bosses will invariably have different expectations of how the new executive should behave, what type of leader is needed, or even the strategic direction the company should take. This view ignores the degree to which work is accomplished through relationships and how long it takes to build those relationships when you are new. Furthermore, this perspective disregards the role organizational culture plays in an executive's ability to perform. Like building relationships, it takes time to learn how to navigate any organizational culture, regardless of whether you are the "right" person for a job and have the requisite experience, track record of success, or skills. A leadership behavior that was extremely effective in a hierarchical or mechanistic culture will be a disaster in a fluid, matrixed one. Most of us know, from our own experience, that starting a new position in a new company requires us to learn not only about the job we are tasked with, but also about the company, the people we will work with, and how things "really get done around here." When we see our own colleagues stumble, it is rarely due to a lack of technical expertise, but more often a result of their inadvertently stepping on others' toes or into political potholes.

This common wisdom has been supported by research that suggests that the entry of even a single new person into an organization has tremendous ripple effects. For example, Michael Watkins (2003) found that executives estimated the average number of people affected by a single transition to be more than twelve. For a business to truly capitalize on the benefit of a new executive, it naturally follows that those affected by the transition should be involved during the onboarding process. This is particularly true given that within the executive ranks a leader's performance is determined more by the degree of alignment and support granted him by the organization than his actual technical skill.

Accepting the view that transition is a collective process that involves the executive's team, peers, and stakeholders is crucial to the success of any executive transition. Likewise, helping the new executive understand the varying expectations placed onto him or her by others (i.e., what direct reports want, what behaviors the boss expects, etc.) will also greatly increase the new executive's success.

With this in mind, it is not hard to understand how managers and HR partners who take an individual orientation to onboarding (i.e., believe that the new hire will handle his or her own onboarding or that the job is done once the hiring decision has been made) have been frustrated by high turnover and failed transitions. Similarly, individuals new to an organization who place too much emphasis on their own capability, intelligence, or leadership skills will likely be frustrated with their inability to accomplish their objectives as quickly or as successfully as they had anticipated. This is most easily seen in cases where a new hire has been told that he or she has been brought in to "fix" an area or act as a change agent. With such a mandate, these individuals are reluctant to listen to their colleagues, seeing them and their viewpoints as part of the problem rather than as partners. These hires are more likely to feel pressure to implement change quickly or act in ways that they believe will demonstrate their expertise, intelligence, and authority. As a result they will, more often than not, fail to build the alliances and organizational support needed to be effective.

Role of Talent Management

Perhaps one of the most productive roles that talent management can play in helping an outside hire to be successful is that of an educator. Helping new executives and their managers understand what a successful transition can and should look like, setting expectations around the typical length of time it takes to transition, and distinguishing onboarding from orientation are practical and specific ways that talent management can strengthen the talent pipeline.

Successful onboarding can be defined as the point at which a new executive has been fully accepted by the organization, understands how to navigate the culture, and has produced positive results. The steps an individual goes through to obtain this success vary, but generally involves the following: (1) identifying those individuals who will play a part in his or her success, (2) clarifying his or her role, (3) identifying the norms and expectations of the organizational culture, and (4) demonstrating some concrete signs of achievement.

It is important to note that of these four steps, only one specifies action, while the other three stress learning. Learning is a critical aspect of any leader's success, but it is even more so in times of transition. For new executives, the risks of misperception, misunderstanding, and even stereotyping are high. Taking the time to ask questions, investigate, and, above all, listen is crucial. For those executives who are particularly keen to act or demonstrate their competence, if talent management can position learning, listening, and the building of relationships as "early wins," they can dramatically increase the chances of the new executive's success.

Most executives consider three months to be the amount of time it takes to transition into a new role. While it is undoubtedly true that the first three months are critical, the expectation that an executive can be fully up to speed in only ninety days is erroneous and potentially harmful. An effective transition for an external hire typically takes closer to six to nine months. It is only after this length of time that most people can begin to be fully accepted and productive in their roles.

Many organizations confuse effective onboarding and orientation—assuming that a basic presentation on the company's history and strategy is enough to prepare new executives. However, orientation programs do not typically help executives clarify their roles, help them get to know their colleagues or direct reports, or help them establish credibility—steps that are essential to early success. Additionally, orientation typically occurs only at the initial stage, as the new executive has joined the organization. At this point, the executive is likely still in the "honeymoon" stage and unaware of the potential difficulties and challenges he or she will face. The executive is not likely to be as well tuned into this information as he or she will be later when experiencing his or her first failures.

Best Practices for Transitioning External Hires into an Organization

Factors such as organizational culture and the level of entry of the executive affect what type of onboarding process should be utilized. Five common elements have been identified and, in general, every successful onboarding process should include these:

1. *Gain Alignment for the Role.* A successful transition is dependent on an executive and stakeholders having a clear understanding of their roles and mandate. The more clarity the organization provides for the executive's role and the more alignment that exists, the better the odds of the new executive's success.

2. *Anticipate Difficulty.* Clues that a new executive will have difficulty transitioning to a new role typically appear during the selection process. Prior to hiring, it is important that the organization identify the aspects of the transition that will be the most difficult. This can be done by asking questions about the executive's past experience with transitions (what worked and what didn't), identifying how similar or different his or her current work culture is from the one being entered, and clarifying his or her expectations of the role (how similar or different these expectations are from others).

3. *Put a Plan in Place.* Regrettably, many organizations do not develop an assimilation plan for new executives; instead they expect the new executive to successfully navigate the transition on his or her own. However, developing

a plan is a critical step in ensuring that the new executive spends sufficient time learning about the organization and the new role. It has been shown that another important aspect of a successful plan requires involving the manager in its creation, since this gives the new executive "permission" to spend time developing relationships and learning without moving into action too quickly.

4. *Explain the Culture.* Because they are new to the organization, most executives will undoubtedly have at least some difficulty reading their new environments. With few strong relationships yet in place, if any, the new executive will also receive little feedback concerning how his or her actions are perceived in the new culture; at a time when he or she needs it most. Providing feedback on the organization's culture, identifying "hidden norms," and helping new executives better understand what people are expecting from them can go a long way to ensuring that they get up to speed quickly.

5. *Develop an Early Warning System.* Organizations that establish regular "check-in" sessions during an executive's transition are more likely to identify problems while they can still be corrected. Interviewing the new executive's team members, manager, and other key stakeholders to provide feedback can help address any missteps before it is too late.

Transition into a New Leadership Role: Preparing High-Potentials

As businesses try to better manage their leadership development costs, more and more companies are targeting their investment on individuals who demonstrate both high performance and the potential to move into leadership roles. Allocating resources in this way allows the business to take a more "calculated" risk on talent and increase potential return on investment. But while targeting development for high-potentials makes sense on the surface, this approach raises many questions. For example, what is the most effective method or point in time for developing this population? Should development be tied to a role, a level, or leadership philosophy? Should development happen early in the pipeline to create a firm foundation of leadership skills within the organization? Or, given the increased rate of job and company turnover, are development initiatives aimed at the upper echelons of the hierarchy a better investment? At what point are executives most open to development?

Just as targeting development dollars to a specific population makes sense, I would argue that targeting the development of high-potentials around critical transitions makes even more sense. The rate of job transition in today's corporate environment is unprecedented when most executives today spend only two to four years in a senior management role. These executives must be prepared to adjust to change rapidly and effectively. And despite being internal, the challenges of a new position for high-potentials remain strong. In short, internal leadership transitions represent an opportunity to develop executives at the point in time when they are both poised to make a significant impact on the business and are most open to learning.

Like external transitions, internal promotions represent a challenge and a development opportunity for an executive. Despite this, someone who is promoted from within is typically seen as a "known" quantity who understand the company culture and will be able to get up to speed quickly in the new leadership role. This assumption, unfortunately, is often incorrect. High-potentials may understand the company culture; however, they are often unaware of their new role requirements, underestimate new behaviors they will have to adopt at a specific level, or fail to see the group dynamics and politics present at the level to which they are promoted. Additionally, these individuals may have to deal with complicated dynamics with past colleagues (i.e., being the favored child) and new authority dynamics (shift from peer to boss).

In their book *The Leadership Pipeline,* Charan, Drotter, and Noel (2001) present six critical career passages that individuals experience, such as being promoted from a functional manager to a business manager. Each of these passages or transitions represent "strategic investment" opportunities for every business, since each has challenges associated with it that can be anticipated. For example, the new executive who has recently been promoted to a business management position must abandon a functional mindset and instead focus on the business more broadly. He or she will have to manage more complexity and learn to value all functions, not just the previous one, equally. He or she will undoubtedly have to make tradeoff decisions that have a negative impact on the previous function, a decision that could negatively impact important relationships with former peers. He or she will have to become more strategic and be seen as a steward of the entire business—promoting growth and financial viability across the enterprise. No matter how high his or her level of performance in a previous role as a functional leader, the shift to a business leader will represent a difficult transition. Helping him or her anticipate and prepare for this shift will increase the chances of success just as he or she is poised to make a greater impact on the business.

Focusing on preparedness for new leadership roles is aligned with what we know works in leadership development: helping executives *learn from their own experiences as they occur.* Transitions are undoubtedly stressful and challenging, but they also hold great promise for learning. These moments represent a choice point (choosing something new over the old, choosing to be seen in a new light, choosing new relationships, etc.) and as such encourage reflection. Transitions invite us to question our past behavior and beliefs. Taking advantage of these opportunities represent great opportunities for development.

Best Practices for Preparing High-Potentials

Many of the best practices identified earlier for preparing new executives also apply to high-potentials in new roles. However, with high-potentials the focus shifts to increasing their understanding of the targeted role or level, rather than the organizational culture. Initiatives that develop behaviors required for the targeted role *before* an executive is promoted into the position are typically most effective. These initiatives can take the form of individual mentoring, job rotations, coaching, or executive education. Whatever shape or form they take, the following elements will be particularly successful:

1. *Identify Role Requirements.* Identifying the abilities, experiences, and/or leadership competencies required of a specific level allows the business to develop high-potentials in the most effective way possible. For example, if a business determines that future growth will come from developing markets, it could require business managers to take on an international assignment prior to being promoted to group manager.
2. *Give Examples.* Learning by example is critical to targeted development. Having senior leaders articulate what they expect from employees at a specific level (i.e., what is required to be a manager) can help executives better understand what they will need to do in the future and plan their development accordingly. In the same way, hearing senior leaders articulate what they themselves learned while being in that role in terms of the successes they had or any missteps they made can prove to be similarly beneficial.
3. *Provide Exposure and Access.* Providing high-potentials with exposure to those at the targeted level or above also helps them see the relationship networks that exist at that level and build alliances, sponsorship, or relationships with their future peers and colleagues.
4. *Capitalize on Just-in-Time Opportunities.* Executives are most attuned to learning when they can link the experience to their current challenges. Development opportunities that occur six months prior to, or following, a critical transition will have the most impact.

Conclusion

Diversification has always been one of the most effective ways of managing risk, and this is equally true when considering how best to ensure a healthy leadership pipeline. Preparing high-potentials for their transitions into new leadership roles at each passage of the pipeline is strategic. Such an approach allows a business to develop its leadership in a focused and targeted manner. But perhaps even more importantly, such an approach supports what many of us have learned from our own experience: While it is easy to attribute someone's success or failure to individual ability, the truth is that success in a new role is complex. It has as much, if not more, to do with how ready an organization is to support a new person in that leadership role.

References

CEOs: Hello, you must be going. (2007, February 12). *BusinessWeekOnline*.

Charan, R., Drotter, S., & Noel, J. (2001). *The leadership pipeline: How to build the leadership-powered company*. San Francisco, CA: Jossey-Bass.

Ciampa, D., & Watkins, M. (1999). *Right from the start: Taking charge in a new leadership role*. Boston, MA: Harvard Business School Press.

Watkins, M. (2003). *The first 90 days*. Boston, MA: Harvard Business School Press.

Stacey E. Philpot is a principal with Oliver Wyman and a member of The Executive Learning Center. She consults to senior management on leadership effectiveness, succession planning, and the behavioral aspects of strategy implementation. Her expertise is in the identification and development of executive talent, with particular emphasis on helping executives transition into senior roles effectively. She has coached numerous executives of Fortune 50 companies with their integration into new organizations; helping them to be more successful in their roles, faster. Dr. Philpot has also developed customized executive education programs for high-potentials in the healthcare, energy, pharmaceutical, and consumer-products industries. She holds a doctorate in organizational psychology from Rutgers University and is a licensed psychologist in the State of Pennsylvania.

CHAPTER 22

ACTION LEARNING: CREATING LEADERS THROUGH WORK

Jim Noel and David Dotlich

When Bank of America was faced with significant business issues that would affect its future, senior leadership decided to try action learning to find solutions to the challenges—an approach that was, at the time, innovative and ground-breaking. After identifying sixty of the most high-potential people in the organization, the bank began to put them in real business situations where they had to perform the tasks of executive leadership—solve problems, choose people, take a stand on recommendations, and work as a team, among other things.

The program was rigorous and stringent. Participants went through coaching on strengths and weaknesses, and to make the program even more challenging, participants knew they were being watched and evaluated. When the smoke had cleared, not only had the teams involved in the action learning program made recommendations to solve some of the bank's toughest issues, but the bank had identified ten of those original sixty who had the skills and knowledge to become the bank's executive team of the future.

Action Learning Today

When we began using action learning in the mid-1980s, we weren't doing anything that hadn't been around for years already, in a sense. People learn best by doing, after all, and action learning at the basic level is really just learning by doing in a controlled environment. Through a process of teaching and learning the finer points of action learning ourselves, we evolved and refined the methodology and implemented it at dozens of companies, and eventually wrote a book based on the methodology. *Action Learning* first debuted in 1998, and since then, we've seen it successfully implemented in companies all over the world.

As successful as these programs were, however, we could not have foreseen some of the significant changes and challenges that the business world would experience in coming decades, nor did we foresee how well action learning would evolve and adapt to that changing world. Finally, we missed a very important link in those early programs—namely, how large a role action learning plays in developing leaders who have the head skills to run a business, the heart skills to communicate and collaborate with a team, and the guts to make quick, tough decisions while under scrutiny.

Action Learning Revisited

Over the last nearly ten years, the theories around action learning haven't changed. It's still recognized as one of the most important tools for developing leaders and solving business issues. Some of the practical aspects are still the same as well; action learning is still expensive and time-consuming, and it still requires the right project. Even with the new technologies available, the expense and time commitment of action learning can mean it is probably not a good fit for companies looking for a quick, cheap fix to leadership pipeline challenges. And, when it comes to choosing projects, participants have to feel as if they're working on something important—something worthwhile—in order to volunteer to be observed in an action learning environment. Companies that can't choose the right projects will probably not have a lot of success in implementing an action learning program.

The significant change around action learning has come from outside the methodology: the business environment. Action learning has stood the test of time in this changing, sometimes volatile, environment, evolving to meet the new environment in some important ways.

When we wrote *Action Learning* in 1998, we specified a twelve-step framework for designing and implementing an action learning program. Now, ten years later, we can say that the basic framework still works—but with some evolution and modification.

1. *Sponsor:* In the past, we said that executive sponsorship was necessary for any action learning program to succeed. Now, sponsorship might not be the CEO—it might be someone else, and that person takes on more of a coaching role. The role of protector that used to be necessary for action learning teams is now less important, and today, sponsors take on the task of helping teams figure out the environment, etc.

2. *Strategic Mandate:* It used to be that companies that wanted to implement an action learning program had a business imperative that needed to be addressed. Today, there are so many things that clamor for the attention of leaders within the company that it's more a matter of choosing the most relevant issue among the many "squeaky wheels." With today's demand for change and adaptation, most companies feel the pressure of multiple business imperatives that need to be addressed; action learning can be an excellent tool to process some of these imperatives.

3. *Learning Process Roadmap:* In our book, we described this piece of the framework as a written chronology and description of how the action learning process will play out within the company. Today, this piece of the framework is no longer realistic. Action learning teams just don't have the luxury of sitting at a three-week program as they used to; for action learning to make sense today, we have to create the chronology as we go.

4. *Selecting Participants:* In general, participants should be selected from a variety of backgrounds, functions, business units, and levels of responsibility in order to create the tensions that facilitate learning. But it's also important not to select just anyone for an action learning program; these programs should target participation by the highest-potential leaders in the company. We still recommend the same basics when advising on how to select participants, but we emphasize the importance of diversity as part of the learning process. With the growing global environment, it's of critical importance to select participants from the broadest mix possible—across cultures, countries, functions, genders, everything.

5. *Forming Learning Teams:* We used to recommend including in these little "leadership laboratories" the people within the organization who were naïve, but gifted—those who had a lot of the raw skills to succeed, but needed to grow and stretch. Now, because of time pressures, it's often necessary to accelerate

the team and include people who have a greater depth of expertise. In fact, we often accelerate learning by importing experts.

6. *Coaching:* While we still need coaches in an action learning program, it's more important than ever for the coach to be very sophisticated and add significant value. If coaches don't add value today, teams move past them.

7. *Orientation to the Issue:* This is the traditional educational component of action learning. In years past, it was a more passive piece of action learning, and we would collect information to disseminate to the action learning participants. Now, we act more as a catalyst to accelerate discovery and insight. This shift also applies to the phases of data gathering and data analysis.

8. *Data Gathering:* Designed to create in participants a gut-level understanding of an issue, the data-gathering component of action learning can often be very uncomfortable. However, this discomfort serves a purpose: It forces people to consider a different perspective and look at a new way of thinking by getting them face-to-face with the data. The key to data gathering is to get participants out into the field—somewhere in a different culture and environment where they are out of their comfort zones and forced to stretch and grow. This kind of growth and development can only come from a position of discomfort, so it's vital to create that position.

9. *Data Analysis:* At this point in the action learning framework, participants have been in the field gathering data and come back to their teams energized and anxious to share knowledge and apply it to their work projects. Debates at this stage can often become heated, intellectually rigorous, and confrontational. But these sessions force participants to stretch and deal with difficult problems and work together to integrate their findings into a whole. This piece of action learning creates a group dynamic that involves tension, sharing ideas, resolving issues, confronting one another, and whatever else it takes to come up with solutions to the challenges presented to participants.

10. *Draft Presentation:* In 1998, we emphasized the importance of the draft presentation and discussed how important it was to consider it a dress-rehearsal for the final presentation to the company CEO or board. Today, many of our draft presentations are much more informal. They often take the format of a dialogue, and they are less of a test than they used to be.

11. *Presentation:* The final presentation is the culmination of knowledge gained from weeks of action learning. Again, today, it's often more informal, more oriented to dialogue.

12. *Reflection (Debriefing):* Reflection is the piece of action learning that distinguishes it from normal work, and this process hasn't changed much in the last ten years. Through a series of tools and questions, we encourage participants

to think deeply about how the action learning process has changed and influenced them. This is their opportunity to sit back at the end and ask what they have learned, to find out from trusted and respected teammates how they have changed, how they haven't, and where else they should. If anything has changed, it's the emphasis we put on this stage as key to the entire process. We've recognized how critical it is to the development of leaders to spend time in reflection to make the rest of the process really worthwhile.

The bottom line is that action learning today is more nimble and flexible; we have opportunities now that we did not have in 1998 to incorporate technology, ways to connect and communicate, and globalization. Today, instead of surrounding the team, we surround the individuals; instead of having a topic assigned by CEO, today's action learning teams choose their own projects. Today, rather than a team of people in a room together meeting regularly, the individuals are more loosely linked. They reconceptualize the business and build new business in their projects—find extensions of a line or something else that helps grow the business or extend the business—rather than try to solve a problem that's already within the boundaries of the business.

In one program we ran for a major pharmaceutical company in 2007, we were able to really see the evolution of action learning over the last ten years. In the past, under normal conditions, we would have walked right through that standard framework to design our program. Now, much of what we do involves providing a framework of growth, some tools and insights around growth leaders, and some diagnostics, and then the leaders at the pharmaceutical created a program of their own. The pressures of today's business world mean that it's hard for teams to meet in a traditional way and difficult to clearly define issues in business units. Getting the right boundaries around the business challenge is more difficult than ever.

Action learning programs we ran at Nike were another case in point for the evolution of the technique. Of course, Nike is recognized as hugely successful with phenomenal market pull, strong branding, and strong leadership, great stock, growing like mad—really, at the peak. The leadership at Nike asked, "When you're at the peak, how can you look at business differently and challenge the existing model?" Action learning teams at Nike have each been asked to challenge the existing model in some way—for example: What about a low priced shoe in developing markets? What about redesigning the supply chain? What's the golf apparel market going to be in ten years? In China, an action learning team is looking for the right approach to integrate businesses in China. Each of these teams works five months with a sponsor and looks at different aspects of the model that are changing, whereas most teams ten years ago didn't challenge the business model but looked at extending it. Today, action learning is a tool to challenge basic business models—and it's making a huge contribution to business.

Perhaps overall we've discovered that designing an action learning program is really an art, and the art of the design today is a collaborative effort between leadership development professionals and the companies they work with. The design is really the key—we have to create this temporary system whereby we introduce new values, behaviors, beliefs, and influences, and then we ask people to live in that system. Our systems have to allow people to discover and explore new ways of behaving and responding, and within those systems, people will learn and change.

Head, Heart, and Guts: The Link We Missed

It's recently have we recognized the link we missed in the action learning programs of the past: The link to developing complete leaders—those with head, heart, and guts.

Head skills are the obvious component of action learning. In fact, we are now seeing that, as valuable as they are, programs that focus on theoretical, classroom-only learning are outdated. On the other hand, focusing on only heart skills—compassion, understanding, collaboration—or guts skills—ethics, decision-making skills, and courage—would result in incomplete leaders without the business skills to lead an organization. The balance lies in developing leaders who have all three types of skills.

In thinking about action learning programs we've conducted over the last two decades, several cases stand out as excellent examples of where we could see the head, heart, and guts aspects of leadership stand out.

Head

Although a large piece of action learning is developing the head knowledge to lead a business, it goes further than just objective skills. Action learning involves taking people who are potential business heads and giving them a project that requires them to take a business issue, reduce it to pieces, and develop a complete business strategy from the ground up. The process means that these high-potential leaders can go from being someone who follows someone else's strategy to someone who has a strategy of his or her own. Potential leaders have to challenge the strategic assumptions of current course, challenge conventional wisdom, really drill down into the business. They have to think about the future and how the business will evolve and face the competition—in other words, what levers to pull to make execution happen. People need to be thoughtful, curious, and insightful. (Can you think of someone who really came into his or her own in terms of head skills through an AL program?)

Heart

Another aspect of action learning is taking a person who already has a lot of the head skills necessary to lead and tempering those skills with some of the other heart and guts skills. In action learning, people have to learn to work with a team, accept their own and their team's flaws, understand diversity, and really learn to look at people's strengths and build on them. Through the crucible of the program comes a degree of authenticity, love, respect, appreciation that just wasn't there before.

I (Jim) remember a young person in an action learning program who was an MBA from Columbia University. He was very bright, assertive, and aggressive, and others in his group would often defer to him. However, he also had a slightly obnoxious air about him; he had very little self-awareness or empathy, and he had a habit of alienating people through self-centered behaviors such as parking his car across three or four spaces.

On the last day of his action learning program, when the group gave feedback to each other, the older, more mature members of this man's team gave him some strong feedback about his behaviors and attitudes. They were honest, open, and candid, and told him that his behaviors would end up being career stoppers if they didn't change. When I talked with this young man later in his career, he confessed that that day was utterly devastating to him at the time, but it became the stake in the ground around which he began to change his behaviors. Although the feedback was tough to hear, he used it to consciously start developing the heart skills that he would need to further his career.

Action learning can also serve to encourage commitment through the desire not to let others on the team or in executive positions down. Commitment and collaboration are heart skills that we've seen developed in significant ways. In one action learning program held in 1989 at General Electric, Jack Welch formed six teams of six to seven potential general managers, each to investigate opportunities to invest in China, India, and the then Soviet Union. The two teams slated to investigate opportunities in China arrived on the same day as the Tiananmen Square protests. In addition to having their project uprooted by circumstances completely out of their control, the teams had to deal with the ambiguity of being in the midst of the dangerous and world-changing events happening around them. They were able to leave China without incident, but also without completing their research.

The really significant piece of this story for these teams happened four months later. Although no one expected them to, they returned to China basically on their own to complete their project. They completed the research they set out to do, and they finished their project. Such dedication shows heart—commitment to a plan and to a team—that isn't part of a classroom learning project. These people had gelled as a team and didn't want to let each other down.

Guts

In an ever-changing business world where ambiguity reigns and often choices are made between two rights rather than a wrong and a right, developing the skills to lead with guts is essential for future business leaders. Action learning programs can help develop these skills in a variety of ways. First, participants are often forced to act on limited information and in ambiguous situations—they have to learn to make tough calls when they only have pieces of information available. Second, participants in action learning programs know they are being watched; working in a fishbowl requires courage, and action learning programs are not for the faint of heart.

Finally, action learning projects often require participants to make tough decisions between right and right that may not be popular or easy. In one action learning program at Washington Mutual Bank, the participants were charged with evaluating a recent purchase by the bank. The bank had inherited a sub-prime consumer credit group in the Southeastern United States through a series of acquisitions, and the action learning team was asked to make recommendations on how to make the group more profitable. Both the head of the consumer group and the head of the bank had charged the action learning team to make these recommendations. The action learning team came to the conclusion that the best course of action for the bank was to sell the sub-prime lender and redeploy the capital to mainstream Washington Mutual businesses. The recommendation did not sit well with the head of this business, but eventually, even he came around to the same perspective as the action learning team. Not only did the team have to make a tough call in front of someone it directly affected, but they also had to stick to their recommendation when it would have been tempting to take the easy way out.

Conclusion

In some ways, we've passed through our own action learning program since we wrote our book in 1998. The more business has changed, and the more action learning has evolved as a methodology and technique, we've realized that it's less about a formal structure or program and more about just creating the temporary systems in which people are allowed to come into their own as leaders.

Confucius is often quoted as saying, "Tell me, and I will forget. Show me, and I may remember. Involve me, and I will understand." Fifteen hundred years later, we come back to that same philosophy in action learning. Teach people through the work they do, and they will understand, create, think, feel, and act in new ways. It's an old idea, but it's true: Given the opportunity, people will rise to the potential within them to be the leaders companies need for the future.

The 2008 Pfeiffer Annual: Leadership Development.

SECTION 6

CREATIVE APPROACHES TO DEVELOPING LEADERS— PUSHING THE BOUNDARY

While it's great to have some tried-and-true methodologies and theories to put into practice, leadership development would never move forward if creative professions weren't always searching for new ways and new metaphors for helping adults learn, think about the world, develop new skills, and practice new behaviors. For leaders, the best insights often come from other places: athletics; poetry, stories, even brain research! In this section, several leading thinkers take us to new places in leadership development and provide some ideas for how we can break out of traditional ways of thinking about learning and search for new models and methods to help leaders grow.

Leader as Storyteller, by Chatham Clarke Sullivan

The Leader as Poet: A Consideration of What Poetry May Have to Offer Organizational Leadership, by Juan Mobili

Choices in Work and in Life, by Neil M. Johnston

The Leading Brain: An Exercise in Self-Coaching, by Agnes Mura

Leading in the Matrix of Today: Integrating Body/Mind/Spirit, by Ginny Whitelaw

Somatics and Leadership, by Susan Nichols

Learning from World-Class Athletes in Managing Performance: Achieving Personal Leadership Excellence Through P⁶PROP, by Christian Marcolli

The Shaping of Successful Careers, by Norman Walker

CHAPTER 23

LEADER AS STORYTELLER

Chatham Clarke Sullivan

In Norman Mailer's *Harlot's Ghost*, one of his characters joins the CIA for her love of spy novels. To her joy, the job succeeds in placing her in situations that resemble those in the novels she's read. Yet she soon discovers that her participation in the story is only partial. Rather than experience the full arc of the narrative, she plays her part only in the middle chapters. She has missed the beginning of the tale, and won't be there for the end. The incompleteness of the experience leaves her deeply unsatisfied. In *The Spooky Art: Some Thoughts on Writing*, Mailer uses the minor tragedy of this character to reflect on his own thinking about the psychology of story:

> "Often, one did not learn how it all turned out. That struck me as being about what life is like: The gun over the mantelpiece does not often get fired. We live in and out of ongoing plots every day of our lives, but they are discontinuous. Our love of plot . . . comes out of our need to find the chain of cause and effect that so often is missing in our own existence." (Mailer, 2003)

Mailer goes on to distinguish between what he calls Real Life and Plot Life, between the fragmented collection of characters and events that comprise our lives and the linear narrative that coheres, unifies, and gives meaning to our

The 2008 Pfeiffer Annual: Leadership Development.

experiences. While we might raise the question of whether life plays out like a story or is random and meaningless, Mailer's simple insight feels deeply intuitive: Humans desire a sense of continuity in life, and story provides the primary vehicle for it. Common sense and now modern science tell us the same: stories are the principle form by which we make life intelligible.

The Rise of Story in the Social Sciences and Business

If story is our basic method for sense making, then leaders, as the primary purveyors of meaning in organizations, must be good storytellers. The popular and scholarly writing concur. Over the past several years there has been a profusion of writing on story. In the social sciences, the writing on story is prolific, so much so that it has generated its own label—the so-called "narrative turn." In the more applied realms of business and management, the trend is similar—storytelling may be on the way to becoming recognized as the preeminent leadership skill. Ironically enough, there is even a story about story. As it goes, six years ago, 3M trained two-dozen rising executives in storytelling as a management tool. So successful were these workshops that today the company teaches over one hundred managers annually. Prompted by their success, Ford, General Electric, IBM, DuPont, and Barclays have followed suit, along with countless other companies (Jones, 2004).

The skeptic in all of us should wonder whether the passion for story borders on faddishness. Perhaps the question is not whether story is in fashion—it clearly is—but whether understanding story actually helps people become better managers. I believe that it does. Story has deep roots in research and powerful, practical implications for how people think and ultimately behave. To take but one tangible example, psychologists have discovered that jurors naturally make sense of a case by constructing stories about what they hear, even if the process occurs unconsciously. Rather than simply iterating facts, trial lawyers who use historical narratives during their opening statements anchor the framework with which the jury later assimilates key information and events of the case. This tactic has been found to be more successful than one in which the lawyer lays out the facts point by point (Pennington & Hastie, 1993). Cognitive psychologists have likewise found that story, parable, and metaphor provide underlying structures for how we store, organize, and remember information. In short, we are now beginning to understand that narrative elements, as well as stories themselves, are crucial elements to the way that we think about and interpret our experience (Schank, 1995; Turner, 1997).

When used authentically, stories also have a natural, timeless feeling to them. Unlike other management fads such as quality circles, reengineering, t-groups, and similar trends, story reaches back as far as we can remember, perhaps as long ago as human consciousness itself. Whether through our religions, primitive myths, or historical dramas, we have always understood ourselves, and the world around us, through stories. It is not surprising, first, that scholarly reflection on story is itself quite old. Aristotle proposed a theory of plot 2,300 years ago. We still use it today.

The Modern Organization—A Perfect Setting for Storytelling

We are bound to lose our way when life comes at us in bits and pieces. Story provides the necessary experience of the whole when only the parts are known. The classic example of the importance of this kind of thinking is the proverbial elephant.

> "Each person standing at one part of the elephant can make his own limited, analytic assessment of the situation, but we do not obtain an elephant by adding "scaly," "long and soft," "massive and cylindrical" together in any conceivable proportion. Without the development of an over-all perspective, we remain lost in our individual investigations. Such a perspective is a province of another mode of knowledge, and cannot be achieved in the same way that individual parts are explored. It does not arise out of a linear sum of independent observations." (Orenstein, 1972, p. 10)

Perhaps nowhere is the need for this type of thinking more manifest than in many of today's organizations. The modern organization has grown increasingly complex over since the industrial age. Contemporary organizations look distinctly different from their forebearers. From hospital systems, to pharmaceutical companies, to owner-led businesses, modern organizations feel less like a single coherent body than a band of loosely knit together units, authorities, and relationships. Although these structures have created new possibilities for organizations to meet the demands of an equally complex market, they carry a burden for the individual, as well as the organization. Members of organizations who work across roles, businesses, functions, divisions, and geographies can easily feel beholden to many masters. Relationships intensify, politics become more complicated, and individuals and groups press for, and must accept, the claims, demands, and experiences of more stakeholders (Hirschhorn, 1993). Across this more multidimensional terrain, the pulls for fragmentation are strong while the forces for integration are very weak. Stories provide a natural antidote to this condition. And they do so for both the individual member and the organization-as-a-whole.

Like individuals, organizations create mental frameworks such as stories that allow the collective body to assimilate and consolidate a wide range of diverse experiences. Stories make sense of the world, guide action, and allow the individual to understand his or her relation to the whole. Good stories have enough integrity to give the community a sense of its own unity and the mental frameworks needed to interpret multiple, sometimes conflicting realities within and outside organizational boundaries. For without these frameworks, the collective mind loses its capacity to understand, adapt, and take initiative. Interestingly, these frameworks do not always have to be accurate. Take, for example, Karl Weick's famous concept of a cognitive map. Like a story, a cognitive map consists of a configuration of ideas, entities, and relations that enable individuals to interpret their experience and take action. Maps are realistic to the extent that they are logical and useful in that they contain the uncertainties of a particular situation. To illustrate his idea, Weick retells the true story of the Nobel Laureate Albert Szent-Gyorti (Miroslav, 1977, in Weick, 1995):

> The young lieutenant of a small Hungarian detachment in the Alps sent a reconnaissance unit out onto the icy wasteland. It began to snow immediately, snowed for two days and the unit did not return.
>
> The lieutenant suffered: he had dispatched his own people to death. But the third day the unit came back. Where had they been? How had they made their way?
>
> Yes, they said, we considered ourselves lost and waited for the end. And then one of us found a map in his pocket. That calmed us down. We pitched camp, lasted out the snowstorm and then with the map we discovered our bearings. And here we are.
>
> The lieutenant borrowed this remarkable map and had a good look at it. It was not a map of the Alps, but of the Pyrenees.

One way of thinking about story, like the Szent-Gyorti's map, is as a frame for making intelligible the uncertainty and complexity of modern organizations. While the modern organization is less fraught with danger than the icy wasteland of the Alps, there is a similar need to integrate the seemingly independent and disconnected experiences parts of the organization have of their past, present, and future.

Leadership and the Strategy Story

Given the importance for people to negotiate a shared interpretation of their work and the organization—to see the whole elephant in Orenstein's language—stories have become recognized as the preferred "sense-making currency" within organizations (Boje, 1991). The leader, as the voice of the organization both externally and internally, is by all accounts its chief storyteller. Externally, the CEO must tell the company's story to its shareholders, the financial community, partners, and other stakeholders. Internally, the story is equally significant: How do you provide meaning for, persuade, and inspire, your own people? The story-teller role is also played by senior managers. Unit and business leaders stand on the boundaries of the respective units to define goals among staff and communicate the group's purpose to the larger organization.

Even though they may be good storytellers in the social sphere, leaders often find that learning to craft and execute good organizational stories can be challenging. I see this most often in learning situations. When I teach executive education at the Wharton School, I find that a participant's ability to synthesize an experience or situation into a meaningful, coherent story is not only a powerful persuasion tool, but a form of communication that typically helps the entire class learn. I often discover that the best storytellers are the most influential among their peers. But the ability to tell stories can be quite uneven across a group of managers, even senior executives. With a group of regional executives of a large healthcare company, a colleague and I once asked volunteers to stand up and articulate a story of how their organization provides value to the consumer. We were surprised by their reactions. Few of the participants felt certain enough to stand up, even though the group had been vocal throughout the session, and participants who made the attempt found the impromptu speech a challenging exercise.

Among the most important stories that a leader, particularly an executive, must tell is the *strategy story*. As Barry and Elms (1995) state it, if stories are a preferred "sense making currency" in organizations, then "strategy must rank as one of the most prominent, influential, and costly stories told in organizations." In our work with strategy, we find that stories offer leaders the opportunity to think about strategy in a fundamentally different way. For example, crafting stories of different strategic scenarios is a powerful device to help leaders appreciate and understand the choices they make. A strategy story highlights the underlying economics of the business, the assumptions that the organization has about its environment and itself, the steps that it will take given its choices, and why it will take them. This approach shifts leaders out of the conventional paradigm for thinking about their business while simultaneously giving them a more authentic and natural picture of the organization.

Story is also a natural medium for strategy. At the heart of any good business model is essentially a story about how you provide value to the customer given the context in which you compete. Because a pro forma is only as good as the assumptions that go into it, the essential task of developing the strategy story is marrying the numbers to the narrative. The question isn't just "Do the numbers add up?" it is also "Does the story hang together?" (Magretta, 2002). The strategy story is a way for stakeholders to feel, "in their bones" as one of my colleagues likes to say, the implications of their decisions. A narrative articulates how different parts of the system have experienced the past and what the strategy story means for the future. This allows leaders to test whether a strategy will or won't work and anticipate what will be needed to help others support it.

Given strategy's prominence within the executive's needed skill set, learning to tell the strategy story can be a crucial part of leadership development. We have found that telling the strategy story is something you can't learn from a textbook, but only through experience. The premise of "learning by doing" is crucial for this work. For example, a colleague and I ran a year-long action learning project during which teams of senior managers had to apply their learning to an actual business problem. Each team led a project with significant financial consequences—the stakes were high and the learning very hands-on. The biggest challenge for the teams was presenting a logical, economically sound, and coherent business case about what they planed to do for their projects.

One of my teams, a group of unit managers from a large real estate firm, was having difficulty turning their idea into a compelling case that would gain the support of their executive sponsor. Their idea was ambitious and important: to implement sustainable development methods across all the company's projects. (Sustainable development is an approach to construction that protects the human, environmental, and communal capital potentially at risk during the building process). At first the team emphasized the abstract qualities and lofty merits of sustainable development; however, they did so as if they were divorced from the very real needs of their own company. For this reason, to the coaches, the CEO, and the participants, the case never fully hung together. While the team's idea was indisputably potent, the argument was weak. In comparison to the significance of what they were contemplating, the case felt resoundingly academic.

To solve this situation, we asked the team to dig deeper into the issue through the lens of a narrative. What they found upon further diagnosis was a meaningful and compelling story that they could rally around. Here is the story, condensed and disguised:

> Over the last five years our company has created some of the most ambitious real estate developments in our geographic region. In fact, in the last five years our projects have become iconic symbols of the city's growth and ambition. As we and others have prospered, the local real estate market has become a driving force for sustaining the region's growth. But there's a rub to our situation. As the region grows, the outside world has begun to look upon our achievements with far greater scrutiny. More than ever before, we must take extra care to assure

the quality of our construction and its impact on the environment in order to protect our brand and our community. Sustainable development therefore is not only a crucial component of our own success but for the continuing success of the region.

During their narrative diagnosis, the participants began to appreciate how closely tied the image of the city was to their own construction projects, which had played such a significant role in the historical development of the city. The insight for them, now clarified through the story, carried with it a different type of relationship to their project. The team felt in their work the weight of their responsibility for future generations. The story became a meaningful way for the team to understand their own participation in the building of a city. Unlike Mailer's spy, the team experienced how their role fit into the larger and much more important narrative.

Telling a Story: From Simplicity to Complexity

So how does one go about learning how tell a good story? The simplest expression of narrative useful to leaders consists of three acts (Atkins, 2005; Shaw, Brown, & Bromily, 1998).

Act I. Set the Stage. In Act I the characters and setting are introduced. In the film industry, a key part of the first act is "establishing the shot." If the scene will take place on a battlefield, you may see a shot of a map that then fades into the field where the action takes place. Setting the stage begins with describing the context and naming the protagonist.

Act II. Introduce Dramatic Conflict. In the second act, something changes that produces a clear dramatic conflict for the protagonist, an imbalance in the world that demands attention. Often the second act includes an "inciting incident" that sets the story in motion. Most importantly, the second act highlights the tension between the protagonist's desire for a goal and a force that obstructs it.

Act III. Reach Resolution. The protagonist finds a way to overcome the obstacle or conflict to restore order to the universe. In the process he or she has changed in some important way.

The three acts are a helpful organizing principle for the creation of stories. Yet they are but a foundation for good story telling. As Mailer reminds us, life does not fit neatly into a three-part plot. The challenge of creating organizational stories is that the author must condense the multitude and complexity of a situation into a medium that people can understand, doing so by honoring the many voices and experiences that are part of any story. This requires that leaders "listen in" to their organizations and empathize not only with their target audience, but with the different people and groups that make up the story. The American playwright David Ives nicely communicates the need to hear and understand when crafting story:

> "I think of theater as an arena for communal empathy. To write for the theater, you have to have a kind of imaginative empathy for people in order to understand how and what they feel. You then bring that to an audience. The audience has to empathize with what you're saying, and the actors have to empathize with what you've written, and all the people who put on a production together have to empathize with each other. I think of theater as this giant civilizing arena where people find a common ground. It's where, in one way or another, we realize that we're in the same leaky boat, and we realize it in person."

Finally, good stories are fundamentally about transformation. Abraham Verghese (2001), the physician author, highlights James Joyce's belief that every story ultimately requires epiphany, the raison d'etre of the story itself. Anne Hunsaker Hawkins (1997) suggests, quite beautifully, that the storyteller's job is therefore to address the *epiphanic*: "Narrative, then, whether in literature or in life, could be said to move through nodes of the epiphanic; it moves toward and then away from moments of recognition, insight, and the sudden apprehension of meaning."

Cautions to Leaders Learning Storytelling

> "We have, as human beings, a storytelling problem. We're a bit too quick to come up with explanations for things we don't really have an explanation for." (Malcolm Gladwell, 2005)

Storytellers, particularly if they are in positions of power, have the great responsibility to speak the truth. The good storyteller places in high regard the effort to accurately reflect the facts, events, and experiences that comprise a real story. The willingness to do so is not simply an ethical position but a component of good storytelling.

There are two reasons why storytellers should seek the truth. First, most people find that only painting a positive picture of a situation doesn't ring true (McKee, 2003). This is bad for the teller's credibility and bad for the story. Spin makes for poor story because it doesn't capture the uncomfortable tension between the protagonists desire and reality, however cruel it may be (McKee, 2003). As everyone knows, it's exactly this tension that makes for a gripping story. But organizational leaders are wary to take these risks, even if they should profit from them. As Robert McKee, the famous screenwriting lecturer has said of executives, "Most companies and executives want to sweep the dirty laundry, the difficulties, the antagonists, and the struggle under the carpet" (p. 7). McKee argues that, as a storyteller, the leader ought to position the problems in the foreground, for the drive for life comes not from its pleasantness, but from the suffering and struggle that forces people to live more deeply.

The second reason for respecting the truth is that stories have a profound effect on framing public discourse. Like a trial lawyer's opening statement, stories naturally select which pieces of information to highlight and which to exclude. The intentional use of framing and stories to shape, and sometimes manipulate, discourse rarely works over the long term. Not only do these attempts restrict the open flow of information and consequently the range of possible solutions, but people respond strongly when their reality is interpreted for them. One hypothesis of why public dissatisfaction with the Bush Administration so clearly hurt congressional elections is that the Iraq war had lost its narrative. People no longer felt that the story told matched the reality on the ground.

The rule for good storytelling is that leaders should take their time, listen in, and understand the complexity of a situation as the first step for creating their stories. This demands a skill that the poet Keats called "negative capability": the capacity to be in a state of uncertainty, doubt, and unknowing without reaching immediately for a conclusion. In modern organizations, where we are constantly having to hold multiple, sometimes contradictory, opinions and ideas in our heads at the same time, it is best to appreciate all the data fully before crafting the story. Leaders should spend as much time crafting their stories as telling them.

References

Atkins, C. (2005). *Beyond bullet points: Using Microsoft PowerPoint to create presentations that inform, motivate, and inspire.* Redmond, WA: Microsoft Press.

Barry, D., & Elms, M. (1997). Strategy retold: Towards a narrative view of strategic discourse. *Academy of Management Review, 22*(2), 429–452.

Boje, D.M. (1991, March). The storytelling organization: A study of story performance in an office-supply firm. *Administrative Science Quarterly, 36*(1), 106–126.

Gladwell, M. (2005). *Blink: The power of thinking without thinking.* New York: Little, Brown and Company.

Hawkins, A.H. (1997). Medical ethics and epiphanic dimension of narrative. In H. Nelson (Ed.), *Stories and their limits.* New York: Routledge.

Hirschhorn, L. (1993). *The workplace within: Psychodynamics of organizational life.* Cambridge, MA: MIT Press.

Ives, D. (n.d.). *The captive audience.* New York: Dramatists Play Service.

Jones, D. (2004, September 19). Indian art of storytelling seeps into boardroom. *USA Today.*

Magretta, J. (2002). What management is: How it works and why its everyone's business. New York: The Free Press.

Mailer, N. (2003). *The spooky art: Some thoughts on writing.* New York: Random House.

McKee, (2003). Storytelling that moves people: A conversation with screenwriter coach. *Harvard Business Review.*

Miroslav, H. (1977, February 4). Brief thoughts on maps. *The Times Literary Supplement, 118.* In K.E. Weick (1995), *Sensemaking in organizations* (p. 54). Thousand Oaks, CA: Sage.

Orenstein, R. (1972). *The psychology of consciousness* (p. 10). New York: Viking Press.

Pennington, N., & Hastie, R. (1993). The story model for Juror Decision Making. In R. Hastie: *Inside the juror: The psychology of juror decision making* (pp. 192–221). New York: Cambridge University Press.

Schank, R.C. (1995). *Tell me a story: Narrative and intelligence.* Evanston, IL: Northwestern University Press.

Shaw, G., Brown, R., & Bromily, P. (1998). Strategic stories: How 3m is rewriting business planning. *Harvard Business Review.*

Turner, M. (1997). *The literary mind: The origins of thought and language.* New York: Oxford University Press.

Verghese, A. (2001). The physician as storyteller. *Annals of Internal Medicine, 135,* 11.

Chatham Clarke Sullivan is an organizational psychologist and an associate at The Center for Applied Research (CFAR), a private consulting firm that spun off from the Wharton School at the University of Pennsylvania. Chatham specializes in strategy and large scale organizational change. Drawing on training in psychology and business, Chatham's work focuses on the intersection between business economics and organizational dynamics. In addition to his work at CFAR, he teaches negotiation, organizational change, and action learning in executive education programs at Aresty and the Leonard Davis Institute of Health Economics at Wharton.

CHAPTER 24

THE LEADER AS POET: A CONSIDERATION OF WHAT POETRY MAY HAVE TO OFFER ORGANIZATIONAL LEADERSHIP

Juan Mobili

Over the last decade the new literature on business leadership, more than ever before, seems to have expanded its search for models it may learn from, beyond the traditional confines of its own field. Fields as apparently unrelated as Eastern philosophy, Sir Edmund Hillary's expedition, the work of William Shakespeare, or Chaos Theory have been the inspiration for books attempting to shed light on or establish universal principles of leadership that could enrich the capacity of business leaders to fulfill their missions in leading organizations toward sustainable growth and market leadership in their respective industries.

Whether or not these explorations have resulted in measurable results or concrete business applications is somewhat debatable. Nonetheless, I believe that the very pursuit of such "non-business" sources for leadership lessons is critical to leaders for rethinking what their jobs are and, more fundamentally, what kind of thinking a leader must be adept at to continue providing new opportunities for organizational sustainability.

More than ever before, given the velocity and depth of the impact of changes occurring in the global business landscape, it is my contention that business leaders must recognize, as Einstein supposedly said, "The significant problems we have cannot be solved at the same level of thinking with which we created them."

I believe poetry may be one of those potential paths to this higher level of thinking that Einstein is warning us to consider.

A Working Definition

The very first obstacle with even considering the words poet and leader in the same sentence—to consider that a meaningful relationship between these two figures may exist and be worth exploring—can be traced back to what and how we learned about poetry, early on in our education.

By and large in our schools, poetry has been reduced to learning by rote and the reduction of interpretations to a single one to be considered the "real" one. Endless memorization and the search for the "right meaning" have been the basis for learning poetry. In other words, many of us have been, to paraphrase Toni Morrison (1993), *"stuffed like geese"* with words we were never invited to make ours, or subjected to some sort of game-show mischief where opening only one door will offer some big prize.

Now poetry, as far as I'm concerned, is none of that. Although definitions abound, I'd like to offer one here that will be most relevant to what *the leader* can learn from *the poet*.

The definition of poetry I'd like to begin with comes from another great American poet, Robert Frost: "To be a poet is not a profession, it's a condition," to which he added elsewhere that "Poetry is when an emotion has found its thought and the thought has found words" (Parini, 1999).

I believe there are two important elements in what Frost says that are worth stressing. First, Frost's suggestion that a poet is not so much something one does, as it is a dimension of how one sees the world. Poetry, perhaps more than any other genre, affords us the freedom to look at things anew, to consider even what's familiar in ways we have not considered. Writing a poem is a very personal act of observation, it's about noticing how else the facts of a situation might connect or be approached, beyond accepted definitions. As Yogi Berra (1998)—someone who is a poet in his own way—says, "You can observe a lot by just watching."

Secondly, the success of a leader in moving an organization in new and possibly uncertain directions largely depends on her or his capacity to relate with and include those people who will execute the strategy. What Frost points to, I think, is that such a task requires a certain kind of language, words that can achieve a distinct tone—a precise point of view—and at the same time, that speak in terms that are meaningful to others, that address what people care about and hope for.

Ultimately, poetry is a not just a literary genre for "sensitive" people but a linguistic discipline that requires a number of abilities that are key to a business leader too—specifically, a capacity to reflect on what you experience and how it could open new worlds of action, and the competence to articulate what you've concluded in ways that may be of value to others, whether they are employees or customers.

What Could Poetry Teach Leaders?

Poetry has much more to offer and its message is far more urgent than we may have given it credit for. The American poet Williams Carlos Williams (1991), who in addition to his significant role in this country's poetic tradition was a medical doctor and as deeply committed to science as he was to art, declared: "There is no news in poetry/yet people die miserably each day/of the lack of what is found there."

What may account for such urgency? The way I see it, there are at least two key challenges to leaders everywhere, to which poetry has something fundamental to offer:

- The capacity to see future possibilities—beyond accepted and obvious interpretations—as the basis for true and *lasting innovation*.
- The development of an authentic, distinct point of view and the ability to inspire others to embrace it, which is at the core of *motivating people* to action even in the midst of uncertainty.

The Challenge to Innovate

"You can't depend on your eyes when your imagination is out of focus."

—MARK TWAIN

I can't imagine anyone reading these words who may not already agree with the imperative necessity of organizational renewal—internal processes that are the basis of efficiency and quality as well as products and services customers are expected to purchase—an ongoing endeavor. Yet, over my twenty years as an organizational consultant, I've witnessed the recurrent struggle businesses face between "thinking out of the box" and minimizing risks. The wish behind reconciling these two valid concerns may boil down to what one of my clients once told me: "I'd try something new as long as I know it'll turn out well."

Poets face a similar dilemma; the words they use are the same words human beings have used for thousands of years. It's old stuff, used over and over. Whether it's poems, services, or products, the same questions come up: How can I make something original from something so common? How can I offer something no one has ever offered with something everyone uses?

Stanley Kunitz (1993), another great American poet, in an interview some years ago, had an answer: "A little doubt is all you need to know."

Whether this may initially strike the reader as flippant or merely catchy at first, there's a fundamental truth to what Kunitz points to here. There's no innovation without uncertainty, no new poem that begins anywhere else but on a blank page, no new initiative in search of the new breakthrough product without tremors and fear of failure.

Perhaps the poet who taught the strongest lessons about these perils was William Stafford who, in addition to a vast number of published poems, spent most of his adult life teaching in American universities and wrote at length about the creative process itself. Although the following quote is directed to writers instead of leaders in business, I'd suggest that you read it with the word "leader" in mind, rather than "writer":

> "A writer is not so much someone who has something to say, as he is someone who has found a process that will bring about new things he would not have thought of if he had not started to say them.

> "I must be willing to fail. I am following a process that leads so wildly and originally into new territory that no judgment can at the moment be made about values, significance, and so on. I am making something new, something that has not been judged before. Later others—and maybe I myself—will make judgments. Now, I am headlong to discover. Any distraction may harm the creating." (Stafford, 1978)

In business terms, it is this commitment to the process "that will bring about new things" that a leader must vow allegiance to. Originality, by definition, is paradoxical, it points to a beginning and it hints to something that has never been before. The "process" may vary, but one task is indispensable: It must balance bold thinking about new offerings and loyalty for what a company's values. As David Wagoner (1999) says, when it comes to the future, "You must treat it as a powerful stranger."

The Challenge of Motivating People

Every experienced and successful leader knows that to underestimate either the importance or the difficulty of inspiring people's commitment toward the organization's bold, strategic goal is to navigate dangerous waters. At the root of the success or failure of a well-executed vision lies in the capacity of a leader to speak articulately and authentically about the future.

One need not look too far to find many painful corporate examples where great ideas and the significant investment of time, capital, and the effort of many were reduced to the label of "flavor of the month" by a company's own employees, and cost its leaders precious credibility.

Poetry has to do with images, images that appear before us—in us—and carry us forward. This capacity to imagine has to do with articulating one's intentions, desires, and commitments.

Poetry is a way of "seeing," a way that might yield new insight into a dilemma we face or a future we can only glimpse. Great poets illuminate aspects of what's already there that might not be apparent through the way we've been looking at them.

In the vocabulary of leadership, one of the common words is "vision." Yet, in my experience, many organizational visions lack the appeal to those who must eventually carry them into existence. These vision statements might point quite clearly to desirable results, yet don't evoke the commitment and passion in the "readers" that made the "writers" gather to write them.

A poem—and I suggest it's the same with an organization's vision—draws its power from allowing others to find where and how they belong in it. A great poem, and a powerful vision, begins with the careful and honest writing of it, understanding that most of its depth and its future depend on its readers.

Charles Olson (1997), in his short poem "These Days" has some important advice for poets that applies quite directly to any organization's leaders:

"Whatever you have to say, leave the roots on, let them dangle/And the dirt/ Just to make clear where they come from."

In my professional experience, ignorance of such advice has cost many leaders and their companies very dearly. There are two common mistakes worth mentioning, that could have benefited from Olson's warning.

There's a historical tendency in large corporations to delay the announcement of significant changes to the organization's future for fear of causing confusion and unrest. As noble as this might sound, it causes problems of its own, namely the proliferation of rumors throughout the organization that, lacking facts, devolve into negative stories that circulate widely and cause a general mood of fear and cynicism. If you "leave the roots on," people might appreciate even more what a leader is up to and, most importantly, the urgency of that future direction the organization is embarking on.

Secondly, people's buy-in and willingness to tackle organizational change is intimately related to a leader's credibility—namely her or his ability to evoke trust and confidence in the new, stated direction. As important as the value of a well-crafted message and an impactful presentation is, the potential to sound like everyone else—whether the language is "corporate speak" or the corporate campaign resembles a SuperBowl commercial, or worse, to sound like someone the leader is not—can cause exactly the opposite result to the one planned. The message itself, then, becomes a distraction to true alignment, and the emotional connection without which trust and a motivated workforce is lost.

As much as corporate strategies may resemble each other within any given industry and the language used may not be utterly original, the roots and dirt are never the same from leader to leader. Leave them on.

A Suggestion Rather Than a Conclusion: Listen Deeply

It has been said many times that with power comes great responsibility. I believe this is the case, and I also believe that most leaders I've met know this and make a genuine effort to be true to such a statement. Yet, a noble intention does not always result in the impact it intended.

For the sake of offering a practice, a way to explore what I've proposed throughout these pages, I recommend that you read some poems, whether they belonged to poets you already love or "surfing the net" for choices. Reading poetry is, to me, akin to listening deeply.

In "listening" to the poems you choose, notice what their words evoke in you, and avoid trying to figure out what the poet must have meant by them. The power of a poem is in encountering what it calls in you, what it tells *you*.

When you read a poem, you don't read the words of another person as much as you meet language at the intersection of two lives. This is where the reader and writer meet; words no longer belong to one or the other alone. Poems are communal epiphanies. Thinking that there is a "truer" or "real" meaning to their words is sailing based on the tattered corner of a map. What the poet meant is only one possible path through a poem; look to go off road.

So roam freely through their words, notice which ones call you and where they take you. Some poems will speak to you with the precision of oracles, others may disturb you, and some will even leave you seeing more clearly—although you may not be able to explain it.

Read each poem several times, read them aloud, savor the music of each line, appreciate pauses, cadences, and punctuation—notice your breath, particularly the breath a line requires—and consider that, at least when it comes to great poems, no noun, verb, or preposition is a coincidence.

I suggest you read poems as one may embark on a journey without a stated destination. The storyteller Michael Meade (1997) said, "When you know where you're going, it's called commuting, not poetry."

Pack light.

References

Berra, Y. (1998). *The Yogi book: I really didn't say everything I said.* New York: Workman.

Kunitz, S. (1993). *Interviews and encounters with Stanley Kunitz.* Lebanon, NH: The Sheep Meadow Press.

Meade, M. (1997, September 20). Excerpted from a lecture. The Spirit of Inspiration—The Soul of Learning conference, San Francisco, California. Available in audio form from Oral Tradition Archives.

Moncur, M. *(Cynical) Quotations.* www.quotationspage.com

Morrison, T. (1993). Nobel Prize Lecture. Available: http://nobelprize.org/.

Olson, C. (1997). *The collected poems of Charles Olson.* Berkeley, CA: University of California Press.

Parini, J. (1999). *Robert Frost: A life.* Markham, ONT: Fitzhenry & Whiteside, Ltd.

Stafford, W. (1978). *Writing the Australian crawl: Views on the writer's vocation.* Ann Arbor, MI: University of Michigan Press.

Wagoner, D. (1999). *Traveling light: Collected and new poems.* Chicago, IL: University of Illinois Press.

Williams, W.C. (1991). *The collected poems of William Carlos Williams, Vol. 1: 1909–1939.* New York: New Directions Publishing Corporation.

Juan Mobili has been a leadership development consultant and coach for global organizations throughout the Americas and Europe for the last eighteen years. His work has been in designing and delivering programs at the executive and middle management levels that take into account the importance of personal character and vision as much as the capacity to produce significant and sustainable results. Juan is also a published poet, music critic, and the director of *Alter*, an international book collection dedicated to reconciling our sense of personal authenticity and ownership with the obligations of being a leader in business.

CHAPTER 25

CHOICES IN WORK AND IN LIFE

Neil M. Johnston

Charles, a senior executive in a large North American Bank, moved to the West Coast after many years on Wall Street. He comes into the office at 6:30 in the morning to talk with his friends as the markets open on the East Coast, reads the papers, has coffee, and starts his daily round of meetings. At about 6:00 in the evening, his day quiets down and he works on his emails, voice mails, and other administrative tasks. Often around 6:30 or 7:00 P.M. he calls his wife and says, "I'm really busy and I will be home later."

Busy is an interesting word in our lives. Busy can be good. We have many challenging tasks to complete, many demanding but enjoyable activities to fit into the day or week. We feel energized by achievement and success. Busy can be a regular way of life, a day-in/day-out flow of activities that have to be completed almost without thinking. There is routine. At the end of each week, there is tiredness and marginal satisfaction of time well spent. At the beginning of each week, there is a determination to use time better.

There is overwhelmingly busy. Everyday events seem to move faster than we are capable of addressing. There is a relentless flow of work interrupted by additional demands. Technology and global operations allow managers to make themselves available twenty-four hours a day, seven days a week. Nothing ever seems to be fully completed. There is a growing sense of frustration, which in the extreme may lead to burnout.

But let's return to Charles.

> After calling his wife, he leaves the office and arrives home around 9:00 in the evening when his two young girls are about to go to bed. Excitement that Dad is home delays their bedtime and minimizes time with his wife to discuss family issues.

What is wrong with this picture? There are three major concerns—organizational, professional, and personal.

Charles is not a good role model for his organization. As executives move up the corporate ladder, they need to recognize, at each transition, that there are processes and skills they need to continue using. There are new processes and skills that need to be assimilated. Most importantly, there are activities that they need to stop doing.

His style of working is probably setting unrealistic expectations down the organization of what it takes to be successful, in terms of hours of work and involvement in detail that is no longer appropriate. Professionally, he is not spending his time on the more strategic aspects of his job, where his contribution is needed.

From a personal perspective, his family is becoming increasingly disenchanted with his workload. Every evening there always seems to be something that keeps him busy in the office. The word "busy" in many ways is an excuse for not facing reality. Charles' coach suggested to him that he substitute the word "priority" for the word "busy" when he called his wife in the evening. So instead of saying, "I'm really busy and I will be home later" he was asked to say, "It's not a priority for me to have dinner with you and the girls tonight."

As you can imagine, the effect was dramatic. Charles discussed the approach with his wife. They agreed that a firm commitment to come home early one night a week was a good starting point. Once this had been converted into a habit, it has an overflow effect on the rest of the week. Within a year, Charles was just as effective with significantly less time in the office.

It is not a priority. The word priority implies choice, discipline, a careful weighing of all the options. It brings into play the value system of the person based on his or her experience, background, and personality. In fact, individual personality plays a much larger role in day-to-day decisions than many senior executives care to admit. More than 50 percent of the time allocation of a senior executive is determined by his or her personality, rather than by the demands of the job itself. This is equally true down through most management levels. We know that if we take a manager out of his or her job today, and the job does not change at all, the next manager in the position does not allocate his or her time in the same way.

If priority setting denotes such a deliberate approach to workload issues, why do so many managers accept that they live in organizations where the priorities are not clear? Why is there an increasing groundswell of concern about the quality of working life? Why do the discussions on "balance" feel so difficult to have in many organizational settings? Why is every activity a priority, so that in essence there are no priorities?

There is a conspiracy of silence among managers in these situations. In one large international organization, managers have become successful over the years by developing extensive networks of relationships on which they can call in reciprocal fashion. This has become known as a "top of" organization. A manager asks another manager for assistance. She explains that the work involved is not so great. Rather than formalizing the work demands so a priority discussion can take place, the workload is minimized and seen as a small extra task "on top of" everything else the manager is doing.

Since the managers in this organization are dedicated professionals, well-meaning individuals, and collaborative colleagues, the response is more often than not a "yes." There is little familiarity with the word "no," let alone a discussion around whether the requested task fits in with the priorities.

> John is a dynamic fast-rising executive in a Midwestern company. He has a lively personality, enjoys the immediate operational nature of his job, and runs from crisis to crisis with well-practiced ease. The downside of his daily choices is that his workload is constantly rising, yet because he is so busy he does not have the time to use the support that is available to him. On first meeting with him, he was having difficulty getting his enlarged responsibilities accomplished. As an example, he was speaking with his assistant and setting his agenda for the day before lunchtime on less than 25 percent of the occasions he was in the office.

> Kathy is a senior executive in a slow-growing distribution company who has all the facts of the business at her fingertips. In fact, there is no one in the company with her grasp of the detail of all the internal processes and external relationships. All questions in her area of responsibility rise up to her desk. The CEO wants her to contribute in a more strategic fashion to the company. Kathy does not see how she can fit one more activity on her plate.

> Eduard works in the European subsidiary of an American high-tech company. As the General Manager, he has the potential to be a successor to the European Vice President, but he needs to develop his abilities to look more

broadly at business and organization development. How does he develop the processes and skills to do this when those around him have grown with him in an operational role? How does he value being more strategic when he has been rewarded over his career for being an excellent operational manager?

In all these cases, the managers are faced with critical choices about the way that they use their time. Time is the only resource for an executive, and they have to be extremely jealous about how they manage it. With the help of his assistant, John started making it a priority to speak with her as soon as he arrived at the office. After six months, he was achieving this on 84 percent of occasions. The priority became a habit, and his calendar and workload more manageable. Kathy realized that she needed to prioritize her monthly strategic sessions with her CEO before all her other activities, to fit into his calendar, and to delegate more to her team. Managing up has been a mantra in many a management-training program. Eduard recognized that he needed to read more widely about strategic business issues to expand his knowledge base so that he could actively engage his boss in conversations that demonstrate how he is developing his own mental model of how to lead the business in the future.

The discipline that is needed in these cases can be used on the broader issue of choice in how we approach work and life in general. The debate in recent years over work/life balance has not been productive. Balance is a very individualistic concept, time dependent, and culturally and organizationally variable. At different stages of life, balance can have different meanings. Balance can be in the hour, day, week, month, year, or longer. Balance in the United States can be different from balance in the Philippines. Balance in an exciting, forward-looking, high-tech company can be different from balance in a declining rust belt environment.

Some months ago during a forum between a group of managers and their CEO, the question was asked of the CEO: "How do you balance the demands of the job with the demands of your own personal life?" The CEO answered "I don't." There was a stunned silence in the room. This was certainly not the warm and fuzzy or the circuitous response that the audience was expecting. It was not the golden insight into balance for which they may have wished.

The CEO went on to say that many years earlier he had discussed his career with his family. He enjoyed his work, wanted to progress to a senior position, and felt he had a major contribution to make to the impact the company could have in the health field. Together with his family, they made the joint decision to pursue his career and that he would be supported in that objective.

Regardless of the individuals who may be dependent on any manager, the key issue is that a deliberate choice on priorities is made and the consequences understood. Choice and priorities—everyone has more choice and is more capable of deciding priorities than he or she currently believes.

Work/life balance is too limiting a concept for the foreseeable future. There is a continuum from separation through balance to integration that needs care and attention every day of the week and every week of the year. This is not an individual activity, but one that engages those around the manager. At work it can be defined as those who give you 360 degree feedback. Outside work, it is all those for whom you care and who care about you.

In some jobs it is quite possible to have a complete separation between work and personal life.

> For example, a retail pharmacist working in one of the major chains is part of a team providing full twenty-four-hour coverage, seven days a week. When a shift ends, the work is over. It cannot be done at home, and when the pharmacist returns to the next shift all the problems have moved on. Of course, the professionalism of a caring service professional will ensure that there is some mental effort given to a decision outside of the work hours. In general, despite the pressures during working time, there is a deliberate separation between work and personal life.

Balance is a much more difficult discussion, as most often it comes from people who, for whatever reason, feel that they have lost control over their working days. Each morning they set off for work with a list of action items to be achieved. At the end of the day, they feel fortunate if they have addressed half of these. Frustration at the lack of personal discipline to get to grips with their workload can lead to a downward spiral in performance and or relationships.

> Many young parents have a clear role model in their minds of their parents, who were not at home or not focused during critical periods in their upbringing. A Californian study on self-esteem painted a picture of a ten-year-old girl who was very proud that her career mother was always at her Saturday soccer games. Her disappointment was that every time she looked at her mother during the game, her mother was talking on her cell phone.

On the other hand, many managers take pleasure and satisfaction at balancing all aspects of their lives. They use modern technology to enhance their lives and to obtain full value out of their days and weeks.

George is the most senior project manager in his company and travels to work by train for approximately an hour each way. He uses the time to do nothing but emails, plus another hour in the middle of the day, and nothing more. People who work with him know that this is an unfailing daily pattern and know how and when to communicate effectively with him. During the week he is always available on his cell phone, but he will only listen (not reply) to messages after 7:00 P.M. on a Friday evening until 7:00 A.M. on a Monday morning (unless it is a critical emergency).

Modern technologies have made a reality of integration. This allows managers to go beyond balance and recognize that the boundaries between work and not work are too blurred to be meaningful. Studies have shown that managers are spending on average more than an hour a day during "working time" to support non-work-related activities. More time is being spent during "non-work hours" in supporting work-related activities.

Leila is a senior scientist working on secret projects for the U.S. government. The nature of her job is such that her creative ideas and resolution of challenging intellectual dilemmas cannot be contained within the concept of a normal working day. As a result, there are no boundaries to any aspect of her life. Some weeks she may not even go into the office; some weeks she may not go home for several days. She has access to equivalent computing power at home or at the workplace. The integration of her work and non-work lives is complete, satisfying, and very productive.

Many years ago in 1964, an article appeared in the *Harvard Business Review* with the title "The Power to See Ourselves," which initiated the interest in getting feedback from those around us. This concept is even more relevant today in terms of looking at ourselves in our own mirrors. A manager's day-to-day actions create the climate in an organization that leads to greater or lesser productivity. Under the continuous pressure of events and activities, it is too easy to be carried along with the flow. Managers at every level always have the choice of creating priorities for themselves and their people in their work and in their lives.

Neil M. Johnston, an international consultant who develops learning strategies to accelerate the achievement of business results, is president and managing partner of Orbis Learning. He has worked on major action learning and 360-degree feedback initiatives. Neil has a distinctive business-driven approach to his executive-coaching assignments. He has extensive experience in education and human-resource management, initially with British Airways, Furness Withy, a diversified international shipping group, and finally with Hewlett-Packard. As Hewlett-Packard's first director of corporation education, he was instrumental in creating an integrated approach to education, developing a comprehensive executive/management development framework, initiating major programs in corporate culture development, and creating learning-technology strategies. Neil has a BA (honors) in geography/sociology from the University of London King's College and the London School of Economics and Political Science, a postgraduate diploma in Management Studies, and a master's degree in management learning from Lancaster University.

CHAPTER 26

THE LEADING BRAIN: AN EXERCISE IN SELF-COACHING

Agnes Mura

Neuroscience, the frontier discipline that studies the brain and the mind, continues to surprise us every day as it unravels the interplay between our biology and our experience, ultimately examining how our brain helps and limits our evolution. A leader's knowledge about the expanding field of brain research, coupled with keen self-awareness moment by moment, is foundational for successful personal transformation. It enables the act of self-coaching, a use of self as an ongoing growth tool that builds and expands.

As president of an international not-for-profit consortium, I have often tripped over obstacles of my own making when confronted with the challenge of addressing a particular segment of members or contributors, designing a truly strategic board discussion, or writing the tone-setting piece for a new directional change initiative. How do I know that such barriers are of my own making? I know because I usually overcome them with little external intervention.

As I consider writing this article, I am confronting some inner hurdles once more. I am therefore facing the same need for self-coaching that I confront many times as a leader in everyday life. I will take this self-coaching opportunity, as leaders often must, and simultaneously apply the many insights that have recently become available from what we now term social neuroscience: insights, among others, about why it is so hard for human beings to change, how our interpretation of reality shapes our experience and why, and how stress—in turn—stimulates and potentially destroys us.

I have not written about this subject in a while, let alone in the context of such illustrious co-authors as this volume brings together. As I approach the task, my mind, therefore, creates a gap between what is and what will be, more importantly, between what I think I need to produce and what I think I am capable of producing. (High achievers have typically low self-esteem; that's why they strive so hard, Dr. Vance Caesar discovered in his doctoral work.)

> I'm self-aware enough to notice that I have a gap to bridge, but that the nature of the gap may be different from what I first feel. I may have an opportunity to change how I operate by adjusting how I hold myself, my strengths and my capabilities in relation to the task.

The mind doesn't like gaps. It doesn't like things it can't connect. When it receives information, it first attempts to relate it to something it recognizes, and the rest is pretty much dismissed. Then, as an added, provocatively unfamiliar data element is introduced, for example, a powerful coaching question or a challenge to act, the brain starts to work on creating connections that will resolve the open tension, the cognitive dissonance. In that sense, my challenge to write for you is a good stimulus for something new to happen. New synapses have an opportunity to fire.

But wait, I am under time pressure. Because I procrastinated.

We procrastinate when closing the action gap is not easy, when we are required to get out of our mental comfort zones (when we are confronted with what feels like change!). So how did I get myself to act at all, and sit down to write? One crutch I used is the behaviorist approach: the trick of writing deadlines into my calendar. But that only got me to sit down and "try."

> A glass of water is at the ready. I start reading literature about my subject. All interesting and stimulating, but ultimately tiring for my eyes and brain. I'm "efforting" (if there is no such verb, there should be) and not making much progress on my change path.

> It's quiet, I have closed my door. I feel stiff; I get up, aware of the struggle I am getting away from, I walk around, look out the window. My mind wanders to the building under construction across the street. I am not consciously trying to do anything right now, although a part of my mind knows what I need to solve. I can trust it to be working on closing the idea-gap, the task that irks me.

We operate at several levels simultaneously. A fundamental assumption of mind-body correlation is accepted almost universally in today's neuro-physiological research: Conscious thought is a result of processes within the cerebral cortex. But the cerebral cortex is continuously receiving messages, directly and indirectly, from the brain's lower levels: From sub-cortical centers such as the amygdalae, hippocampus, and basal ganglia; from still lower levels such as the hypothalamus and central grey matter; from yet lower nuclei located in the brain stem. As studies by today's foremost neuro-physiologists—Edelman, Rolls, Damasio, LeDoux, Heilman, Valenstein, or Jeffrey Schwartz—are showing, cortical processes of the brain are riding on top of multiple sub-cortical and lower brain processes. In the February 17, 2006, issue of *Science*, Amsterdam University psychologists demonstrate that conscious thought may be best suited for simple decisions, but that complex situations are better served by "both minds"—the conscious *and* the subconscious.

I am an executive coach. I know, experientially, how to engage as much of the whole brain as possible. Inducing lateral thinking and big-picture visioning can help allow the moment in which several levels of the brain fire up and an insight is created. I ask myself: "What would it mean to you to have this article published?" "Why not just give up? It's an option." "What's going on with you right now?"

Attempting to answer, my mind begins to let go of the immediate task at hand, seems to slow down. At some level, it's dreaming of what can be, and my immediate environment is fading from my view. I'm elsewhere.

The state is introspection, reflection. Whatever term we use for that state in which the auditory and the visual cortex quiet down, it is preparing the conditions for a different kind of mental event.

Pop, electrical impulses connect across new neural pathways. . . . The insight appears: "Write about this very process of writing an article!"

Moments of insight are the gold we all mine for. For years I have known, and many formidable leaders have told me that "changing one's mind," "thinking a new thought" is a favorite thrill of theirs. The studies that have observed brain activity at the time of insight show the brain "lighting up" with pleasure, you might say. In accordance with the length of time and the effort we had been deploying in seeking the insight, either a smaller of a more substantial burst of adrenaline, dopamine, and other stimulating hormones create a cocktail that courses through our bodies, and we perceive it as excitingly delightful (similar, apparently, to hearing and getting a great joke).

I ride the excitement of my first insight for a bit, sketch out some ideas for an outline. "Some of them are not so hot," a voice says in my mind. It finds contradictions, mistakes; it questions my knowledge. My energy is beginning to wane. Where does this "voice" come from that zeroes in on my inadequacies?!

The emotional mind, according to LeDoux, is deeply wrapped up in the working of the amygdala. It is what Freud and the psychodynamic theorists were primarily referring to when they described the multi-tiered functioning of the mind. They proposed that many cognitive structures and functions in the mind are devoted primarily to the management and control of the powerful emotions that are embedded in past experiences (especially from childhood) and, perhaps, even in archetypal, inherited images that are strongly associated with intensive, often primitive feelings.

Successful performance and leadership have a great deal to do with which internal voices we choose to listen to and which not—because there will always be voices! An adaptive characteristic we as humans developed as we evolved on the Savannah is to store unfathomable amounts of data in our long-term memories, thus creating huge efficiencies in processing and storing information. Parental and societal input, wrapped in our interpretations, is tucked away in our long-term memories. And this data self-organizes, in dialogue with our rational minds and with our continuous experiences, into "templates" that show up as assumptions, conclusions, beliefs, or preferences. So to expect ourselves or others to operate without involuntary references to such templates is illusory.

Moreover, our brains cannot distinguish well between an internal reality of its own making and external events it responds to. So my self-criticism, just like "feedback" by others, engenders a powerful, visceral negative template-reaction in my brain. Naomi Eisenberger and Matthew Lieberman at UCLA scanned people's brains during episodes of rejection and found that the areas of the brain activated by rejection (emotional distress) are similar to ones that respond to physical pain. So the poets were right: There is real pain in a broken heart.

I freeze. "This isn't going anywhere," I think. My own mind has created a judgmental evaluation, and I am experiencing all the stress reactions that are to be expected. My heart starts beating with worry; my shoulders are tightening. The idea flow has stopped. I'm thrashing about, trying to "fix my mistakes," scavenging through books. and wasting time.

"Break the mood, break the pattern!" I self-coach. Stepping out of the office, I automatically approach the coffee maker, and the cookies that someone kindly laid out.

A post-modern trap we have built for ourselves in the last century or so is no longer to view discomfort and pain as an acceptable part of living. We seek immediate relief. Tired and overworked? Grab caffeine. A conflict gave you tension headaches? Grab an analgesic. Too wound up to fall asleep? Grab a sleeping pill. And the circle replays itself next day. John Preston has written many best-selling books on depression, psychopharmacology, and the emotional healing process and faults this type of vicious circle for many chronic ills the workforce is developing. Foremost among them is a lack of connection and awareness of our bodies' messages, masked as they are by foreign substances. Another is the long-lasting, perhaps permanent damage caused by a combination of stress and caffeine, in particular. Researchers of the effect of sustained stress on the brain and on the body speak of the cortisol effect, a complex downward spiral by which hormones like cortisol repeatedly wash through the physical system and engender physiological stress responses, accompanied and followed by deeper and deeper brain "ruts" of depression or anxiety. Robert Sapolsky describes this rutting process:

> "Stress responses tend to spiral up and down. First we are triggered. Then, we react to being triggered with confusion, humiliation, and even anger (I'm angry because you scared me). This becomes a spiral of stress. For intense stressful events, we create an Engram [memory] that never goes away."

This effect is turbo-charged by caffeine. John Preston suggests that therapists and coaches might need to first ensure that their clients are not consuming more than 250 milligrams of caffeine a day, before even attempting an intervention.

> I don't even much like the taste coffee. Why then do I crave it every day, particularly in times of stress? What's an alternative to such a habit? Another voice, one of reason—sounding much like my colleague Jim Loehr's—reminds me that if I want to perform at my highest capacity as a "corporate athlete," I have to train accordingly. Like making a licorice tea right now . . . and perhaps, starting tomorrow, turning the coffee maker off for the day after one morning cup.

Training means using the little bit of working memory and willpower that *is* under our control to establish consistent positive rituals, like having five, small and balanced meals during the day, instead of starving the brain during the day when it most needs glucose (and oxygen!) and overeating at night.

> Armed with a fresh cup of tea, I follow another performance-physiology prescription. Oscillate! Don't keep doing one type of activity for more than ninety to 120 minutes. After so much writing and reading, I stretch for a couple of

minutes. Nothing indecent, just a few arches and curls of the spine, sitting in my chair, and a few gentle twists, looking all the way behind myself. My back and my brain have received rushes of oxygen due to the movement; my eyes have stretched and rested.

I am now writing with intensity and ease. Someone wants to interrupt me, but I cherish the momentum and keep going.

Such sustained action holds in place the new brain circuits created by the insight, hardwiring them, as the authors of *A Brain-Based Approach to Coaching*, David Rock and Jeffery Schwartz, would say. If I want to write with increasing ease, I have to write now and stick with it. Knowing what we are up against in creating lasting behavioral and cognitive change, executive education is therefore increasingly pushing into action learning methods. The results of several days of training have long been recognized to remain in the 20 to 30 percent range of effectiveness against objectives, unless followed by customized coaching, mentoring, and active application.

I won't finish this today. As I look at my agenda and envision the next oasis of time I can dedicate to this, waves of anxiety rush through my mind and body. But I know that I have to block a daily amount of time and finish this soon. "You should finish it soon," I hear myself saying. That doesn't sound like fun to me. My mind doesn't grab on to the intention, I can't fool myself. Yes, I can calendar it to make sure I don't forget, but, saddled with that "should," will I be back to square one when I sit down?

We can change the behavior associated with our motivational mind (LeDoux) through reinforcements, rewards, and punishments, but our motivations are often deeply "rutted" and tend to re-engage old behaviors once the reinforcements (crutches) are withdrawn. It helps enormously to engage another part of the brain that responds to social motivation.

So I pick up the phone and tell an esteemed colleague about my beginning article. I know that if my colleague sounds encouraging and excited about the project, my mind will resonate with his optimism . . . especially since I'm a woman. And my colleague Bill does me one better. He tells me of a series of speaking engagements (my favorite professional activity!) that he can arrange for me on the basis of this article. I am emotionally high. It will be no effort for me now to remember my task, nor to return to it daily for a few days.

The colleague's input helps the brain release endorphins, which, in turn, disinhibit the release of a dose of wonderful dopamine. The hormones have the effect of what we call a positive emotional state. We remember and are motivated to act not only based on social connections but when we are affected emotionally.

A male colleague, who just phoned, hears the tale of my findings. He voices a different perspective: It is his sense that he personally would have felt more stimulated into writing if the challenge had included a competitive element instead of just positive reinforcement.

His act of self-awareness surfaces something that brain research confirms: In men, cortisol does, in moderate amounts and when not induced too often, increase alertness and excitement, moving them to action. Much of the workaholism we encounter might be explained by various levels of addiction to such hormones generated during a high state of stimulation at work. In women, on the other hand, cortisol interacts with estrogen and progesterone and may shut a person down, which is why competition may not be the best stimulant to high performance for women. One of the key skills leaders have to develop is to rightly calibrate the degree and the duration of the challenges they impress on the individuals they lead, as well as on themselves.

So it won't become immediately natural for me to keep writing. But the power of positive emotional states, generally healthy mental and physical habits, and the consistency of practice will be helpful.

In addition to actual experiences, every occasion when we just speak of an emotional event reactivates the circuits related to it in our brain, ensuring retention in memory. Otherwise, the news about our attention span isn't good when it comes to creating enduring change. If you have taken a crash course in a computer program and didn't use it regularly, you know that retention was minimal. A very few minutes a day of consistent, practiced attention to a new idea, behavior, or attitude work wonders, compared to an hour a week or even a one-time full-week experience.

However, most helpful of all in my progress, will be my willingness to let my mind float laterally, obliquely, in its own time, through its own free associations to activate the unexpected connections I so long to generate.

The end of "efforting" is near.

References

Caesar, V. (2005). *The high achiever's guide to happiness*. Thousand Oaks, CA: Sage.

Eisenberger, N.I., Lieberman, M.D., & Williams, K.D. (2003). Does rejection hurt? An FMRI study of social exclusion. *Science, 302*, 290–292.

Lieberman, M.D. (in press). Social cognitive neuroscience: A review of core processes. *Annual Review of Psychology, 58*.

Kounios, J., Frymiare, J.L., Bowden, E.M., Fleck, J.L., Subramaniam, K., Parrish, T.D., & Jung-Beeman, M. (2006). The prepared mind: Neural activity prior to problem presentation predicts subsequent solution by sudden insight. *Psychological Science*.

LeDoux, J. (1998). *The emotional brain*. New York: Simon & Schuster.

LeDoux, J. (2003). *Synaptic self: How our brains become who we are*. New York: Penguin.

Loehr, J., & Schwartz, T. (2003). *The power of full engagement*. Glencoe, IL: The Free Press.

Bergquist, W., & Mura, A. (2005). *Ten themes and variations for postmodern leaders and their coaches*. Sacramento, CA: Pacific Soundings Press.

Preston, J. (2002–2004). Lectures on behavioral neurobiology delivered at The Professional School of Psychology, Sacramento, California.

Rock, D. (2006). *Quiet leadership*. New York: HarperCollins.

Rock, D., & Schwartz, J. (2005). A brain-based approach to coaching. *The International Journal of Coaching in Organizations, 3*(2).

Sapolsky, R. (1998). *Why zebras don't get ulcers*. New York: W.H. Freeman and Company.

Agnes Mura coaches and develops Fortune 500 global executives in six languages. In 2002, she earned the *Builders' Award* of the Professional Coaches and Mentors Association, which she had co-founded in the mid-1990s. In 2003, she was invited to the editorial board of the *International Journal of Coaching in Organizations* (www.IJCO.info). In 2004, she became the first president of The International Consortium for Coaching in Organizations (www.CoachingConsortium.org), a worldwide organization of companies, academics, practitioners, and associations dedicated to the success of executive coaching interventions in organizations. Her book, *Ten Themes and Variations for Postmodern Leaders and Their Coaches*, co-authored with William Bergquist, was published by Pacific Soundings Press in 2005.

CHAPTER 27

LEADING IN THE MATRIX OF TODAY: INTEGRATING BODY/MIND/SPIRIT

Ginny Whitelaw

The challenges of leading in today's matrix are greater than ever before: Leaders are being asked to accomplish more with less authority, balance competing perspectives, involve more people in every project or decision, do more with fewer resources, juggle more demands faster, balance driving their own agendas with supporting others, and do all of this while handling a daily drubbing of dozens, if not hundreds of emails, instant messages, calls, and other assorted interruptions.

One doesn't perform well, much less thrive, in this accelerated environment by simply speeding up. Rather it calls a dynamic, versatile quality—where we're firing on all cylinders, using all four energies of whole and balanced leaders. What are these energy patterns? And why are they so essential to effective leadership, sustainable performance, and our own sense of being "whole" in body, mind, and spirit? I can do more than tell you about them; you have the patterns in you right now. Let me take you on a quick tour.

- **The Driver:** Stab the air with your index finger, over and over, like a politician making a point—or an angry coach challenging an umpire's decision. These sharp, thrusting movements bring out the Driver. Direct and aggressive, this is the pathway of people who love to win. Picture Donald Trump as he says, "You're fired!"

The 2008 Pfeiffer Annual: Leadership Development.
Copyright © 2008 by John Wiley & Sons, Inc. Reproduced by permission of Pfeiffer, an Imprint of Wiley. www.pfeiffer.com

- **The Organizer:** Sit up straight and fold your hands neatly in your lap. Like Queen Elizabeth II, the Organizer holds perfect form, with "a place for everything and everything in its place." Moving step-by-step, the Organizer ticks through a project list, doing the right thing and doing things right.
- **The Collaborator:** Move your head or your hips from side to side, and let your whole body follow. You're getting into the swing of the Collaborator, who knows how to have fun and engage people. When Oprah tilts her head, smiles, and draws people into the discussion, she's engaging the pattern of the Collaborator.
- **The Visionary:** Let your arm rise effortlessly, as though it's buoyed by air, and your hand move randomly through space. These hanging, drifting motions bring out the Visionary—like a Tai Chi master—open to anything and sensing the flow. The Visionary is the pattern of possibilities, chaos, imagination and breakthrough.

Nothing happens until something moves.

—ALBERT EINSTEIN

These fundamental energies have been recognized since the 1930s as patterns in the nervous system (Rathbone, 1936). They show up as four distinct ways in which nerves trigger the opposing muscle groups that make our every movement possible. But more recent work, particularly by Elizabeth Wetzig (who termed them Coordination Patterns™), has shown that they're not only physical patterns, but they run through every aspect of our being, as well as in how we do things (Knaster, 1996). Activate the movement of a particular pattern, and you access the feelings, thoughts, and behaviors that go with it. For example, if you jab a finger at someone to make your point, you enter the pushiness of the Driver. You'll likely feel an increased sense of urgency and your thoughts will be sharply focused. By contrast, if you lean back in your chair and gaze out the window, you'll enter the drifting, expansiveness of the Visionary. Here you'll likely see a bigger picture, and ideas may pop in from left field.

Perhaps you've never thought much about how movement and mindset are related; at first this simple idea can be hard to grasp. I've come to think of these patterns as energy that manifests in different, but related ways at every level within us and through our actions. As an analogy, my family has a cabin on the shores of Lake Superior, and I've spent a good deal of time in that magnificent Lake. The energy of the lake shows up in the water as waves and in the sand on the bottom as ripples. The ripples and waves aren't identical because they're different media, but they are interlinked by common energy.

Similarly, the four essential patterns in us show up in the various media or dimensions comprising us. Borrowing a model from Loehr and Schwartz (2003), we can call these dimensions physical, emotional, mental, and spiritual. (See Figure 1.) "Physical" refers to our bodies. "Emotional" and "mental" refer to the feeling and thinking aspects of mind, respectively. And "spiritual" refers to our transformative capacity or connectedness beyond our egos. As Loehr and Schwartz observe, our best sustained performance "requires strength, endurance, flexibility, and resilience in all dimensions." These qualities exactly represent the four patterns running through all these levels: Driver (strength), Organizer (endurance), Visionary (flexibility), and Collaborator (resilience). Out of this mountain of being comes our doing—our behaviors in the world.

FIGURE 1. FOUR LEVELS OF BEING

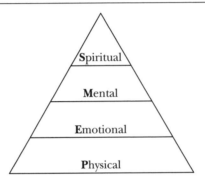

Four Energies Manifest at Each Level

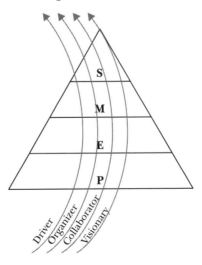

As an example, the Driver pattern shows up physically as pushing or thrusting. Emotionally it emerges as a sense of urgency and intensity. Mentally it manifests as sharply focused, challenging thoughts, and its spiritual dimension is around accomplishing a mission. Driver behaviors, as a result, are pushy, fast, and direct. Since our actions—and everyone else's—emerge in these patterns, the world around us similarly reflects these same four energies. Driver art, to continue the example, is bold and edgy (think Picasso). Driver companies are fast and measure everything (think Dell). Likewise, all of the energy patterns have a signature at every level, as shown in Table 1. Understanding these linkages is a gateway to

TABLE 1. EXAMPLES OF THE ENERGY PATTERNS AT EVERY LEVEL

	Driver	Organizer	Collaborator	Visionary
Physical	Pushing, thrusting	Holding form, posture perfect	Swinging, rocking	Hanging, drifting, extending
Emotional	Urgent, abrupt, quick to anger	Composed, calm, tendency to worry	Optimistic, resilient, warm	Open, detached, spontaneous
Mental	Sharply focused, calculating, competitive	Linear, logical, step-by-step, do the right thing	One thing leads to another, stories, humor, sees both sides	Leaps to new insight, gets to essence
Spiritual	Accomplish the mission	Serve a greater good beyond oneself	Spread happiness to others	Manifest essence and purpose in the world
Leadership Behaviors	Focus on priorities, action, outcomes, bottom line	Establish orderly processes, clear roles, responsibility	Oriented to customers, employees, loyalty, fun	Create the future, think outside the box
Workplace	Bold, no-frills architecture, cubicles	Orderly; quiet spaces to think. A place for everything	Colorful, common places to gather, exchange ideas	Places to network, be alone, or be with nature
Work Processes	Minimal, focused on outcomes	Step-by-step, and unambiguous	Practical, oriented toward how people really work	Loose, adjustable to circumstances
Corporate Culture	Winning, competitive, fast, no-nonsense; e.g., "Just Do It"	Stable, dependable, ethical, e.g., "Solid as a Rock"	Fun, zany, family oriented; e.g., the LUV Airline"	Creative, paradigm breaking; e.g., "Invent"

deeper self-knowledge, as well as deeper understanding of the world around us, and every leadership situation we face.

In our own research, we have further established how these patterns link to leadership, and we call ways of measuring one's preferences for them in an instrument the Focus Energy Balance Indictor (FEBI). You may already have some sense of your favorite pattern; the mini-FEBI assessment (see Exhibit 1) can give you a better idea, and you're welcome to take the full instrument on our website (www.focusleadership.com).

The FEBI gives insight into your pattern order, which you can think of as a staircase of four steps. The lowest step represents your favorite, "Home" pattern—the one that's easiest for you to access. At progressively higher energy levels,

---

EXHIBIT 1. WHICH PATTERNS DO YOU FAVOR?

Although not as reliable or detailed as the full FEBI, this mini-assessment will give you some idea of how the patterns show up in you. It's best to answer the questions first—top of mind—before looking at the scoring.

On a scale of 1 (never) to 10 (always), indicate how true the following statements are for you. A "5" means average; this statement is about as true for you as it is for people in general.

1. I'm conscientious about commitments.
2. I am direct and to the point.
3. My moods go up and down.
4. I love to win.
5. I think life is flux, nothing is fixed.
6. When people are upset, I remain calm and rational.
7. I have many stacks of papers, articles, etc., around my office and home.
8. When faced with obstacles, I push harder.
9. I have a hard time attending to details.
10. When facing a big task, I break it down, and take it one step at a time.
11. I often go back and forth on decisions.
12. I enjoy the energy of networking.

To calculate your totals,
    Add your scores for numbers 2, 4, and 8 for **Driver:** _____
    Add your scores for numbers 1, 6, and 10 for **Organizer:** _____
    Add your scores for numbers 3, 11, and 12 for **Collaborator:** _____
    Add your scores for numbers 5, 7, and 9 for **Visionary:** _____

---

you access each of the other patterns. But if the steps are steep, you may not use those patterns when they're called for. And that's when trouble arises.

"Great with the details, *but* not strategic enough."

"Makes war on the numbers, *but* is hard on relationships."

"Great with people, *but* over-commits and under-delivers."

I read comments like these by the hundreds in the programs I teach where leaders receive 360 degree feedback. Here they face the "*buts*" that have trailed them through their careers, often limiting their satisfaction, effectiveness, and advancement. While we are wise to leverage our natural preferences in the way we lead, the absence or repeated misuse of any of these four essential energies creates gaps in our leadership. These gaps are quickly exposed under the pressures of leading in today's matrix. Here's what they look like:

- **Not Enough Driver**—Inability to focus on top priorities, maintain a sense or urgency, hit targets, cut to the point, or tell it like it is; often perceived as lacking clear direction, ambition, or edge.
- **Not Enough Organizer**—inability to get things done, break large jobs into executable tasks, deliver on time, do things right, and do the right (e.g., ethical) things; often perceived as sloppy and undependable.
- **Not Enough Collaborator**—inability to engage with people, care about and influence them, see both sides of an issue, lighten up, and make work fun; often perceived as rigid, insular, and non-team players.
- **Not Enough Visionary**—inability to think outside the box, leap to novel insights, scan the horizon for what to pay attention to, let go, and sense the flow; often perceived as lacking in imagination or not being strategic enough.

Conversely, every pattern is essential for leading in today's matrix:

- **Driver**: Focusing attention, hitting targets, breaking down barriers
- **Organizer**: Managing disciplined execution, doing the right thing
- **Collaborator**: Enlisting support, reconciling competing perspectives, developing people
- **Visionary**: Thinking outside the box, being agile and open

Taken together and used appropriately, these four energies balance one another and generate the behavioral breadth needed for whole, effective leadership. They're also essential to performing at our best for the long run. We know from research around peak performance that it comes through alternating drive and recovery (Benson, 1975; Loehr & Schwartz, 2003), pushing to our limits and then renewing. In pattern terms, this pulse could be skillful use of the Driver pattern, and then letting go with the Visionary. Or it could be stretching ourselves into our weakest pattern, and then returning to our more comfortable "home" pattern.

That's not to say we have to use each pattern equally; we still do well to play to our strengths, using our preferred patterns most of the time. But if we have—or develop—easy enough access to the other patterns, we'll start to notice when we need them and be able to go there. Akin to the adage, "If your only tool is a hammer, everything looks like a nail," if you're only comfortable in the Driver pattern, everything looks like it needs to be hammered. That's when you start hearing things like: "Makes war on the numbers, *but* is hard on relationships." With greater pattern versatility, you gain greater flexibility in action and avoid the tyranny of the "buts."

If we try to change only in our superficial behaviors—not integrated in body, mind, or spirit—we won't be very effective. I was working once with an Organized Driver, John, who wanted to be more influential with his colleagues. At first John set up a series of perfunctory, three-point agenda-driven meetings with several colleagues, but had no real sense of engaging them. The meetings didn't go well, and he grew discouraged. I was trying to help John find the Collaborator pattern in himself (deeply buried, as you might guess). If he could get into the Collaborator frame of body and mind, truly engage the other person, play in the give-and-take of the exchange, emotionally connect with the other's feelings, listen, and build on the other's ideas, then he'd have a real conversation and a good chance to influence. We weren't trying to make Collaborator his favorite pattern, but just give him enough access to it that he could use it when necessary. The research suggests that one's pattern preference order doesn't change from youth. What does change through practice is the ease of access to our less-preferred patterns. In the stair-step analogy, practice lowers the height between steps. A colleague of mine likens this process to learning a foreign language: "I'll never be mistaken for a native, but at least I can order food in a restaurant and get by."

Now here is the revolutionary possibility of these patterns for leadership development: Because every level is linked by common energies, you can use movement to change mindset, to literally move your leadership to a new level of wholeness and balance. In John's case of wanting easier access to the Collaborator, for example, swinging movements help—as in swinging a golf club, swing dancing, slow-and-easy bicycling, or even just rocking back and forth (as you did in touring the Collaborator pattern earlier). John couldn't get his head around taking swing dancing lessons with his wife, but he was quick to pick up on a new reason to play more golf. Ways of stimulating the senses with the right pattern also help, such as music, art, or other elements in the work environment. John put a couple of rocking chairs in his office—more as a reminder at first. "But it's very relaxing," he noticed, "and gives me more patience when people come into my office." He's hardly a native, but John is easing into the Collaborator enough to get by!

TABLE 2. WAYS OF GAINING EASE IN ANY PATTERN

	Driver	Organizer	Collaborator	Visionary
Work Behaviors	Know your top three priorities Measure something you're doing—and cut it in half Get to the point Set stretch goals Reduce distractions Enforce clarity and action	Make a list Organize your day Make sacred time for planning Break big jobs down into steps Always know your next step Under-promise and over-deliver	Put fun into your day, celebrate Build your network Build or bond a team you're working with See both sides Find your way around obstacles; work indirectly Work through people	Add spontaneity to your day Make time for reflection Brainstorm Widen your perspective (e.g., surf the net, solicit many points of view) Create some chaos, stir things up
Background	Office: Stark and sparse furnishings Music: Rock & Roll, Rap Art: Sharp, high contrast, sports posters, "Winning"	Office: Neat and tidy, a place for everything Music: Classical Art: Still life, perfectly composed, "Quality is…"	Office: fun and colorful, overstuffed furnishings Music: Jazz Art: family photos, comic strip characters, "Hang in there, Baby"	Office: light and airy, harmonious with nature Music: New Age Art: Enigmatic, evocative, outer space posters, "Invent…"
Physical Activities	Movement: thrust, push Running Karate Weightlifting Cardio machine (hard and fast) Kendo, sword work Bicycling (hard and fast) Aggressive sports Skiing (hard and fast) Tennis Racquetball	Movement: shape, hold form Ballet Yoga Meditation Walking Dressage Ceramics Housecleaning Organizing a space Woodworking Needlepoint Anything done step-by-step	Movement: swing, rock Ballroom dance Ice dancing Aikido Golf (the swing) Skating, rollerblading Swimming Bicycling (slow and easy) Skiing (slow and easy) Weaving Bowling (the setup, social aspect)	Movement: hang, drift Tai Chi, Chi Kung Meditation (samadhi) Sailing Hang gliding Scuba diving Snorkeling Archery Photography (in the moment) Being out in nature

Table 2 gives some suggestions for developing easier access to any of the patterns. If you aren't sure which pattern could help you most, consider the pattern that scored lowest for you in the mini-assessment, or think of the most troubling or recurring "but" you've heard in your own leadership, and start with the pattern that would erase it.

So how do these patterns help leaders handle the complex demands of today's matrix? The Driver's determination and the Organizer's ability to get things done have long been valued in organizations—and continue to be indispensable in a matrix. For example, the Driver's energy focuses attention on critical issues and sets clear direction. The Organizer's strengths are called on to break large tasks down into steps that can be executed throughout the matrix and manage the interdependent project plans that link work together.

But it's the other two patterns, the Collaborator and Visionary, that become even more necessary in a matrix than in the hierarchical organizations of old. The Collaborator's gift for engaging and influencing colleagues, rather than relying on authority, becomes the new currency of power in a matrix. Also, this pattern is a natural at seeing both sides of an issue and being able to bounce back and forth, balancing the competing demands of multiple reporting lines. The Visionary comes to the fore its ability to "chill" in the midst of frenetic activity, to "hang" with chaos and ambiguity, rather than try to figure it out or eradicate it. And when it comes to speed, even the Driver's fast action and the Organizer's efficiency are no match for the Visionary's gift for scanning and intuitively leaping to what's most essential.

In total, the patterns are a leader's essential inner team for wholeness, balance, maximum effectiveness, and deep personal satisfaction. Vertically they link body, mind, and spirit, allowing us to integrate our actions with our heartfelt intent, our walk with our talk. Taken together, they cover the breadth of versatile action needed to lead effectively in today's complex matrix. And because they link brawn to brain to behavior, they open up new ways of expanding leadership capacity. Integrating our whole self, we are able to lead in whole, new ways. That's how we meet the challenges of today's matrix: not by speeding up, but by opening up to the fullness of who we are.

References

Benson, H. (1975). *The relaxation response.* Boston, MA: Harvard Business School Press.

Knaster, M. (1996). *Discovering the body's wisdom.* New York: Bantam.

Loehr, J., & Schwartz, T. (2003). *The power of full engagement.* New York: Simon & Schuster.

Rathbone, J. (1936). *Residual neuromuscular hypertension.* New York: Bureau of Publication, Columbia University.

Ginny Whitelaw, Ph.D., is an executive coach, leadership consultant, and co-founder of Focus Leadership. For many years, she has been a principal consultant with the Oliver Wyman Delta Executive Learning Center, a premier leadership development firm, and has served on the adjunct faculty of the Columbia University Senior Executive Program. A biophysicist by training, Dr. Whitelaw worked for ten years at NASA, becoming the deputy manager of the Space Station Program. She has extensive experience in managing large programs and leading for-profit and non-profit organizations. She also has thirty years of experience in Zen and martial arts, holds a fifth degree black belt in Aikido, and is a teacher of Zen meditation. She is the author of *BodyLearning*, and (in collaboration with Betsy Wetzig) *Moved to Greatness: Four Essential Energies of a Whole and Balanced Leader*.

CHAPTER 28

SOMATICS AND LEADERSHIP

Susan Nichols

"All 'graduations' in human development mean the abandonment of a familiar position . . . all growth . . . must come to terms with this fact."

—ERIK H. ERIKSON

"He who feels it knows it more."

—BOB MARLEY

Changing life-long patterns of behavior is difficult. It's a lot easier to write a book about how one needs to be in order to be an effective leader. There are a lot of those out there—many of them very informative. But there are noticeably fewer when it comes to helping us learn the process by which we come to embody those ways of being and acting in the world—the "how" of the how, so to speak.

Goffee and Jones remind us in their book, *Why Should Anyone Be Led by You?*, that leadership is situational, non-hierarchical, and relational. Leadership can (and must) be exhibited at all levels within an organization and it means being able to keenly sense a situation to determine what's needed in the moment to build and maintain connection (relationship) with people in order to fulfill on an endeavor. Further, and very importantly, it requires that leaders authentically embody a wide range of behaviors (commanding, compassionate, casual, authoritative, close, distant, etc.) so that the people they engage with are left with the experience that they are authentic, real, congruent, inspiring, and contactable. Most people are often much more embodied on one end of a behavioral spectrum. How is it that we evolve our patterns and develop greater authentic range as a leader?

The pace of our world is quickening. The pressures and amount of complexity are increasing. We are a world-wide community; there is way more to do than time to do it, and we're being asked to be highly productive in environments in which nothing is predictable. How do we develop employees who can be masterful under these conditions? We suggest that the answer to these developmental questions lies not in reading more books or taking more knowledge into our heads—not that that doesn't have its place, but it falls desperately short when it comes to producing embodied action. Somatics[1] offers a process of development that engages the whole person—the mental, physical, emotional, and spiritual (what we value and care for)—in a way that produces embodiment, that is, that which is "in our body," that we can enact without having to consciously think about it. Throughout this article, we will explore a number of examples that bring to life the process, struggles, and successes of developing newly embodied leadership competencies and one of the foundational practices that makes any learning possible, that is, the ability to let go of what is comfortable and known for the possibility of what we need and want to grow into.

Stepping Up—Developing Leadership Presence

Barbara was a very respected and well-regarded vice president in a large financial institution. She was part of the inner circle of leadership and appreciated for her insights. She had a way about her that was calming, and people liked being around her. When we met, Barbara was being asked to step up to lead a new division for the company, which was a very important new venture. She was going to be reporting to the CEO, taking on the leadership of the entire effort, and sitting on the board of the spinoff division. This promotion required that Barbara "sit at a much bigger table." While she had things to learn about the new business she was stepping into, this was not what challenged her most; she knew her competency in learning a new marketplace. What was more of a "grab" for

---

[1] Somatics comes from the root Greek word "soma," which means "the living body." The discourse of Somatics has been widely shaped and forwarded in the domain of leadership and action by the work of Dr. Richard Strozzi-Heckler of Strozzi Institute (www.strozziinstitute.com). His work with the military now serves as standard leadership training for all U.S. marines and the work inside corporations detailed in *The Leadership Dojo* (release 9/07). The field of somatics touches on the lived internal experience of one's stories, moods, emotions, and sensations; the integrated whole experience of one's mental, physical, emotional, and spiritual bodies.

her was the reality of stepping into the visibility of the president's position and the presence and capacity she would need to embody with the new team she was joining. Until this point, Barbara had been able to lead from a position relatively under the radar. Her division and responsibilities, while important, were not in the main revenue stream of the company and therefore were not in the spotlight. She was recognized for her talent, smarts, and leadership potential though and promoted into this new exciting opportunity.

Barbara is not unlike many people who are good at what they do and then are asked to step up to the next level of management. With that comes more responsibility, bigger stakes, more rigorous conversations, more senior-level people you're engaging with, leading versus managing, etc. She needed to grow her leadership presence and play a bigger game, that is, interact with, have conversations with, and take stands with people (in this case all men) whom she previously had given power to. Now, knowing (intellectually) that she had to do this and being able to do this (in her body/whole self) were like living on two different planets.

Barbara lived in a story that other people had more to contribute than she did. This was one of the things that made her good at her job as the head of a service division. She was in her fifties, which meant that she was brought up in a time when women played more "behind the scenes" roles and did not challenge the status quo. She was very competent at what she did, in sort of a "good girl" way, that is, she would be, it was expected. She was cultured to do her job, do it well, keep things together, and not necessarily to rock the boat. This is not to heavily psychoanalyze Barbara, but to demonstrate that who/how she was in the world had a history that literally and figuratively shaped her. Barbara was average in height but she "kept herself small." She was very contained and moved genteelly. Again, this was partly what people liked about her presence and found easy to relate to, but it was not the presence that was being called for in stepping up to this new position's responsibilities. She needed to access a range of behavior that was unpracticed for her.

You Are What You Practice

"In the heat of the game, we play to the level of our practice."

—RICHARD STROZZI-HECKLER

We relate to the notion of practice most commonly in the realms of sports or the development of some artistic talent, such as dance, music, theatre, or the art. We practice doing something so that we get it into our bodies and we don't have to think about it. But we also practice ways of being, thinking, and interacting in the world; we just aren't aware that we are actually practicing something all the time. This is a new way to conceive of the notion of "practice" that offers a lot of possibility when it comes to developing new leadership competencies.

A "practice," in this sense, is whatever it is you do over and over again such that you come to embody that practice; it's what comes out of you without you even thinking about it and, often, in the way we're talking about it, we are blind to it. An example of this is the person who always says "yes" to requests. This may sound extreme, but I'm sure you all know someone like this . . . it's the person you call when you need help painting your house. He or she finds it very difficult to say "no" to people—bosses, co-workers, friends, family, etc. Another example is the person who always has a reason for why something won't work—a project will never work, the goals will never be met, management will never change, my life is hard and people do it to me, and so forth. These people "practice" a certain mood of defeatism and victimization. We all practice a certain way that we handle (or not) stress when we feel it in our lives. We will talk more about this later when we look at the foundational practice of centering and how to manage ourselves most effectively in stress. The questions for us all to reflect on is: "What are my practices?" and "Do they align with who/how I need to be in order to be the leader I need and want to be?"

Barbara had "practiced" doing her job well, keeping things in order, and staying under the radar. When she thought about being in the kinds of meetings she was going to be in, countering her senior colleagues and challenging the board, standing in front of her organization extending her presence in setting a vision, and so forth, she became very anxious, her face flushed, her stomach contracted, her eyes widened, and she stopped breathing (obviously, not literally, but her breath became very shallow and high in her chest). She became nervous, her voice lost depth, and, in addition to thinking negative thoughts about herself, she retreated into the story that "others are more important/better and I have nothing to say." She did have insights to share though; she was very excited about this opportunity, cared deeply about the opportunity and the people she would work with. She had ideas about where to take the organization, but in these moments her "body" deceived her. She needed to learn "in her body" to make some new moves—to be with a lot more energy moving through her, energy of excitement, fear, desire, possibility, anxiousness, commitment, and so on, and still remain effective in her actions.

The Body We Are Versus the Body We Have

We live, breathe, and take action in the world in a body—a body that is more than just the physical flesh and bones—a body that has energy and life running through it and has a history to it—that has lived certain experiences and been literally and figuratively "shaped" by these events and circumstances. An example of this is the person who lives in the story that "the weight of the world is on my shoulders" and literally his or her shoulders slump slightly forward. These people most often have "weighted," serious looks on their faces. Or the person who is a perfectionist and exhibits a certain (figurative) "rigidness" in the way they interact with others. You've also probably experienced someone who moves with an unimaginable grace—a person who stands tall, is comfortable in his or her own skin, and always seems aware of and in touch with what is most important. We've all learned certain ways of being. We are holistic beings, not independent parts. My mind is not separate from my body; my emotions don't happen independent of my body; what I care deeply about (spiritual) lives in and through my body. The person you are, the way that you are, the Self that you are is inseparable from your body.

Over the course of my working with her, Barbara became aware of both the value and limitations of the "body" she was and took on some new practices for the sake of being successful in her new role. Her commitment was to develop the embodied competence to stand in the face of a lot bigger energy, power, and challenge—the energy of her deep care for the company, its employees, and the future she saw for it; the energy of confrontation with her colleagues or CEO in standing up for what she believed was right; and so on—while she maintained her connection to herself, her ground, her competence, her colleagues, and her vision. For any of you who have made a similar leap in development, you know that this is far more than an intellectual exercise. She had to literally develop the "body" that could have that kind of energy running through it (fear, anxiousness, care) and not be ambushed by it.

Embodying New Competence Through Practice

"Knowledge is only rumor until it is in the muscle."

—ASIAN PROVERB

The beginning part of learning this new capacity involved becoming aware of her historical "shaping" in terms of the story ("Others have more to contribute than I do"), the mood ("Do it right"), and the physical sensations ("Stay small, contain yourself, contract, be under the radar"). She could then begin to see all of the ways this showed up in her life (how she "practiced" this at home, at work, at the grocery store, etc.) and begin practicing over time being more direct in conversations, stepping into the limelight, having attention on her, challenging her husband and colleagues more, and practicing the behaviors she was working to embody.

Additionally, she took on two somatic practices. These were practices that engaged her whole body, her whole self—physical, mental, emotional, and spiritual—against the background of a commitment to develop these new competencies. The first practice was to do a certain repeated movement kata (a series of movements) in an exaggerated, "big" way. In other words, if she was "comfortable" (practiced) doing the movement at one level of "volume" so to speak, we asked her to exaggerate the movement size by two to three times. This meant taking bigger steps, taking up more room, allowing her arms to extend fully and going at a faster pace than she was used to. The practice was intended to have her experience taking up space, being the center of attention, having bigger energy running through her, and maintaining her breath, relaxing her body, softening her eyes, opening her attention, and keeping connected to the ground throughout. Just engaging in this kind of movement brought up the stories and emotional challenge that she experienced when she was in those kinds of circumstances or situations because her body was used to "pulling in" and being small. She didn't feel like herself, she didn't like it, she felt uncomfortable, she felt unsafe and on the edge of a combination of anger, fight, and tears. Inside of these sensations, stories, and emotions, she practiced staying grounded, relaxed, confident, and connected to what she cared about, which was developing her presence and capacity to be successful in her new role.

The second practice she took on was working with a wooden sword, from the practice of aikido,[2] called a bokken. The bokken practice in this case was working two developmental edges. First, just by putting a sword in her hand, it extended her presence and made her "bigger" than she was comfortable with. This, in and of itself, was a challenge and built on the first practice we described. Secondly, a sword represents a symbol of power and cuts right to the heart of things. It's a great practice for developing the ability to be direct, succinct, clear, concise, graceful, and complete in conversation.

Barbara took on both of these practices daily. They didn't take a lot of time (fifteen minutes in the morning). But when she engaged in them sincerely against the background of her care and commitment to embody new leadership competencies, she began to notice over time (and so reported her colleagues) that she was stepping more quickly into conversations that were previously challenging;

---

[2] Aikido is a Japanese martial art founded in the early 1900s by Morihei Ueshiba. It is a non-violent, non-competitive martial practice geared toward the development of the ability to manage oneself in the midst of chaos and conflict and maintain/move to a peaceful resolve. It is considered the martial art of peace.

she began to step more easily to the front of the room to speak to her board and employee base; and she found herself more available, present, and connected to herself, others, and what she cared about in the context of large public forums. She connected her mind, body, spirit, and emotions in a practice over time that enabled the shifting of an old embodied way of being.

Foundational Somatic Practice—Centering

When Barbara engaged in the bokken and movement practices, her old stories, moods, emotions, and sensations (that is, her body/self) triggered her. Her fifty-year history wanted to "shape" her in a way that would not produce the results she was looking for in this new leadership role. She needed a practice that helped bring her back to a centered, present state where she could make a different choice (versus going into the conditioned way of responding that she had—contracting and being small). She had to learn in her body how to maintain her composure and remain present and extended when she was uncomfortable.

Centering is the foundational somatic practice for developing the capacity to be in choice versus run by our unconscious physical, mental, and emotional reactions. Being centered allows us the best possibility for effective action in the moment; it makes possible the notion of "situational" leadership. When we are off-center, we are in some form of reaction and, therefore, not fully present to access how we need to be in the moment to produce the result we intend. It is the "practice of all practices" because it is the physical, mental, and emotional experience of being present (in the moment/aware), open (to possibilities, ideas, other people, and choice), and connected (to self, others, and what is important). It is the doorway into being able to manage ourselves effectively in the midst of stress, anger, discomfort, change, transition, difficult conversations, learning something new, and so forth, and is the foundation for developing a leadership presence.

The practice and embodiment of center enables us to be with (tolerate, breathe through, and open to) the sensations in our bodies that accompany the stories, moods, and emotions of what makes us uncomfortable. And, as we have said in this article, it is not an intellectual concept: It is a somatic, whole-body experience that one feels and others can see and experience. When taken in as a whole, the diagram in Figure 1 provides an overview of the physical, mental, and emotional states associated with being centered.

The practice of centering is a life-long practice. We get knocked off-center, "grabbed" by life all the time—things change, stuff happens, bosses call, kids get sick, people cut you off on the highway, FedEx doesn't deliver the package when you need it, events don't go as planned, we become nervous, we miss planes, you

FIGURE 1. OVERVIEW OF BEING CENTERED

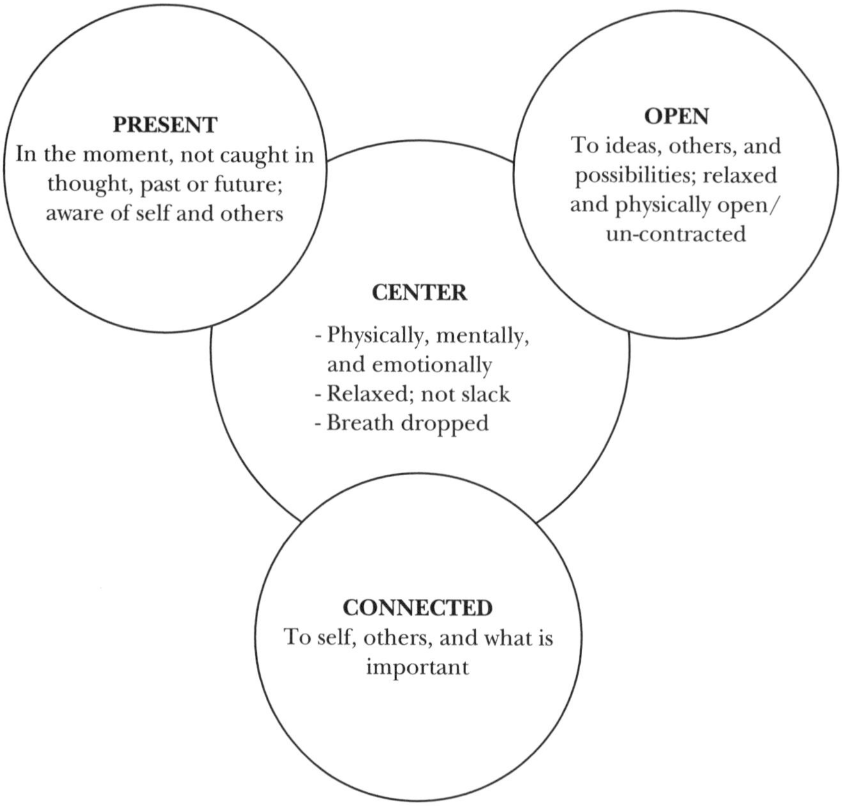

PRESENT
In the moment, not caught in
thought, past or future;
aware of self and others

OPEN
To ideas, others, and
possibilities; relaxed
and physically open/
un-contracted

CENTER
- Physically, mentally,
  and emotionally
- Relaxed; not slack
- Breath dropped

CONNECTED
To self, others, and what is
important

receive the promotion ("grabs" aren't always negative). A "grab" is anything that takes us off-center, out of the moment, away from our focus, and into a reactive state that "has us more than we have it." The practice is becoming aware of when we are off-center—that is, lost in thought, not present, worrying, tense, angry, frustrated, overly excited, in some kind of state unproductive to what will serve us where we are—and being able to, through the practice of centering, bring ourselves back to a productive, open, choice-full state.

Experiencing Center—The Practice

The place to begin to understand the experience of "center" is with the physical body. This is not to imply that centering is a solely physical process. It is not. A person who is centered is mentally, physically, and emotionally present, open, and connected. However, we are generally much more "practiced" at being in our heads/thinking and are often out of touch with our physical and emotional bodies. The physical state of being centered is one in which the physical body is relaxed but not slack; open and un-contracted versus tense, contracted, or rigid; and energetically aligned along the three spatial dimensions of *length* (up and down, feet to top of head), *width* (side to side), and *depth* (front to back). This means that:

- The head rests comfortably on the spine,
- The chin is level,
- The body is upright but not straining to be tall,
- The breath is dropped into the lower abdomen,
- The head, shoulders, and hips are vertically aligned,
- The knees are unlocked, and
- The skeletal system is actually supporting the physical structure versus the muscles being engaged—eyes, jaw, shoulders, belly/abdomen, pelvic region, legs are all un-contracted.

When we encounter some form of stress (learning something new, being in the discomfort zone, having a difficult conversation, etc.), our bodies react. Often, we are unaware of the physical reactions we have to stress. It is more difficult to think and be in relationships with others when we are contracted. When we relax the contraction, we have more possibilities available to us. People engage differently with someone that is stressed/off-center versus relaxed, present, and openly engaged. We suggest that you take on the practice of centering in your work and everyday life; it will make an immediate impact on your health, vitality, and effectiveness.

Begin by paying attention to your physical body in the way we have described—aligning along the dimensions of length, width, and depth, dropping/ deepening your breath and relaxing along the vertical line (eyes, jaw, shoulders, abdomen, legs). Practice paying attention to where you contract in your body in times of stress or challenge and notice what happens to your breath. For example, some people tighten their eyes and faces and find later that they suffer from headaches. Others clamp their jaws unknowingly or experience shoulder and neck problems or stomach ulcers or digestion problems from holding stress in those areas. When taking on any new practice, it's helpful to have a specific time that you engage in the practice so that you remember to do it and it becomes embodied over time. Since centering is a life-long practice to be engaged in all the time, it's useful in the beginning to choose a specific event that will trigger your awareness. A few suggestions are any or all of the following:

- Every time you walk into a meeting,
- Before you answer the phone,
- Every time you interact with a person you have a hard time with,
- In the morning as you go to work, at lunch, and again in the evening before you transition to your home life.
- Set a recurring reminder in your calendar.

Summary

We're suggesting that the ultimate effectiveness of a leader is in the "Self" that he or she is—the congruency and impact of "how" he or she is in the world.

"Who (how) a person is will ultimately determine if their brains, talents, competencies, energy, effort, deal-making abilities, and opportunities will succeed."

DR. HENRY CLOUD, *INTEGRITY*

"Who (how) you are speaks so loudly I can't hear what you're saying."

RALPH WALDO EMERSON

And that "how" you are comes out of and from your "body"— not just your physical body, but the somatic whole of how you are, the experience that I have of you, the mood that you are, the way you interact with others, the dignity that you are (or not), the actions you take (or not). In our example, Barbara had to learn through her whole body (her story, mood, emotions, and sensations) to be able to take new actions and interact more powerfully in order to be effective in her new leadership position. This kind of development doesn't happen overnight, in a seminar, or by reading a book. It happens over time through intentional practice.

At a time when things are getting more complex, faster, and more intense, and the success of a brand is being driven out to the customer service rep on the phone (one bad experience equals one lost customer and potentially many more through communicating via the Internet), we need to be able to develop leaders at all levels of the organization who can manage themselves effectively in the midst of stress, chaos, and change—employees who can have a lot going on, be stressed, and still slow down to create relationship in any moment; employees who can experience failure, think on their feet, and move generatively to take the next productive step; employees who can manage themselves in the "discomfort zone" and lead others in the process.

Somatics offers a process of self-development that acknowledges that we are more than just intellectual beings. Learning new embodied behaviors means triggering the old. This challenges more than just our intellect; it challenges how we've known ourselves to be. Evolving old behaviors and ways that have historically shaped us requires that we consciously take on whole-body practices over time. Developing ourselves to be able to be fully present with the person on the other end of the line, listen wholly, and manage ourselves skillfully when things inevitably become challenging, in a way that allows us to produce continued connection and relationship, requires that we learn through our whole bodies—our mental, physical, emotional, and spiritual selves. Somatic practices take this from being an intellectual exercise to a holistic process for producing sustainable results.

Susan Nichols is a coach and consultant specializing in a somatic approach within her leadership development practice. She works with individuals and teams to take on the practices to embody their leadership potential and coordinate effectively in action. She is a master somatic coach and teacher for Strozzi Institute, www.strozziinstitute.com, the premier training institute for embodied leadership. She brings over twenty years of her own experience as a leader in the private sector, is a committed student of aikido, a life-long athlete and student of personal development.

CHAPTER 29

LEARNINGS FROM WORLD-CLASS ATHLETES IN MANAGING PERFORMANCE: ACHIEVING PERSONAL LEADERSHIP EXCELLENCE THROUGH P⁶PROP

Christian Marcolli

Working with world-class athletes, as well as with executives, has led me to formulate an answer to what I see as the key question for anyone seeking excellence in what they do: What does it take to be able to perform consistently at one's personal best in an ever-changing environment? Whether the pursuit of excellence manifests in that millimetre difference in a serve, or leading a board through a crisis meeting, there are six key components that together make up the P⁶PROP (The Six P's [Passion, Precision, Perception, Peace, Presence, Persistence] Personal Resource Optimizing Performance) model of Personal Leadership Excellence. P⁶PROP is designed to help to turn great corporate leaders into excellent "business champions."

A Holistic View of Excellence

In business the term "excellence" has been applied for many years concerning many different contexts. Almost every publication on business excellence focuses on two questions namely: (1) What enables you to become great at what you do? and (2) What allows you to perform at the highest levels of excellence? While there is no doubt that discussions on high performance must include these two aspects,

I believe that the concept of excellence should be viewed in a more holistic way. The major question regarding excellence is not so much how you become great at what you do, but rather additional dimensions reflecting the whole person:

- What does it take to harness your full potential in your chosen field?
- What does it take to perform at your personal best consistently over years regardless of changes to your environment and circumstances?

The P^6PROP model of Personal Leadership Excellence directly links the concept of excellence to one's individual potential for performance. This leads to a new, more holistic understanding of excellence: it is about harnessing one's potential as fully and consistently as possible. That is the only way to become great and stay at the top. In other words: Even though situations and environments change constantly, excellent performers become and remain great as a direct consequence of their passion for and pursuit of excellence. This passion and ongoing quest differentiates the business champion of today from the corporate leader of yesterday.

Why Do Business Champions Have to Display Excellence?

The corporate world has become an arena that demands high performance, and this will only intensify in the future. Inspired by the work of Jack Groppel (2000) and Jim Loehr and Tony Schwartz (2003), I have worked to transfer insights from my experience as a sport psychologist with some of the world's best athletes to my work as an executive coach for corporate leaders. Through long-term work with excellent athletes who were, and often still are, the best and most successful in their fields, I have found astonishing parallels across the various disciplines. These parallels stand out despite the diversity of individual differences and personality traits, as well as the factor of whether athletes are training for individual or team sports. The building blocks of excellence are always the same, and they comprise the dimensions that make athletes successful and empower them to stay at the top of their sports over time. Once these building blocks are understood, as is the way they interact, it becomes easy to assess whether one is capable of excellence or not.

The corporate leader of many *Harvard Business Review* reviews (1998) has evolved into a "business champion" whose success as a leader depends on his or her pursuit of personal excellence. In the future, business champions will have to be able to perform consistently at a world-class level, and their performance will need to be comparable to that of the very best athletes. They will be exposed to heavy competition (within and outside their organizations), have to manage an immense workload, and still be able to stay calm and focused under pressure in order to get the best out of their people and themselves. These pressures will grow even more in the future. Pressure will come from matrix corporate structures with increasingly complex operating environments, leaner teams, enhancements in information technology that increase the speed and volume of business, while under budget constraints to perform ever faster yet always delivering high quality. In addition, business champions are expected not only to deliver outstanding personal performance on a regular basis, but also to achieve top results with their departments or teams by providing effective leadership.

Meeting these high standards consistently and reliably requires more than "a favorable phase" or "everything just coming together right now"—it requires personal leadership excellence.

Personal leadership excellence describes the basic mental attitude that is central to building a successful professional career. It involves the determination to invest all one's efforts into getting the best out of oneself, one's staff, and the situation one is in. For executives, the desired predictability, control, and constancy is central to the concept of success; it is the basis from which they deliver peak performance.

The P⁶PROP Model of Personal Leadership Excellence

The P^6PROP model of Personal Leadership Excellence provides business champions with a framework within which they can learn to understand themselves, their way forward, the rules of the road, and the tools they need to accumulate to arrive successfully.

Personal leadership excellence is the key to continuous high performance and effective action as a business champion—to be the best you possibly can be all day, every day. If excellence can be achieved on a daily basis, the chances of becoming great at what you do increase dramatically. The earlier in a career that this is applied, the higher the chances that a business champion will make it to the top and stay there. The components of P^6PROP are discussed in the following paragraphs.

P^1: Passion—*Are You in the Right Game?*

The prerequisite of excellence is passion, and that is only present if you are in a game that is right for you as an individual. Passion is crucial because it gives you the energy for creativity, innovation, and perfection, as well as the power to persevere in difficult situations. Excellent performers are absolutely convinced that they are in the right place doing what they can do best. For business champions, this implies they are in just the right job, function, or role and that leadership is their game and therefore they have the dedication and commitment for continuous personal improvement.

P^2: Precision—*Have You Mastered the Techniques of the Game?*

The second component of personal leadership excellence is precision. Excellent performers have managed to automate the skills necessary to perform at their level. This provides them with the resources to assess situations accurately and apply the right skills at the right time. In addition, excellent performers are able to apply alternatives and tactics depending on the situation. They understand the systems and politics around them, but do not let them negatively interfere with their performance. On top, they are able to apply all the skills with a high level of quality, but also with the right timing. The degree of precision they apply determines their potential for execution, in and with this, the level of performance they can achieve.

In the corporate world, as a business champion, this means having the necessary job skills to perform in a given role or function as well as the necessary leadership and management skills. The business champion must also be able to identify and work with the dynamic of the system as well as the politics in play.

One factor that determines how quickly you can acquire P^2 (Precision) is how fast a learner you are (that is, your adaptability)—especially if you are required to change role, function, level, or even your job, which in today's corporate world can happen at very short notice. This is clearly recognized as an influencing factor in the learning process, but is viewed as a stable factor of an individual's personal make-up and will therefore not be discussed further.

P^3: Perception—*Do You Have a Stable Environment That You Fully Trust?*

Another component of personal leadership excellence is perception—how you perceive your external environment. It is the ability to identify which people you can trust fully (at work and in private), the knowledge that you have the full support of a handful of people, and that you are loved as a person no matter what happens to you (job loss or any other issue). High performers are exposed to their limits and need an emotional and social "safety net" where they can share their inner thoughts and feelings.

This is crucial to peak performance because it provides the strong feeling of emotional belonging and bonding. The relationships that form this safety net are a source of honest and open feedback about how one is perceived, which, in turn, helps one to grow continuously. This, ultimately, allows a person to develop the ability to trust and let go.

P^4: Peace—*Do You Know Yourself Inside Out and Appreciate Your Uniqueness?*

The fourth component of personal leadership excellence is inner peace. Put simply, inner peace is being in harmony with yourself and your perspective on life. From a more technical viewpoint, inner peace is a result of a high degree of self-awareness and self-acceptance. Knowing and accepting yourself allows you to be grounded within yourself, to remain confident, and to develop optimal behaviors of personal effectiveness. This level of self-insight means that you, the individual, must first know your personal preferences, your strengths, and your weaknesses, as well as how you come across.

Then you must clearly identify your "good habits" for sourcing and managing your energy (physical, emotional, and mental) and know when and where you have to make an effort to stay in control of your impulses. This involves developing a complete set of behavioral alternatives for situations that require responses that are not a standard part of your behavioral preferences.

Finally, in order to reach inner peace, it is important that you reflect on and appreciate your personal history and that you have a clear understanding of your vision, where you want to go, and what you want to achieve.

P^5: Presence—*Are You Authentic?*

Presence is the fifth component of personal leadership excellence. Presence is one of the most admired characteristics of excellent performers. Based on the four underlying components of personal leadership excellence, excellent performers have the confidence to be authentic and the courage to be unique and do things in their own way. They can live and show their passion as well as harness it as necessary.

Presence allows performers to fully engage and connect with people in any given situation. It gives them the ability to focus on and be completely in the moment and behave absolutely authentically. This means they act honestly, instinctively, and, as a result, display charisma.

P^6: Persistence—*Are You Disciplined with Good Habits?*

The final component of personal leadership excellence is persistence. What impresses me most about world-class performers is their ability to reproduce excellent performance over and over again. Over the long term, peak performance is exhausting. This last dimension of peak performance addresses the ability to recharge energy on a continuous basis; excellent performers constantly work against the exhaustion factor. They are champions in executing "good habits." They follow tailor-made routines and rituals designed for maintaining their physical condition, for controlling their breath, diet, and sleep needs, and they have efficient ways of managing stress and anxiety. In addition, they maintain a consciously applied balance between performance and recuperation, that is, they are able to switch off from their work on a regular basis. All this together gives them not only the necessary basis of emotional stability to perform consistently in extreme situations, but also the focus to experience quality time and interactions within and beyond their jobs.

Excellent performers call on this emotional stability when they experience failure ("You cannot always be a champion, but you can always behave like one") as well as when they experience success—they are able to resist the temptations of success such as a sense of complacency.

PROP: *Personal Resource Optimizing Performance*

PROP stands for **P**ersonal **R**esource **O**ptimizing **P**erformance, and P^6PROP can best be visualized as the six blades of a propeller—each corresponding to a P component—that provide maximum thrust and forward drive when angled optimally. The effect of the six blades is not cumulative per se but a weighted additive, and to be at your best all the blades must work together.

The way each blade is angled determines whether that dimension has a positive impact on your performance, a neutral, or a derailing, negative impact. The components of the P^6PROP model are interrelating, and thus the component scores from P^1 through to P^6 are key to understanding the overall P^6PROP score and the business champion's overall potential for excellent performance.

The P^6PROP Inventory

The P^6PROP Inventory, which can be self-administered or given to others, can be completed by individuals close to the person being profiled (a peer, report, or manager) and a person in a position of trust outside work. A score is calculated for each dimension and sub-scale. By weighting the answers and combining the individual P scores following a validated algorithm, an overall P^6PROP score and profile is created, allowing the individual and coach insight on each dimension.

The Goal of Personal Leadership Excellence: Harnessed Passion

The ultimate behavioral consequence and goal of personal leadership excellence is "Harnessed Passion." This means that a business champion is passionate about what he or she does, has the necessary skills to perform at a high and effective level, works within an environment that allows him or her to perform and grow, leverages inner peace through being in harmony with him- or herself, has a strong authentic presence, and is able to reproduce peak performance on a regular basis because he or she is persistent in recuperating his energy. Figure 1 illustrates the

FIGURE 1. THE P⁶PROP MODEL OF PERSONAL LEADERSHIP EXCELLENCE—OPTIMAL SCORE (HARNESSED PASSION)

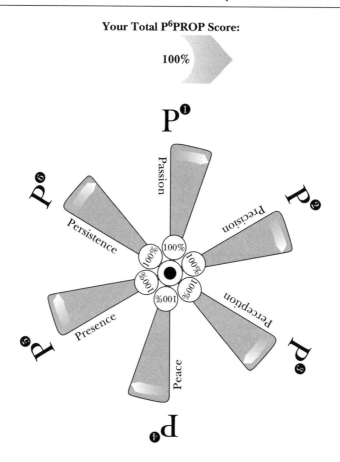

optimal level of Harnessed Passion with the corresponding scores in the P^6PROP Model of Personal Leadership Excellence.

P^6PROP in Action

The pattern most often found in beginning work with corporate leaders is that a number of the six components are well developed, while others are neutral, and some are low. Figure 2 shows an example of how a diagnostic P^6PROP profile might look.

FIGURE 2. EXAMPLE OF THE P^6PROP MODEL OF PERSONAL LEADERSHIP EXCELLENCE AS A DIAGNOSTIC TOOL

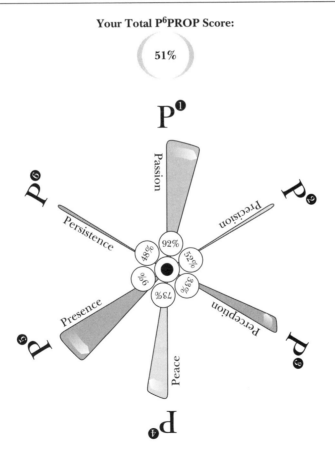

In the above example, the client scored high for passion (92 percent), meaning that he was clearly in the right job and position. It was also obvious that he had a rather high degree of self-awareness, which gave him inner peace (73 percent). However, when it came to understanding his impact on others, he was unsure about how he came across, especially when he was under pressure. Regarding precision, it turned out that he was not at the top of his game—he was able to perform averagely well, but not to excel (52 percent).

But the three areas that were actively working against him were perception (33 percent) and presence (9 percent) and persistence (48 percent). He did not have a stable environment, and he felt he was on his own with no one he could trust. He did not have the kind of relationships that would have allowed him to feel appreciated and loved (emotional and social safety-net), that would also have provided a source of feedback on how he was perceived. All of this was having a negative impact on his self-confidence. At work, he over-compensated for his low self-confidence by trying to identify behaviors that made his colleagues successful, and then he copied them. The result was that his behavior was no longer perceived as authentic or genuine. Although quite self-aware in regard to his own strengths and weaknesses, he had little presence and did not make a positive impact on people. It was clear that his lack of perception was holding him back from transforming his self-awareness and inner peace into authenticity because he was afraid that he would not be accepted and supported when being himself.

In addition, his score in persistence was at a lower level (48 percent). Although he was having normal sleeping routines and he was not smoking or drinking alcohol in an excessive manner, he was not maintaining a healthy lifestyle in other aspects—in terms of physical activity, he was not following any kind of regular fitness program. He did not have an established stress management routine and as a result often felt tired and wasn't always fully alert in important meetings.

The client's total P^6PROP Score (51 percent) indicated that, despite his high level of passion for his job, he had not developed the other components to the extent that they were working for him in order to perform excellently on a regular basis. In fact, the combination of all the P-components indicated that the thrust for personal leadership excellence was neutral and therefore not supporting him displaying excellence and helping him to be a business champion.

The client's P^6PROP profile identified his strengths, as well as neutral and low-performing areas. This diagnosis allowed me as his coach to clearly identify and prioritize the areas of concern—presence, perception, persistence, precision, peace—and plan the coaching process accordingly.

References

Groppel, J. (2000). *The corporate athlete.* Hoboken, NJ: John Wiley & Sons.

Harvard Business Review on Leadership (1998). Boston, MA: Harvard Business School Press.

Loehr, J., & Schwartz, T. (2003). *The power of full engagement. Managing energy, not time is the key to high performance and personal renewal.* New York: The Free Press.

Dr. Christian Marcolli works as an executive coach, consultant, lecturer, and sport psychologist. His focus is on the nature of leadership as well as on strategies designed to foster and achieve peak performance under difficult, changing conditions. He holds a doctorate in applied psychology and was a professional athlete. He has extensive experience as a sport psychologist for a number of world-class athletes.

CHAPTER 30

THE SHAPING OF SUCCESSFUL CAREERS

Norman Walker

We all intellectually understand that our success at work is far more than the skill sets we bring and is the outcome of our diversity of experiences, our interactions with colleagues, and—very importantly—our bosses, the situations we have faced, and how we have dealt with adversity. We know that our success involves quite a lot of luck, being fortunate to be in the right place at the right time, having a boss who saw something in us we were perhaps unaware of. We also know that the path of a successful career rarely moves smoothly upward. It is more often a path that takes detours and side turnings, and occasionally goes backward. It is also very rarely clear in terms of its direction, bringing to mind the old saying that it is better to travel hopefully than to arrive. Indeed the energy and effort placed by some companies in trying to anticipate and plan career paths with the certainty that their predecessors forty years ago were able to do is thus rather surprising.

I am not suggesting that companies should be anything other than passionate and wholly committed in their pursuit of developing people—just that the acceleration of organizational change within a company, even before we consider the impact of external drivers of change, which can range from technological to the arrival of Private Equity, necessitates development not for specific positions but as part of organizational capability building and a preparedness to deal with change and its accompanying uncertainties.

These are some of the themes that run through much of the leadership literature, which places so much emphasis on a range of competencies needed to achieve success and which so many companies blandly follow with exhaustive inventories of how to be successful in their companies. I would suggest that much of this work, thorough and professional as it is, does not really reach the fundamental issues that drive the acceleration of development at a personal level.

In the book *Leadership Passages*, Dotlich, Noel, and Walker were attempting to understand what it was about successful leaders that had allowed them to negotiate key professional passages, for example, the first time they assumed the role of a manager or the first time they became a general manager or the first time they worked abroad. These are very common transitions, but they wondered whether there was a common thread among successful managers and, if so, what it was.

This was the genesis of the book, but what became clear as the first of some seventy-five CEO interviews took place was that there was a very different dimension to these successful careers that was being emphasized repeatedly: Their success had been shaped not only by their jobs and career paths but just as much by factors and influences outside the workplace, their families and friends, the emotionally charged events of divorce, death, and serious illness. These were the events that were shaping successful leaders. And one further uncomfortable event—failure. This was brought home to the authors in an early interview with a very successful, high-profile CEO of a large company who was profiling his top team. As he spoke, he outlined their background and experiences. It was an impressive group. He was then asked whether there was a common characteristic that they all shared. He paused and replied: "At one point or another, each one of us has been fired."

The authors thereafter took a different direction and considered both the professional and personal transitions people face if they work and live long enough.

As Table 1 suggests, the passages shown can serve as a roadmap to describe the likely events faced by people in their careers. Contrary to conventional wisdom, and certainly contrary to where most corporations place their efforts in developing people, there is a lot more to managerial development than work assignments, crucial as they are. The combination of diversity and adversity of experience, in combination with personal and professional experiences, drives leadership learning and personal growth. This also requires a leader to reflect on those experiences. Unfortunately, corporations rarely encourage this.

While I was working recently with a group of senior HR leaders, my colleagues and I put this to the test, asking them to reflect on the pivotal developmental points in their careers to date. When they started to recount their stories, it was most often with the job or assignment. A significant promotion within the same company but to a different country, a new assignment the individual felt he or she

TABLE 1. LEADERSHIP PASSAGES

	Career Work	Life Relationships (Family)
Adversity	Failure/difficulty at work or in leading others	Personal upheaval, death, divorce, loss of meaning
Diversity	Range of interesting stimulation projects, assignments, and roles	Breadth of life experience: living in unique places, family, culture

was not ready for in terms of experience, or a new job that felt like a stretch—and on arrival the new boss was taken ill, leaving this individual in charge of a very difficult labor relations situation.

These were the usual professional challenges, but when we probed further to understand why these situations were so demanding, the personal side emerged very strongly.

For example, the individual transferred abroad felt extremely vulnerable in a foreign country, although she spoke the language, as she missed the network, relationships, and support structure—but crucially, she had a very ill mother back home who was a constant source of worry to her.

The leader who had to face the extremely demanding labor relations situation was not just dealing with a professional challenge, but it became extremely personal and quite literally close to home, as he was being targeted with abuse and threats from the militant wing of the trade union he was dealing with.

So we see that the most demanding of challenges often are accompanied by two other factors. First, there is the psychological and emotional component of the challenge and second, and directly related, the very real possibility of failure.

On this second point it is interesting to understand how much we do to put ourselves under this pressure. In talking to leaders about the need to accelerate the development of their talent, I often ask them whether they have ever entered a new job and not felt fully confident about their ability to rise to the challenge and succeed. Most self-aware leaders will acknowledge this. The message here is that, while they may not have been fully confident, someone, normally their immediate boss, most certainly did have that confidence and trust in them. Their bosses believed they could succeed or would never have appointed them. That is not to say that there was not some risk attached and the possibility of failing is a specter that could emerge.

The next question we asked the leaders was how often they take risks to develop their talent. Are they being cautious—like the high-flying marketing executive who was asked what experiences would be necessary to qualify someone to do his job? He reflected carefully on the question and then began to list the experiences he believed would be essential to give someone the requisite experience. We added up the years necessary, and in his case he would have had to start work at the age of fourteen to meet his own criteria. This example underlines the propensity leaders have to overstate the experience required and underestimate the amount of stretch proven professionals can take in growing into new assignments.

In thinking about "stretch" to go into a position, I would like to share with you the case of Thomas Ebeling, the CEO of Novartis Pharmaceuticals. Ebeling is a psychologist by education, and his early career was in fast-moving consumer goods companies, where he had a very rapid rise, becoming the PepsiCo General Manager for Germany before joining the Consumer Health Division of Novartis, initially managing a number of businesses and then as head of the division. In 1999 he was moved to the flagship Pharmaceutical Division, initially as COO but within a matter of months as CEO. Today his division of some 54,000 employees has revenues of over $22 billion and an operating income of $6.7 billion. In every year since he took over responsibility, top and bottom line have grown by double digits.

How many bosses would have taken the risk of appointing a thirty-eight-year-old to their flagship business? Perhaps a few. How many would have appointed a consumer marketer to such a scientific business who had no scientific background and was certainly not trained as a medical doctor? Very, very few.

Clearly this was an audacious appointment by Daniel Vasella, the chairman and CEO of Novartis. I would venture to suggest that Vasella, who had enjoyed a similarly striking career acceleration, from being a medical doctor to running a significant pharmaceutical company in a matter of only a few years, was more open to taking the risk with others.

At the time of the appointment, the water cooler gossip was that Ebeling would surely fail—knowing nothing of the science, never mind the other complexities of the pharmaceutical industry. That he has been so extraordinarily successful is a testament to Vasella's instinct, judgment, and risk aversion and to the exceptional qualities that Ebeling has shown in mastering a new business area, building a team on which he is not the subject expert, and a good old-fashioned focus on execution.

In passing, both Vasella and Ebeling display one characteristic that seems to be common among the most successful leaders: an appetite for learning and willingness to test new boundaries almost on a daily basis.

Most people don't think of events such as divorce, serious illness, loss of a loved one, problems with adolescent children, or even financial difficulties as having anything to do with leadership. These tend to be categorized as private matters that, if discussed at work at all, are dealt with very superficially. It is rare for leaders to share their feelings on these issues and how much upheaval these events are having or have had on their lives. To do so would be seen as signs of weakness in the corporate world, where professionalism is defined as the absence of emotion and where the ups and downs that are a reality in all our lives have no impact or relevance to our work performance.

This deeply engrained attitude, which is particularly prevalent in older executives whose bosses have been tough and militaristic in style, denies the reality that our professional lives and our personal lives are connected and entwined and one will certainly influence one another. They cannot be compartmentalized, no matter how hard we try.

Daniel Vasella, whom I mentioned earlier, is one of the rare examples of a chairman who has been public about the challenges he had as a child and how these have affected the way he thinks and operates today. At the age of eight, he had tuberculosis and meningitis and was kept out of school for a year convalescing in the mountains of his native Switzerland. When he was ten, one of his sisters died of cancer. His father died when he was thirteen, and a few years later another sister died in a car accident. These childhood traumas may well have helped determine his choice to become a medical doctor and underpin his passionate drive to help and cure illness that remains the underlying purpose of his firm.

In the mid-1990s, I was fortunate to have as a boss Ray Viault at Kraft Foods. Viault went on to become Vice Chairman of General Mills until his retirement last year. He is a very wise man who fully understands the links and influences we are discussing here. He relates his own story:

> The biggest setback I ever had in my life was my divorce from my first wife. That was a big one. It was not only that, it was that I was then separated from my three very young children. I was just getting going and building some assets, and they were all stripped away. At the end of that process, I was divorced; I tried a reconciliation with my wife, and she had no interest whatsoever. I had lost all my assets, and I was living in a rooming house. I still had my job, and my children were living about an hour away. I was still in a formative part of my career. I had no money for a house or anything. I would visit my children every weekend, and there was no place to go because I didn't have a home. That was my situation, and I went through a whole process of wondering: What am I trying to do? Where am I going? What is important? What is not important? How am I going to behave?—all of that, as well as examining what were the aspects of myself that contributed to the situation. It had to do with What is my attitude and my attitude toward my ex-wife? What am I trying to do with the three children? What am I trying to do with my career? Where does it all fit together? I would say of all the things in my life, that was the fork in the road.

Both Daniel Vasella and Ray Viault are examples of individuals who experienced hardship and extreme emotional distress, but who reflected on it, grew stronger as a result, and are mature enough and self-confident enough to share their experiences with us.

Individuals and corporations continue to stress the separation of work and life outside work in the continuing debate. Indeed, consider the growth industry of consultants, advisors, and others built around the subject of work/life balance. It seems to me that this artificial division of the two simply continues the thinking that they are somehow unconnected.

If the goal is to achieve an ideal balance between your work and your family, you will likely fail.

Anyone who accepts a senior position in today's work environment must accept that his or her work responsibility comes at a cost to another part of his or her life. At times you may make sacrifices to pursue your career and at other times decide that more time needs to be spent on family, but these must be conscious decisions and you must recognize the implications of each decision.

As much as corporations try to support individuals with programs at the end of the day, it becomes for most a dynamic, values-based decision dependant on individual circumstances.

What becomes clear to many people over time is that there are three concurrent challenges in our lives. The first is the management of our work and careers. This typically takes most of our energy and effort. It is where we spend most of our time, and our "success" is the output. The second challenge is our family and friends. When we have exhausted ourselves at work, we return home, expecting "quality time" with our family. It is very often from this area of our lives that the highly emotionally demanding events occur—illness, death, and divorce. The third challenge is managing ourselves. For many of us, there is just no more time to deal with this. We are so busy and engaged at work that whatever energy and time are left over go to our family, so our individual needs are ignored.

Many of the successful leaders I have spoken to reverse this order, placing their own personal needs, be it health, fitness, learning, time for reflection, and simply recuperation at the top of the list on the basis that not to do so will impair their effectiveness in the other two areas.

David Whyte, the poet and philosopher, refers to these challenges as our three "marriages." His ideas resonate so clearly with leaders. His upcoming book, *The Three Marriages*, is an in-depth study of the concept.

It is clear that the challenges, disruption, stress, expectations of self, and expectations of others place a very significant burden on today's leaders. To manage these successfully requires many qualities and experiences, some of which we have covered here. But underpinning all of it for many people is a robust set of personal values that guide them as they go about their business. These values are shown most clearly when a person is faced with critical issues, be they moral, ethical, or just a case of determining "the right thing to do." Values are not just about the big things.

I remember vividly an experience I had as a young man in my early twenties when working for Ford Motor Company in Dagenham, England. I was a labour relations officer in Thames Foundry, which was an intimidating place, dark and acid smelling. Fireworks of sparks showered down from the molten metal being poured. The general foreman of the area of the plant I was working in was a huge, gruff, Irishman named Gerry who was an institution and held in some reverence.

One morning he appeared at my door with a small bunch of flowers, which he had picked from his garden, and said that he and his team had heard that I had just become a father and he wanted to offer their congratulations. For me it was an extraordinary gesture and the fact I am recounting it now reveals how much it meant to me then and has lived with me, underlining as it does, the fundamental human nature of our work.

In making that gift, Gerry laid down a number of things that were important to him. Family was one, recognition another. Understanding what our personal values are is for many a daunting task.

In my work with a leading private equity firm, where I often meet CEOs interested in entering private equity, one of the key questions for me is to determine whether the man or woman sitting opposite me really knows who he or she is and what the person's key learnings and mistakes have been during his or her career. The values of the person are soon revealed. Bill George, in his new book *True North*, explores this in great detail. George underscores how much factors external to our jobs can be the decisive influences in our lives.

If we therefore accept that our careers are inextricably bound together with our private lives, what might we expect the enlightened organization to be doing or considering? Let me suggest a few ideas:

1. Actively discuss setback and failure with leaders in the context of personal development. This is not easy for most companies, but it is where the personal learning is taking place. Simply firing someone for failure removes a previously successful executive from the firm and fails to capture any learning for the firm.
2. Recognize and engage with people going through severe personal disruption. The immediate manager must be the key player here, but good HR departments have a vital role to play.
3. Invest heavily in personal development that deepens the individual's self-knowledge and give assignments that truly stretch people.

Norman Walker advises and consults with CEOs and senior executives on organization and people issues, with particular emphasis on the development of future leaders and implementing business-led people processes. He is the co-author of *Leadership Passages,* which deals with the personal and professional challenges that can make or break a leader. He is a senior advisor to TPG Capital, a global private equity firm. He was the global head of HR at Novartis and prior to that held senior positions at Kraft Foods, Grand Met, and the Ford Motor Company.

SECTION 7

A LOOK TO THE FUTURE

The Future of Leadership Development, by Jim Noel and David Dotlich

CHAPTER 31

THE FUTURE OF LEADERSHIP DEVELOPMENT

Jim Noel and David Dotlich

As she stops to catch her breath between a meeting on long-term capital appropriation and another meeting on defining a new bonus incentive system for Asian business units, Jane takes a few minutes to sit at her desk and contemplate a rewarding moment in her day and her career. This afternoon, her company is wrapping up the third phase of a development process for high-potential future leaders. Yesterday, Jane, the CEO, and the Executive Committee heard a carefully selected team of high-potentials present recommendations to address a key business challenge facing the company.

Several years ago, things were much different for Jane. When she was an early-career high-potential herself, there were few formal development opportunities—and most of them were boring classroom presentations by business school professors. She knew—she'd been to a few herself. Over time, those selected for high-potential programs were removed from their jobs for days or weeks at a time and still expected to return to demanding positions and catch up on work. A few years ago, Jane's company began to experiment with action learning and discovered that focusing high-potential leaders on real issues and learning was beneficial to the learner and produced great ideas for the company. But even with these clear benefits, the demands of running a complex global business made it more difficult to take people away from their jobs and maintain the pace.

Somewhere along the line, it became clear that the company would have to find a way to use the work itself to develop people. It seemed so simple, but it was a necessary solution that, in turn, drove new innovations in action learning. As Jane continued to advance in her own career, she began to believe in the difference using real work for development made—and became an advocate of "experiential learning."

Shortly after she was promoted to Chief Learning Officer, her company—a large high-tech organization—focused on the fact that its R&D costs were going up, and at the same time, new product introductions were going down. The situation was fairly stable at that point, but it would quickly become a business model that the company could not sustain over time. Jane saw it as an opportunity to move forward further into experiential learning, and she set out to design a process that would help the company solve the R&D issue and develop some high-potential people at the same time.

As a group, Jane and the Executive Committee selected seven high-potential leaders from across the company to form a team. The seven-person, cross-functional group was assigned the task of examining the R&D productivity issue as part of their current assignment—their additional job for the next few months—and finding solutions to the problem. Instead of following a designed program, the team just tackled the problem. When they had questions or needed knowledge, Jane's job was to provide just-in-time learning—to find people who could provide answers or learning experiences that would help them understand and better deal with the issues they were tackling. Because they needed to get up and running as a team quickly, she provided help in how to organize and build up the performance of the team quickly. She provided coaches who could work with the individuals on the team to assist them on performance and provide feedback on behavior and leadership, or who could serve as an expert on a needed issue as it emerged in the group.

The last few weeks were the most interesting and exciting to observe. The team had coalesced as a high-performing team—there was palpable energy when she walked into the room while they were working. They were polishing their presentation, and she had provided academics and consultants to be sounding boards for rehearsals. These outside professionals had been able to help create additional thoughts and challenges for the team and had offered some tough feedback. But the team took the feedback well—they would be presenting to the CEO, and the fact that they were working on a issue that was real and relevant to the future of the company gave them all a stake in finding the right solution and presenting it well.

When the final presentation was made, Jane watched as the CEO and senior executive team nodded, frowned, made notes, or tuned out. She listened as questions were asked and feedback presented. And when the presentation was over and the team excused, she was especially pleased when the Executive Committee expressed approval at the quality of the presentation and ideas.

As Jane reflects on the success of the last three months this morning, she is also preparing to facilitate a reflection session for the team to discuss what they learned about business, strategy, leadership, and sustaining a team over time. Jane knows reflection is the heart of the learning process. And while she's glad to finish the program, she's also energized about the real results of the program and the unique learning design, that the company used a real business issue as a learning platform, and that business outcomes and learning and insight all came together to solve a problem and grow the business and leaders.

A Learning Culture in the Making

Does the scenario we paint seem too far-fetched? We don't think so. In fact, this may be the inevitable direction in which leadership development is heading—to organizational contexts in which learning is part of everyday work and work is part of everyday learning; where teams flow together and break apart as needed to solve real business issues and pursue real business results as they develop the leadership skills they need to advance in the company. Learning will be less "events," "packaged," and "programs"—and more embedded in work.

The contributions to this book and the outstanding leadership learning work all around leads us to several inescapable conclusions:

- *People must in charge of their own development.* The future will not be about prescribing training based on a person's position or tenure; rather, it's an attitude and culture that emphasizes learning and adaptability as a key component of performance—which everyone recognizes and values. This isn't to say that associates and employees will be allowed to freely pick and choose any amount and type of development program they find interesting. Instead, it's accelerating the current move toward an organizational environment and culture that encourages people to pursue, with the guidance of their supervisors or coaches, the (development) classes, programs, and opportunities that are appropriate to the career paths they want to pursue.
- *The old paradigm of efficiency over effectiveness doesn't work any more.* Effectiveness is more important than efficiency in today's business environment. Under the old paradigm, learning impact was measured in terms of number of students

taught, classroom days conducted, and even amount of money invested. The complexity and challenge of business will continue to focus on what works, rather than on what's cost-effective, and on what works, rather than on what can be easily taught. In addition, new paradigms for leadership effectiveness and learning are unlimited, and, as evidenced by authors in this book, reach to athletics, poetry, brain research, yoga, energy management, and a variety of other new and breakthrough ideas in the effort to find, in a competitive business environment, new ways for leaders to be effective.

- *Organizational capability will continue to drive leadership development.* Companies are focusing on the importance of results. The requirement now and in the future is building organizational agility, adaptability, and flexibility, which lead to business outcomes, with internal clients for leadership development linking learning with organizational and individual performance. As many authors in this book have pointed out, the importance of learning is not for learning's sake—it is to drive results, which is usually defined as new capabilities.

- *Global skills and global awareness will play a bigger role in leading people and organizations.* Whether or not one interacts with other countries or cultures, the nature of work and organizations will increasingly require global understanding and awareness, at every level, and in every role. Leadership development experts will need to be global experts, wherever they work in the future, because work is becoming globally interdependent.

- *Learning in the group or the classroom will continue to be part of leadership development.* There's no question that a classroom environment has a valuable place in developing people. As a method of developing insights and imparting information, and creating a dialogue removed from the pressures of work—the classroom is often best and will probably always play a role in creating new perspectives and building skills. In fact, because the classroom can create an environment for dialogue, and people like to learn together, classroom learning will always be valuable and useful under some conditions.

- *Breakthroughs in "just in time" technology for learning are also moving from the distant horizon to more frequent usage.* Podcasts, email insights sent to the blackberry, self-paced videos, blogs, and group learning via the web are increasing in frequency, and also relevance for more than skills training or front line supervisors, but finding their way into executive development.

- *The emphasis on experiential learning will grow.* This aspect of development may be the one thing most clearly evident to us after the years of experience we have leading development programs: People learn best through the work (that is, application) they do. It is this aspect of leadership development that we want to emphasize in summarizing this volume.

Work as a Driver of People

As demands on time intensify and focus on results increases, the greatest changes in leadership development may not come in program design or classroom events, but in the workplace. Given that there is less opportunity to remove people from their BlackBerries, cell phones, or constellation of colleagues, customers, and direct reports for days or weeks at a time, the pace of future leadership learning will need to keep up and respond as close to real time as possible. This will require taking advantage of leadership development opportunities within the everyday work that people do.

While this will require real upgrades to succession planning and talent management and cross functional, cross-business and cross-geography assignments—which is happening in most companies today—formal development over the next few years will likely involve many of the same methods and tools that we use now: classroom teaching, coaching, 360-degree feedback, assessment tools, and simulation, to name a few. However, what will change is that more leadership learning opportunities will move down from the top. Companies are heading toward a paradigm shift, in which lateral relationships is how work is done and in which leadership development becomes not just about developing the upper level, high-potential people, but also about developing more leaders who are held accountable for creating environments in which people learn, and for teaching and developing others. In this new paradigm, leadership development occurs at all levels, and more people are defined as leaders and encouraged to be leaders.

Today, leadership development is shifting away from primarily teaching leaders concepts and information and moving toward developing whole leaders who demonstrate head, heart, and guts. This means leaders must not only be insightful, strategic, and analytical, but they must excel in connecting, coaching, and motivating others, or "heart" skills. In addition, leaders must be able to act intuitively, make decisions with little information, and demonstrate unyielding integrity. This focus on relationship skills means that leaders must primarily be coaches of others and that bosses will have measurable responsibility for developing people and departments. Leaders will need the skills to give good feedback continuously, to use everyday work, projects, assignments, and business challenges as a driver of development, and to encourage their people to take charge of their own development. In this manner, everyday work can have the benefits of an action learning environment.

As the transition toward whole leadership and learning through work and experience continues to grow in interdependent, global organizations, there are three emerging conditions for effective leadership development: collaboration, connectedness, and community.

Collaboration

Work now is done across internal and external boundaries, and the old top-down way of allocating tasks, making decisions, and driving results is appropriate to fewer and fewer business conditions today.

Collaboration is now a requirement for most tasks and projects, and it is much more than just working well with others on a team. It means working across the organization—across levels, functions, and cultures to do the work. With the pace of competition as well as technological change, collaboration is not so much a conscious team effort—a situation in which people work together on a team consciously splitting up duties—although that can still be part of it, but now means that everyone participates in unstructured company or group tasks and goals to produce results without being told what to do. In other words, people see what needs to be done and do it without waiting for someone to instruct them or assign a role or task.

Nike is a wonderful example of how collaboration can work when done well, and leaders can lead it.

This type of collaboration means that leadership will become more important than ever at all levels of the company. To take a view that leadership is primarily an executive requirement that will become more short-sighted in the future as leaders and initiators at all levels contribute to the corporate vision and goals by executing as needed, without waiting to be told what to do, which creates more capable and competitive organizations. Of course, leadership from the top will still be needed; strategy, guidance, and vision are necessary elements of the senior executive contribution, to name a few. But when employees across the company are hired in line with that strategy, guidance, and vision, and when they understand it and are trained and developed and enabled to do what must be done, effective collaboration will result.

Some of the ways that companies can encourage collaboration include:

- *Make use of technology tools.* Has there ever been a more exciting time for technology in business than right now? The future promises more technology tools that companies can use to encourage collaboration. Even now, a Nike employee in Sao Paolo can spot a new fashion trend, snap a photo with a digital camera or cell phone, send it to a colleague in design team at the corporate center, and a new shoe or garment can be designed, manufactured, and distributed in a matter of days—fast cycling a response to emerging consumer tastes and trends.
- *Take advantage of action learning opportunities.* Action learning can be a powerful tool for encouraging collaboration, as employees discover together new ways

of doing things and are able to challenge the conventional wisdom or culture in a safe context. This leads to continuous corporate renewal and constructive change in response to rapidly changing environments.

- *Encouraging and enabling cross*-boundary information sharing and connection by developing group based decision-tools, incentives, and information about what is happening elsewhere in the organization to facilitate collaboration.

Connectedness

Much of leadership development in the past has focused on developing the individual in a very compartmentalized way. It's time that companies recognize the value of experiences that take place outside formal leadership development programs. Individuals don't exist in a vacuum; rather, they are connected to each other both inside and outside of the office, lab, or plant, and all of those connections provide experience that can help create leaders for the future.

People are developed as leaders in all areas of life—work, hobbies, education, families, communities, volunteer experiences, and so forth. In fact, because the business context is often so narrowly defined, acceptable models of effective leadership are also narrowly defined, which limits many excellent people from emerging as leaders and often creates the conditions in which companies cannot adapt or change because of rigid definitions of acceptable leadership. Many people perceived as incapable of advancing at work occupy significant leadership roles in volunteer organizations, churches, synagogues, school boards, and many other places, but those leadership skills are untapped at work. We especially need to recognize this idea where women are concerned because, although we are seeing women increasingly in upper levels of business, they are still not represented in the numbers they should be. It's important to recognize and give credit for the value of life experiences outside the work environment, whether it's the experience of raising children, serving in a community, or even traveling and being exposed to different cultures.

In addition to encouraging connectedness to the outside environment, companies need to foster and encourage connectedness within the organization. Of course, in a global environment, it's tough to make connections across boundaries, but some companies are achieving success in this area. Nike, for example, is a leader in creating a boundary-less organization and using technology to foster this environment. Increasingly, as people have issues, they seek input and advice across BlackBerry devices, and colleagues offer such input and advice in moments to help resolve issues, which is becoming a design element of leadership development programs and coaching.

Community

Two other aspects of connectedness need more attention for leaders and leadership development. The first is the importance of meaning, which comes from community. Leadership development experts can learn from the military, from firefighters and police, and other situations in which the motivation to undertake difficult challengers, such as war or entering a burning building, is commitment to the mission and to one's peers. This insight is often lacking in impersonal work environments in which leaders don't really understand why people come to work or challenge themselves.

The shift toward greater integration across functions and hierarchies results in a philosophy of the corporate community. As lower-level people step across boundaries to do the jobs they know and CEOs and others create blogs that encourage input and commentary across the organization, this trend will continue to develop. Communities of consumers, interest groups, friends, and colleagues are now creating connectedness, but also achieving the "wisdom of crowds" in which the best insights are gleaned from large numbers of people inputting their views. It's an important shift; when people are part of a community, they are invested in the community's vision, strategy, and success.

Also, the satisfaction derived from family and friends is a motivator to work, so work/life balance must be respected and built into company policy and leadership expectations. People are better contributors and leaders are more creative when they are regularly in touch with what is meaningful in their own lives through greater balance.

Where Does All of This Take Us?

After reflecting on the ideas and insights of the many excellent contributors to this book, we hope you come away with some answers to current leadership challenges, but also with some questions that will encourage new thinking and development in this field. Some of the key questions we hope you will contemplate:

1. *Do we really constantly need new ideas?* This is a field that keeps looking for the next new thing. In fact, we are much like the fashion industry—despising last year's model or trend only because we're familiar with it. We wonder: Do we really need to be driven by "leadership trendiness"? We have a rich history and some wonderful tools already at our disposal—maybe we just need to adapt and refine what we have in order to build a respected tradition of

methods and approaches like the finance function has done over the last two hundred years.

2. *Do we need to regularly invent new tools in order to be respected?* In reading this book, it's clear that many companies are using what works, rather than what's new. If we can turn daily work into real learning, the need for new learning tools will become less of a driver. Opportunities to learn are all around us, often not requiring the latest method or tool, but more creative reflecting, processing, and insight.

3. *Do we need to separate learning from work?* As we indicated earlier, time is increasingly expensive, and embedding learning within work will be the expectation and the norm. Leadership learning doesn't need to be "big events," but with more creativity we can move closer to the work itself.

4. *Should we acknowledge that leaders are not continuously successful, or successful in all environments?* Just as we are learning that much of what we thought was learned behavior has a genetic component, should we come to accept that, rather than "changing" or "developing" leaders, we should find the right context or environment for them to succeed?

5. *Should we eliminate leadership development as a function?* As we read what the authors in this book have written, we are struck by the thought that because continuous learning and development is so important in a competitive, technology-driven business environment, it may be too important to assign to any one function or group, and rather be the responsibility of leaders, just as business results are the responsibility of leaders. This will be a challenge, but worth putting our creativity and problem-solving ability toward addressing.

CONTRIBUTORS

Marijo Bos
Blanca de Navarra, 3
Madrid 28010
Spain
  +34 (91) 391 4417
  Marijo.Bos@affiliate.oliverwyman.com

Mario Castaneda
Boulevard de Constance
77305 Fontainebleau
France
  +33 (160) 72 42 78
  Mario.Castaneda@StratX.com

Ram Charan
12655 North Central Expwy., Suite 103
Dallas, TX 75243
  (972) 490–9040
  office@charanassoc.com

Anthony V. Codianni
2 Musick
Irvine, CA 92618
  (949) 462–6160
  Anthony.Codianni@tabs.toshiba.com

Jill Conner
27 North Moore, Apt. 9B
New York, NY 10013
  (212) 941–6409
  jtconner@aol.com

David Dotlich
1631 NW Thurman Street, Suite 100
Portland, OR 97209
  (503) 243–3476
  David.Dotlich@oliverwyman.com

Brian Fishel
100 S. Tryon Street
NC 1-002-34-40
Clarlotte, NC 28255
  (704) 386-7585
  Brian.Fishel@bankofamerica.com

Neil M. Johnston
P.O. Box 1693
Palo Alto, CA 94302
  (650) 903–9982
  orbis@compuserve.com

Thomas R. Knighton
584 Hickory Road
Glen Ellyn, IL 60137
(630) 469–9598
Tom.Knighton@oliverwyman.com

Terry Kristiansen
2 Musick
Irvine, CA 92618
(949) 462–6160
Terry.Kristiansen@tabs.toshiba.com

Jean-Claude Larreche
Boulevard de Constance
77305 Fontainebleau
France
+33 (160) 72 42 78
JCLarreche@Insead.edu

Zohra Jan Mamod
Boulevard de Constance
77305 Fontainebleau
France
+33 (160) 72 42 78
Zohra.JanMamod@StratX.fr

Christian Marcolli
Inwilerstrasse 22
Baar 06340
Switzerland
+41 (41) 760.3903
CH.Marcolli@marcolli.com

Ken Meyers
216 Wagner Road
Northfield, IL 60093
(847) 501–2731
Ken.Meyers@oliverwyman.com

Juan Mobili
60 Lakeroad
Valley Cottage, NY 10989
(845) 268–8185
JMobili@aol.com

Alaric Mostyn
1 Grosvenor Place
London SW1 7HJ
UK
44 (0) 20 7343 9507
Alaric.Mostyn@oliverwyman.com

Agnes Mura
2417 34th Street, Suite 18
Santa Monica, CA 90405
(310) 450–5035
agnes@agnesmura.com

Susan Nichols
2433 NW 83rd Place
Portland, OR 97229
(503) 807–8096
susienic@earthlink.net

Jim Noel
P.O. Box 592
Rindge, NH 03461
(603) 899–3021
JNoel6775@aol.com

Eric Olson
505 N. Alta Vista Ave.
Monrovia, CA 91016
(626) 484–7456
Eric.Olson@oliverwyman.com

Adam Ortiz
7200 Swansea Lane
Cornelius, NC 28031
(704) 248–0863
adam@edc-llc.com

Stacey E. Philpot
208 Burrwood Ave.
Haddon Township, NJ 08108
(215) 806–5261
Stacey.Philpot@oliverwyman.com

Alice Portz
2620 Evergreen Point Road
Medina, WA 98039
  (425) 453–6302
  Alice.Portz@affiliate.oliverwyman.com

Stephen Rhinesmith
86 Capri Lane
Chatham, MA 02633
  (508) 945–7399
  Stephen.Rhinesmith@oliverwyman
  .com

Robert A. Stringer
200 Clarendon Street, 11th Floor
Boston, MA 02116
  (617) 424–3933
  Bob.Stringer@oliverwyman.com

Chatham Clarke Sullivan
Four Penn Center
1600 John F. Kennedy Boulevard,
Suite 600
Philadelphia, PA 19103
  (215) 320–3224
  CSullivan@cfar.com

Tim Sullivan
187 Steep Hill Road
Weston, CT 06883
  (203) 227–7883
  TChassulli@aol.com

Jim Sutton
1 SW Bowerman Dr
John McEnroe Building, 3rd Floor
Beaverton, OR 97005
  (503) 671–6806
  jim.sutton@nike.com

Vera Vitels
One Time Warner Center, 16th Floor
New York, NY 10019
  (212) 484–7869
  Vera.Vitels@timewarner.com

Norman Walker
Holzlistrasse 56
Binningen 04102
Switzerland
  +41 (61) 683 5055
  N.Walker@normanwalker.ch

Frank Waltmann
Corporate Human Resources
Lichtstrasse 35
Basel CH-4002
Switzerland
  +41 (61) 324 3444
  Frank.Waltmann@novartis.com

Kevin D. Wilde
General Mills, Inc.
No1. General Mills Blvd
M03-13
Minneapolis, MN 55426
  763-764-3398
  Kevin.Wilde@genmills.com

Ginny Whitelaw
1029 Park Road
Crownsville, MD 21032
  (410) 923–0286
  GinnyWhitelaw@aol.com

ABOUT THE EDITORS

Jim Noel is an independent consultant and leadership coach. He is the former manager of Executive Education and Leadership Effectiveness at GE's famed Leadership Institute in Crotonville, New York, and later Citibank's vice president of Executive Development. Early in his career, Jim was assistant dean of the College of General Studies at The George Washington University in Washington, D.C. His consulting firm, Noel and Associates, assists companies in the selection, assessment, and development of key leadership teams. He is the co-author of three books on leadership, including *The Leadership Pipeline* with Ram Charan and Steve Drotter.

David Dotlich, Ph.D., is a senior partner with Oliver Wyman, a founder of The Executive Learning Center, and former president of Mercer Delta Consulting. He consults to executive committees, CEOs, and senior leaders in the areas of leadership, business strategy, and executive coaching with companies such as Johnson & Johnson, Nike, Nordstrom, UBS, Bank of America, Sara Lee, Time Warner, and Novartis. He is a certified psychologist in career development, life planning, and numerous psychological inventories. Dr. Dotlich was formerly corporate vice president of human resources for Honeywell International, Inc.

Dr. Dotlich is a co-author of six best-selling books, including *Why CEOs Fail, Unnatural Leadership, Leadership Passages,* and, most recently, *Head, Heart & Guts: How the World's Best Companies Develop Complete Leaders.*

Dr. Dotlich was an Edmund James Fellow at the University of Illinois, and while working on an MA in race relations from the University of Witwatersrand in Johannesburg, South Africa, he conducted survey research on racial attitudes in the African townships and began an overland tour company After returning to the United States, he joined the U.S. Department of Commerce as a training director assigned to Minneapolis. While there, he completed his MA and Ph.D. at the University of Minnesota and was selected Outstanding Graduate Student of the University. He has also completed the INSEAD Executive Program.

HOW TO USE THE CD-ROM

System Requirements

PC with Microsoft Windows 98SE or later
Mac with Apple OS version 8.6 or later

Using the CD With Windows

To view the items located on the CD, follow these steps:

1. Insert the CD into your computer's CD-ROM drive.
2. A window appears with the following options:
   Contents: Allows you to view the files included on the CD-ROM.
   Software: Allows you to install useful software from the CD-ROM.
   Links: Displays a hyperlinked page of websites.
   Author: Displays a page with information about the Author(s).
   Contact Us: Displays a page with information on contacting the publisher or author.
   Help: Displays a page with information on using the CD.
   Exit: Closes the interface window.

If you do not have autorun enabled, or if the autorun window does not appear, follow these steps to access the CD:

1. Click Start→Run.
2. In the dialog box that appears, type d:\start.exe, where d is the letter of your CD-ROM drive. This brings up the autorun window described in the preceding set of steps.
3. Choose the desired option from the menu. (See Step 2 in the preceding list for a description of these options.)

In Case of Trouble

If you experience difficulty using the CD-ROM, please follow these steps:

1. Make sure your hardware and systems configurations conform to the systems requirements noted under "System Requirements" above.
2. Review the installation procedure for your type of hardware and operating system.

It is possible to reinstall the software if necessary.

To speak with someone in Product Technical Support, call 800–762–2974 or 317–572–3994 M-F 8:30 A.M.–5:00 P.M. EST. You can also get support and contact Product Technical Support through our website at www.wiley.com/techsupport.

Before calling or writing, please have the following information available:

• Type of computer and operating system
• Any error messages displayed
• Complete description of the problem.

It is best if you are sitting at your computer when making the call.